# Parenting Teenagers

# Other works by the authors

*The Effective Parent* (Don Dinkmeyer, Gary D. McKay, Don Dinkmeyer, Jr., James S. Dinkmeyer, and Joyce L. McKay)

*The Encouragement Book* (Don Dinkmeyer and Lewis E. Losoncy)

*Parenting Young Children: Helpful Strategies Based on Systematic Training for Effective Parenting (STEP) for Parents of Children Under Six* (Don Dinkmeyer, Sr., Gary D. McKay, and James S. Dinkmeyer)

*The Parent's Handbook: Systematic Training for Effective Parenting* (Don Dinkmeyer and Gary D. McKay)

*PREP for Effective Family Living* (Don Dinkmeyer, Gary D. McKay, Don Dinkmeyer, Jr., James S. Dinkmeyer, and Jon Carlson)

*Raising a Responsible Child* (Don Dinkmeyer and Gary D. McKay)

*Taking Time for Love: How to Stay Happily Married* (Don Dinkmeyer and Jon Carlson)

*Time for a Better Marriage* (Don Dinkmeyer and Jon Carlson)

SYSTEMATIC TRAINING FOR EFFECTIVE PARENTING

# *Parenting Teenagers*

## Systematic Training for Effective Parenting of Teens

# DON DINKMEYER & GARY D. MCKAY

**AGS** ®

American Guidance Service, Circle Pines, Minnesota 55014-1796

**AGS**® staff participating in the development and production of this publication:

### Project Team
Marjorie Lisovskis, Managing Editor
Mary Kaye Kuzma, Production Coordinator
Julie Nauman, Designer
Steven Moravetz, Marketing Associate

### Product Development
Dorothy Chapman, Instructional Materials Director
Lynne Cromwell, Publishing Services Manager
Bonnie Goldsmith, Acquisitions Editor
Charles Pederson, Assistant Editor
Maureen Wilson, Art Director

### Illustrations
Jim Johnston

### Cover Design
Terry Dugan, Terry Dugan Design

Second edition ©1990 **AGS**® American Guidance Service, Inc.
First edition ©1983, under the title *The Parent's Guide*.

Printed in the United States of America.

A 0 9 8

Library of Congress Catalog Card Number: 89-82447
ISBN 0-88671-404-4

To our wives—Elvira Jane and Joyce—and to all the other STEP parents who've encouraged us along the way.

To Don, Jim, Robert, Kristin, Jennifer, and Mike, and to all the other teenagers—past and present—with whom we've lived and worked.

# Contents

# Introduction

Parenting teenagers is one of the most challenging tasks of raising children today. Rapidly advancing social changes have made the job increasingly difficult and confusing. Compounding this are other factors: societal pressures, well-meaning friends and relatives, and conflicting theories presented in books and magazines, on television, and through other media.

To provide guidance through the often turbulent adolescent years, parents need a practical, down-to-earth philosophy that can help them understand the motivations of their teens. The area of discipline with teenagers is a sensitive but important one; it requires careful consideration and a lot of follow-through. Learning to encourage and to communicate openly with teens presents yet another challenge requiring effort, understanding, and commitment.

*Parenting Teenagers,* the parent's guide of STEP/teen (Systematic Training for Effective Parenting of Teens), is based on its predecessor, STEP, one of the most widely used parent-education programs in the world. Over one million parents have found STEP effective in improving parent-child relationships. STEP/teen has been written in response to requests from many of those parents for a STEP-like approach to improving relationships with teenagers.

The amount of success you achieve with STEP/teen will depend on how much effort and commitment you put into applying the suggested procedures. *Parenting Teenagers* is designed to provide *systematic* training for improving parent-teen relationships. It needs to be studied and applied one step at a time. Plan to spend at least a week with each of the ten chapters. At the beginning of the week, read through the chapter carefully. Then study the questions and charts. The personal development exercises provide a chance to work with concepts before putting into practice the weekly activity. From there you'll need only your own willingness to work at putting your new skills to use.

You may wish to further enhance your experience with this book by joining a STEP/teen parent study group. In a STEP/teen group, you'll meet with a group leader and other parents. Together you'll listen and respond to recorded family situations on audio and video and work at skill building exercises. Most important of all, you'll have an opportunity to discuss the ideas in STEP/teen and to find support and encouragement from the leader and other group members. Turn to page 197 for more information about parent groups and about the complete STEP/teen program.

Whether you're studying this book alone or participating in a group, we wish you success in your efforts to make your relationship with your teenager more rewarding and satisfying. Our experience has shown that when parents really work at applying these principles, they *do* become more effective parents. We believe that STEP/teen can help you reach this goal!

**Don Dinkmeyer, Ph.D.**
Diplomate of Counseling Psychology,
    American Board of Professional Psychology
Diplomate, American Board of Family Psychology
Clinical Member, American Association for
    Marriage and Family Therapy
President, Communication and Motivation
    Training Institute, Inc. (CMTI) Coral Springs, Florida

**Gary D. McKay, Ph.D.**
Educational and Psychological Consultant
Clinical Member, American Association for
    Marriage and Family Therapy
President, Communication and Motivation
    Training Institute-West, Inc. (CMTI-West)
    Tucson, Arizona

# CHAPTER 1

●

# Understanding Your Teenager and Yourself

Many parents enjoy their children's infancy and childhood but find their teenage years a time of conflict. How many times have parents said to their teenagers, "Look at what I've done for you! The least you could do is . . ." There are probably as many ways to finish that statement as there are parents!

Parenting today's teens is more difficult than in previous years because of far-reaching technological and sociological changes that have occurred. Teenagers have always been exposed to activities, information, and people that challenge their families' standards and values—but never so much as today. Parents whose own teenage years don't seem so very long ago are finding their children growing up in a changed world. These changes have brought great benefits to society, but problems too.

Perhaps most influential of all the changes is what we will call the democratic revolution. In recent decades various people have sought to be treated as equals: labor, ethnic, and religious groups, women, older people, and others. Institutions, values, and traditional concepts of authority have been challenged and in some cases changed. No two people are likely to hold the same attitude toward these changes. It is likely, though, that people in our society will continue to demand to be treated as equals. The democratic revolution may ebb and flow, but it won't disappear.

Families have not escaped the changes taking place in the rest of society. Parent-teen relationships have been dramatically affected—so much so that today's parents are generally not able to control their teenagers easily and effectively. The demanding approach that may have worked for *their* parents simply doesn't work as well for today's parents. And those parents who have thrown up their hands and let their children rule the roost have found that approach equally ineffective.

Some of the problems facing parents come from outside the family, from society at large. Others are unintentionally of the parents' own making. Sometimes there is a self-fulfilling prophecy at work: if parents expect their teens to cause problems, the chances are good that problems will arise. Parents' expectations are extremely powerful in teenagers' lives. Teens know when their parents expect them to try out for sports, join the band or choir, wear the "right" kind of clothes, be elected to an honor society, or become popular at school. Similarly, teens know or sense when their parents expect them to do poorly in school, join the "wrong" group of friends, abuse car privileges, use tobacco or drugs, or generally behave in an irresponsible manner. A teen, or even a younger child, doesn't need radar to pick up a parent's signals.

As you begin STEP/teen, take a moment to think about the expectations you have for your teenager. Are they realistic? Do they fit your child's abilities, interests, and goals? Or are you setting standards for your teen that you yourself were unable to meet when you were that age? Ask yourself if the standards have more to do with your own desires than with your teen's.

We believe that teens need to develop realistic standards and expectations for themselves based on their own abilities, interests, and values. If they don't, teenagers learn to please only their parents. They don't learn to think for themselves, set goals, and take initiative. They learn how to satisfy their parents' dreams, and not their own. If you modify the expectations you have for your teenager, you will overcome one of the greatest roadblocks to effective parenting. And teenagers whose parents help them learn to set their own standards will overcome one of the greatest challenges of becoming an adult—learning to take responsibility for oneself.

Given the changes that have occurred because of the democratic revolution, human beings need relationships based on equality and mutual respect. People have chosen, consciously or unconsciously, to value democratic attitudes. Of course, this democratic ideal does not imply that people are exactly the same. All people, including teens and parents, have different abilities and responsibilities. Democratic equality implies that people are of equal value as human beings. For parents and teens, this means that neither is superior or inferior to the other—that they, like all people, are of equal human worth. It takes courage to put this equality into action and behave democratically. STEP/teen gives parents that courage.

# Ineffective Methods of Parenting

Almost all parents want to improve their relationships with their teenagers, but many don't know how to proceed. Misunderstandings and lack of information abound. Some parents assume that teens are rebellious by nature and impossible to live with. These parents think the best approach to living with teenagers is to hold tight and weather the storm—and hope they can get their bearings after their teens leave home.

Other people assume that teenagers can be forced to obey a parent's will. Family harmony, they think, can be achieved by getting tough, giving lots of orders in a loud voice, and making sure teens follow those orders to the letter.

Our years of experience point to one conclusion: neither "weathering the storm" nor "getting tough" will improve most parent-teen relationships. In fact, both approaches probably guarantee that family life will deteriorate. Why? Because neither approach encourages teenagers to become responsible for themselves.

We call parents who let their children run roughshod over them permissive. Those who run roughshod over their children we call autocratic. Permissive and autocratic parenting differ greatly, but they share an important characteristic: they're both ineffective.

Permissive parents generally are afraid to take a stand on things they believe in. Rather than risk being attacked verbally by their teenagers, they offer no opinions and make requests that can be easily ignored. They avoid conflict at all costs.

Permissive parents usually see themselves as powerless in relation to their teenagers. Often they feel overwhelmed by an array of problems and activities that have become associated—rightly or wrongly—with the teenage scene: alcohol and other drug abuse, sexual promiscuity, disrespect for authority, vandalism, and lack of cooperation. Some parents believe that negative, rebellious teenage behavior is inevitable. It's almost as if these parents are saying, "There's a time when every teenager is bound to behave badly. Parents have no power to prevent this from happening, and so it's best to act as if everything's okay." Divorce or child-custody fights can lead parents to believe they have to make things up to their children. Parents involved in custody proceedings often crave their children's approval.

Many adults have bitter memories of being raised in environments laden with restrictions and punishments. Such parents may believe that setting limits and establishing guidelines actually harm a teenager's development. Our experience, however, indicates that most teens view limits and guidelines as proof of their parents' concern for them. A seventeen-year-old told us that he was sure his father didn't care about him because his father had said nothing to him after he'd regularly broken curfew by over two hours. The teen reasoned that if his father loved him, he would have said or done something that showed he cared. In this case a parent's failure to be firm was perceived by a teen as a lack of love.

Teens often interpret permissiveness as a sign of weakness. And they can be quick to seize any power given up by their parents. After all, permissive parenting gives teens an excuse for rebelling or showing disrespect for parents. It's an open invitation that many young people find hard to refuse. Being permissive is like granting a teenager a license to misbehave.

It's important to understand why permissiveness is an ineffective method of parenting. We believe it fails because it takes away respect from *both* the parent and the teen. Teens are treated as uncontrollable and uncooperative family members, and parents behave as if they themselves are helpless, unable to provide guidance or maintain family unity. This attitude of despair and discouragement in a parent can reduce a teenager's self-esteem, because it implies the parent's conviction that the teenager is a "hopeless case," incapable of changing. Teens may feel good if allowed to do whatever they choose, but they usually don't feel good for very long. If they sense that their parents don't respect them, they will find it hard to respect themselves. Thus, permissiveness breeds disrespect and discouragement and invites rebellion. It's a vicious cycle that can create havoc in family life.

Pampering is one of the most common forms of disrespect. Our stand on pampering is based on the philosophy of Rudolf Dreikurs and Vicki Soltz: *Do nothing regularly for people that they can do for themselves.*[1] Pampering handicaps teenagers because it teaches them that they can't handle things on their own. They lose self-confidence and begin to think of themselves as immature, inept, and constantly in need of attention and help. If teens grow used to being waited on and served by parents, they will learn to expect similar treatment from others—from grandparents, relatives, teachers, employers, and marital partners.

There are countless ways in which parents may pamper. Francis Walton has compiled the following list:[2]

- calling teens to get up even when they have alarm clocks
- reminding teens what time it is, as if they can't tell time and figure out whether they'll be late for an appointment
- speaking for teenagers when other people are speaking to them
- selecting, buying, picking up, and laundering teens' clothing
- regularly searching for teens' misplaced personal possessions
- granting special and repeated privileges for the use of the family car
- "snoopervising" homework by asking how much has to be done, checking it, and making sure it gets done

- making money available whenever requested or giving an allowance beyond what is reasonably needed
- taking responsibility for most household tasks
- allowing teens to disregard established curfews
- providing constant chauffeur service

As you can see, some forms of pampering are full of good intentions. The problem with any form of pampering is that it doesn't encourage teens to become responsible for themselves.

Why do pampered teens extract so much service from their parents and gain so much power over them? Because permissive, pampering parents have a faulty set of beliefs. One of the faultiest beliefs a parent can hold is this: "I will lose my child's love if I don't give in on most issues." Nothing could be further from the truth. In fact, pampering usually produces the opposite of the hoped-for effect. Instead of being respected and loved, parents earn disrespect and even contempt.

What happens when parents stop pampering? Frankly, family life can be difficult for a while. Teenagers often become more demanding because they think they aren't getting a fair shake. They may believe that "life is unfair," and try to manipulate parents back into the position of servant. If they become very angry, they may try to get revenge—perhaps by sabotaging a family activity. If all else fails, many teens give up, displaying an "I don't care" attitude toward their parents' expectations. They may, for example, forget important appointments, stop handing in homework, or do chores so poorly that someone else (guess who) has to do them over. The following chapters of STEP/teen can help parents deal with responses such as these, so that teens will begin to take responsibility for themselves.

Equally as ineffective as the permissive method of parenting is the autocratic, "get tough" approach. Autocratic parents believe they know what's good for everybody else, and they try to force their ideas on others. They assume that teenagers will never perform adequately—and never up to parents' standards. Autocratic parents often do the following:

• They are extremely critical of teens' performance.
• They are demanding and threatening.
• They manipulate teens by punishing or rewarding them.
• They remind and nag.
• They become overinvolved in homework.
• They do not trust or respect teens.
• They believe there's one "right" opinion and stubbornly hold to it.

Teenagers respond to autocratic parents in various ways. Some become angry and decide to rebel against their parents. Feeling criticized about themselves and all they value, they may take a stand on issues their parents can't control: for example, choice of friends, smoking cigarettes, amount of effort applied to schoolwork, attendance at religious services, using drugs, or engaging in sex. When an autocratic parent and a rebellious teen struggle for power, nobody really wins. The parent or teen may win a temporary victory, but mutual respect will be lost and their relationship will suffer.

In some families, teenagers respond to threatening and demanding parents by becoming very discouraged. These teens are so sure their parents are "right" and they themselves are "wrong," they give up. To avoid criticism, some may try to please their parents and conform to parents' expec-

tations. On the surface this kind of family life may look ideal—teenagers who aren't constantly testing limits, trying the patience of parents, and engaging in outright rebellion! The parents appear to have "won." But what is the price of the victory? We believe the price is too high if teenagers lose their self-respect and learn to please and conform rather than think for themselves and make informed decisions.

## The Key to Effective Parenting: Equality and Mutual Respect

STEP/teen is the alternative to both permissive and autocratic parenting. Its basic premise is that all family members—parents and children alike—must learn to live as equals.

Living together as social equals is a difficult concept to grasp. Many parents object immediately, saying their children are not their equals. One father told us, "I earn the money, own the car, and make all the major decisions. When my daughter feels she's my equal, it's time for her to strike out on her own—go to college or get a job. Until then, I'm the boss." We told that father that equality is not based on earning power, possessions, experience, physical stature, or age. It's based on the right shared by every human being to be treated respectfully. In STEP/teen, parents have responsibilities that are unique to parenthood: providing guidance and discipline for their teenagers. But they also have a responsibility to respect their teens and treat them as persons having equal human worth and dignity.

Living as equals means that neither parent nor teen tries to be superior, seize power, punish, or talk down to the other. The relationship is democratic: respect replaces rebellion, and cooperation replaces coercion. Often when a parent and teen do not treat each other as equals, each is concerned with getting his or her own way:

**Mom:** Doug, get over to the table. It's time to eat.
**Doug:** I have to make a call now. I promised I'd call before six.
**Mom:** When I say "Come," I don't want any excuses.
**Doug:** Mom, it'll only take a minute.
**Mom:** Doug!

A situation like this is a training ground for developing power-hungry individuals who seek to control others. Doug may obey his mother, but he will resent having to do so. He's learning that the way to keep from being ordered around is to order around other people.

Relationships based on inequality tend to create or maintain distance between family members. If a pampering parent is afraid of a teen, or if a conforming teen is afraid of an autocratic parent, how can the two people become close? Parents and teens must trust and respect each other if they are to overcome this distance. First, they must trust and respect themselves. Both parents and teens have to feel secure about their position and role in the family. That feeling of security doesn't come overnight, but over the course of the following chapters STEP/teen can help you develop it.

Parents who feel secure and enjoy a healthy respect for themselves can establish effective relationships with their teenagers. Free from thinking only in terms of winning, being right, and being in control, they are able to relate to their teens in new ways. These parents recognize two important points: a parent can't really force his or her will on a teenager, and a teenager can't really force his or her will on a par-

ent. *People cannot make others do anything they do not want to do.*

The challenge in parenting teens is to focus on *changing yourself,* not your teenager. Some parents are discouraged when they first hear this. They're interested in changing their teenager—in getting the teen to come home on time, to be respectful and cooperative, to stay away from alcohol and other drugs, and to do well in school. Keep in mind, though, what we just emphasized: you can't make teens do what they don't want to do. You can't change their behavior by giving orders and policing their actions. You can, however, create a change in yourself and in your relationship with your teenager. That kind of change can have a dramatic influence on your teen.

As you will learn through STEP/teen, the responses parents typically give to their teens' misbehavior actually *reward* that misbehavior. A teen who is seeking attention is rewarded as much by punishment or lecturing as by praise. If parents change how they respond, then teenagers no longer receive a reward for misbehaving. Your influence is greatest through changing yourself, not others. As you stop attempting to control your teenager, he or she will no longer reap payoffs for resisting and rebelling. You'll find yourself the beneficiary of better relationships and less tension. These changes won't come overnight, of course. Your teen will most likely test you. But, with time, your teenager will begin to act responsibly, not in reaction to a control pattern set up by you, but by personal choice and free will.

In an equal relationship between parent and teen you will find the following characteristics:

• mutual respect
• mutual trust

- mutual concern and caring
- empathy—sympathetic understanding—for one another
- a desire to listen to one another
- emphasis on assets rather than faults
- a commitment to cooperation and equal participation in resolving conflicts
- sharing of thoughts and feelings rather than hiding them and bearing resentment
- mutual commitment to common goals, but with freedom to pursue independent goals
- support for and acceptance of one another as imperfect people in the process of growing

Begging or commanding will have little effect on a teen whose mind is made up.

We believe relationships based on equality provide the greatest opportunity for personal growth—they're character building. They produce flexibility, open-mindedness, and a desire to understand the other person. Disagreement and conflict don't disappear, because no two people ever think alike or act alike. Why should they? But in a democratic relationship, people with differences of opinion can resolve conflict through negotiation. They don't need to hide or suppress feelings, but can share them, thereby strengthening the relationship. In short, a relationship based on equality encourages both parent and teen

to become the most they can become, and to appreciate, respect, and love each other.

# Adolescence as a Holding Pattern

Take a moment to think back to your own adolescence. Can you remember what it felt like to be suspended somewhere between childhood and adulthood? Today's teenagers are in the same position, although for them the pressures and challenges are even greater. Advertising, movies, television, books, video games, records and tapes, radio—these are all busy delivering messages to teenagers and vying for teenagers' attention and money. They're powerful influences in teenage life.

Do you remember what it felt like to be suspended somewhere between childhood and adulthood?

An even more powerful influence during puberty is a teenager's own body. Emotional changes accompany the physical changes, and both kinds of change occur over a short period of years. It's a time when many teens are in conflict with themselves—one minute they may feel grown up, the next minute like a small child. How teens respond to puberty depends upon how they see themselves and life—their basic perceptions. Not all teens go through the same emotional changes.

Parents experience great anxiety about their teenagers' sexual maturation. Different parents have different worries: that their teens will become sexually active or promiscuous, that they'll be hurt emotionally, that they won't use some form of contraception, that they'll contract a venereal disease. The overwhelming majority of parents do not want to encourage their teenagers to become sexually active. At the same time, teens are receiving messages from their peers and their bodies that may stimulate sexual desire and activity.

Adolescence is a holding pattern, but it can be a rough ride for both parents and teens. In addition to sex, parents have a host of other concerns: their teenager's choice of friends, choice of clothing, choice of entertainment, attitude toward school, spending habits, and hairstyle, to mention a few. In short, the whole range of their teenager's emerging values. STEP/teen doesn't promise to resolve all the conflicts between parents' values and teens' values. But it does offer ways to smooth the ride—ways of thinking, feeling, listening, communicating, and acting. It is a systematic approach to changing family life during your children's adolescence.

## Independence and Responsibility

It is difficult to make the transition from parenting a child to parenting a young adult. Many parents are not only used to taking care of their children, but also take satisfaction in doing so, right down to making their beds, fixing all their meals, and supervising their homework. It can be tough enough to share responsibility with teens, let alone recognize and accept that teens will eventually have full responsibility for their lives.

It is also difficult for many parents to accept their teenager's growing independence. It's hard to feel unneeded! And yet it's a fact that human beings normally seek to become independent as they mature. They want to be more able to make decisions for themselves. It's a sign of mental health that teens want to decide who their friends will be, how they'll spend their time, what they'll wear, what they'll eat and drink, and when they'll turn out the light at bedtime. They're learning how to make decisions and run their lives.

Independence and responsibility go hand in hand; a parent who gives one without the other is asking for trouble. An independent teen without a sense of responsibility is an accident waiting to happen. On the other hand, a teen who's burdened with responsibilities but who has no opportunity to make decisions will probably enter adulthood feeling resentful and victimized. In both instances, the teen will be ill equipped to make intelligent decisions.

Responsibility must accompany independence, but all too often teenagers grab the independence and push away the responsibility. A sixteen-year-old may be eager to take off in the family car but not to fill up the gas tank. And what about paying for the additional insurance needed for young drivers? A thirteen-year-old may want to close the bedroom door and stop parents from supervising homework, but is that teen ready to accept the consequences of failing to turn in assignments? In fact, the message teens' actions often send seems to be "I want to make my own decisions, but I want you to take the responsibility if I make a bad one."

As children grow toward adolescence, parents need to decrease the amount of control they exert over them. At the same time, children need to increase the amount of responsibility they take for themselves. What we're describing here is a lively balancing act that continues for several years. If parents and teens develop mutual trust, parents can allow their teens to begin to make their own decisions. Parents can provide guidance by clearly expressing their own opinions and values. Teens can make their own decisions, within limits, as long as they're willing to accept the consequences—including financial, emotional, academic, physical, and social ones.

The issue of parental control may remind you of your own teenage years. What was your response when your parents tried to control you? How did you feel? We suggest you become aware of how frequently you try to control your teen. Then take the next step, and think about how frequently you and your teen become involved in power struggles. There *is* a connection between using control and getting caught up in a struggle for power. As you reduce your controlling and give your teen a chance to become independent, neither of you will feel the need to get the upper hand. If you find that your teen takes the independence but not the responsibility, you obviously have to provide guidance and discipline. Throughout STEP/teen we will present specific procedures for encouraging teenagers to become independent and responsible. We will also discuss methods of discipline.

## Seeking Significance and a Sense of Belonging

Teenagers are at a time in their lives when they are busy creating an identity—figuring out who they are and what gives meaning to their lives. They're searching for ways to be significant, and they're very interested in being accepted by their peers (friends and acquaintances). To many teens, being accepted by peers is more important than being accepted by parents, and often the desire for peer acceptance becomes all-consuming. This may leave parents, especially those who have previously enjoyed their child's undivided admiration, feeling puzzled and rejected. But seeking significance beyond home and family is a necessary step toward maturing into adulthood.

Significance can be achieved in a variety of ways, both positive and negative. Some teens seek significance through mechanical skills, drama, athletics, music, schoolwork, or volunteer work. They may join clubs or get part-time jobs. Other teens seek significance through delinquency or irresponsible behavior. Sexual promiscuity, alcohol or other drug abuse, reckless driving, skipping school, cigarette smoking, shoplifting, and vandalism are among the negative ways that some teens try to count with their peers. Quite often a teen will seek significance in both positive and negative ways—with some combination of the two that will give the teen a sense of belonging.

Very young children get meaning and a sense of belonging from their parents and siblings. Parents need to recognize that during late childhood and adolescence children shift their focus from their families to their peers. It's part of growing up. It is important to teenagers to dress like their friends, listen to the same music, go to the same movies, and be invited to the same parties. A fifteen-year-old who doesn't get an invitation to a party can feel desperately rejected.

Some parents are mystified by what they see as their teenager's desire to conform.

They wonder why certain kinds of clothes are "wrong" while others are "right." Why can't many teenagers think for themselves rather than follow the herd—dressing, talking, and acting like every other teen on the block? That's a tough question that deserves an answer. We agree that it can be frustrating for parents to watch their children embrace other people's values, but we think it is typical for teens to do this. Even if teens seem to be conforming to the values of their peers, they are learning to make decisions that are different from the ones their parents would make for them. (Most of us did this too, remember?) As long as a teenager's decisions are not dangerous, harmful to self or others, or irresponsible, we think a parent's most effective response is to listen, observe, and try to understand. Many of the issues that cause conflict between parents and teens—such as entertainment, hairstyle, clothing, and music—are best left up to teens. By making decisions involving those issues, they will learn to clarify their goals and values.

## The Goals of Misbehavior

As children mature they develop methods of achieving their basic goal: the sense of belonging. The family atmosphere, the child's position in the family (youngest, oldest, and so forth), the methods of child training parents use, and the child's creative response to the challenges of life all affect how a child behaves. These factors help shape a personality, and they have an impact on the ways an individual seeks a sense of belonging.

Children who misbehave usually do so for a purpose.[3] The term *misbehavior* refers to actions and words that disregard or disrespect the rights or safety of others, or that

are self-defeating or even dangerous to oneself. Misbehavior is disrespectful. Dreikurs and Soltz discussed the following basic four goals of misbehavior:

- attention
- power
- revenge
- display of inadequacy

These are mistaken, or negative, goals because they don't foster a person's development; in fact, they hinder development. If children are busy putting energy into getting power or revenge, for example, they're stopping themselves from pursuing positive goals. They are discouraged children.

To take account of teenage misbehavior, Eugene Kelly and Thomas Sweeney extended the list of goals to include the following:[4]

- excitement
- peer acceptance
- superiority

These goals, combined with the basic four, represent methods that teens use to achieve a sense of belonging. When pursued in excess, or through irresponsible acts, they, too, are based on faulty beliefs and mistaken ideas—they're simply not in teens' best interests.

How do you recognize a goal of misbehavior? *Your own feelings* and *your teen's response to what you do or say* are your best guide to understanding the purpose of your teenager's misbehavior. When your teen misbehaves, consider first your own feelings. Are you annoyed? angry? hurt? depressed? Second, look at how your teen responds when you react to his or her behavior. Does your teen ignore you? scowl at you? argue? momentarily stop the misbehavior, but begin again? By first identifying how you feel, and, second, examining your teenager's reaction to your attempt at correction, you can identify what your teen is after. And once you know your teen's goal, you can learn how to deal with the misbehavior in the most effective way.

The first step, then, is to identify the goal of your teenager's misbehavior. As you'll see, each of the seven goals of teenage misbehavior is associated with a specific feeling or response of the parent and with some typical reactions of the teen to the parent's attempt at correcting misbehavior. In later chapters we'll deal with specific ways for parents to proceed after they've identified the goals of teenage misbehavior.

If you feel annoyed, the chances are good your teen's goal is attention.

**Attention.** Almost all young children seek attention, and the goal appears in teens to varying degrees. If teenagers can't get attention in positive ways, they may seek it in ways that are disturbing and annoying. Like the rest of us, teens want to be noticed! They may try to be noticed by turning up the volume of the television or stereo, or by interrupting conversations. If you're having a conversation with a friend of yours and your daughter suddenly turns on the stereo loudly in the next room, ask yourself how you feel. If you feel *annoyed*,

the chances are good that your daughter's goal is attention.

If you ask her to turn down the volume and she ignores you, turns it down momentarily and then turns it back up, or shuts it off but then does something else to disturb you, your assumption that her goal is attention is probably correct.

**Power.** Power-seeking teens believe they are important when they challenge authority and take control. Afraid that other people are out to boss them around, they look for ways to control every situation. Such teens may try to boss parents. Power-seeking teens want to do only what *they* decide to do. Often when parents challenge them, the parents may win the argument but lose ground in the relationship. Why would parents challenge their teens? Because power-seeking behavior is associated with *anger*. If your son takes off in the family car without asking, you may feel angry and want to fight back—perhaps yell and threaten. If you give in and allow him this freedom, he'll know who's in control. But if you decide to fight power with power, your teenager will probably be impressed with the

Power-seeking teens want things *their* way.

usefulness of power and may intensify the struggle. When dealing with a power-seeking teen, it is best to disengage from the struggle. Who can fight without an opponent? Once you've identified power as your teenager's goal, you'll be able to begin practicing new responses that will not satisfy that goal.

**Revenge.** Teenagers who pursue revenge are convinced they are not lovable. They believe they can find their place in the family or in the classroom only by being cruel and hurting others. A teen who has been involved in a power struggle with a parent and who knows the parent has won can still inflict hurt upon the parent. When faced with revenge-seeking behavior, parents usually feel *deeply hurt*. They may want to get even. But by punishing their teenager, these parents provide a fresh reason for the teen to seek further revenge.

**Display of inadequacy.** Teens who display inadequacy are the most discouraged of all teenagers. Their goal is to see that others expect nothing of them. They show parents (and themselves) that they just can't make friends, gain or lose weight,

Teens may hurt or embarrass parents in order to seek revenge.

figure out homework assignments, or perform household tasks adequately. These teens believe they lack the ability and stamina to perform competently; they have a very low opinion of themselves. Some have the mistaken belief that anything less than the best is nothing. When they don't think they can be the best, they give up. Their parents generally feel *despair* and may also want to give up. They may actually come to agree that their teen is incompetent and inadequate.

Teens who display inadequacy are the most discouraged of all.

Parents of teens usually have little trouble recognizing the goals of excitement, peer acceptance, and superiority. When they aren't exaggerated, these goals can function positively for teenagers. When, however, teenagers believe that pursuing these goals is the only way to be worthwhile, the goals exert a negative influence on their lives. They become disruptive.

**Excitement.** When teens whose goal is excitement use negative behavior to pursue the goal, or seek their excitement to excess, their parents often find themselves on the defensive. Parents may spend half of their time reacting to one exploit and the other half worrying about what's to come. They're usually *shocked* and *surprised* by their teenager's actions, and they often feel *hurt* and *angry* as well.

Some parents are mystified by their teen's desire for peer acceptance.

Parents of teens usually have no trouble recognizing the goal of excitement!

**Peer acceptance.** Teens who seek to be accepted by their peers will get along fine with their parents as long as everyone agrees on the choice of friends. If, however, parents don't approve of their children's friends, they'll feel *anxious* and *worried*.

**Superiority.** Teens who seek superiority—in academics, sports, or other endeavors—

usually receive the *approval* of their parents. After all, many parents believe a teenager's achievements reflect well on their own parenting skills. Even though some parents approve, we think that superstriving may not be healthy for either teenagers or their relationships with their peers. And some teens seek superiority in destructive ways, such as drinking more beer than anyone else, or putting parents down. Striving for superiority needs to be balanced with a desire to cooperate for the common good.

Teens often pursue the goals of peer acceptance, excitement, and superiority outside of the family. But whether pursued at home or away from home, these goals are frequently related to the teen-parent relationship. Often they are pursued along with one of the four basic goals. If a teen attends drinking parties, he or she may be pursuing revenge or power as well as excitement and peer acceptance. The same could be true of a teen who regularly watches gory movies or spends lots of time in video-game arcades. A teen who chooses friends that parents dislike may actually be using peer acceptance to gain parental attention.

If a teenager is a math whiz and Dad can't balance the checkbook, the teen might use superiority for power or revenge. Engaging in sex could be for the purposes of excitement and power in an area outside of the parent's control, or it could be to gain a partner's acceptance. The self-destructive use of cigarettes, alcohol, and other drugs provides not only excitement and peer acceptance, but also a means to seek revenge and exercise power over a parent's attempts to control the teen's activities. When a teen is using drugs as an escape, he or she may appear to be seeking excitement but actually be displaying inadequacy to meet the challenges of living.

Teens are usually not aware of their goals, except when the goal is revenge. But even when revenge is a goal, teens are not aware that they have decided the only way to deal with feeling hurt is to hurt back.

The need to feel superior can be positive or negative.

Teens can change goals, use different behavior for the same goals, or use the same behavior for different goals. The *only* way for parents to determine the goal is by identifying *their own feelings* and *the teen's reactions to their attempts to correct the misbehavior.*

While it's important for you to gain an understanding of all seven goals, it's especially important that you understand the basic four. Why? Because they occur in your relationship with your teenager. By changing your responses to these goals, you can influence your teen.

As you ponder these seven goals of misbehavior, remember that they are found in all teenagers and adults in varying degrees. If you were to analyze your feelings, words, and actions over the course of a week's time, you'd probably find evidence of all seven. Nobody's perfect! The point of exploring these goals so carefully is not to prove how "bad" teenagers are. The point is to understand both their misbehavior and parents' reactions to it. Only by doing this can ineffective patterns of behavior be broken and new, effective parent-teen relationships built.

## Positive Goals

When we say that teenagers' behavior has certain goals, we mean that everything they do has a purpose. A goal is the end toward which all behavior is directed. Just as our destination on a car trip influences our choice of routes, so too does a goal influence behavior. And just as we're able to choose a destination, we are able to choose goals for ourselves as well. In STEP/teen we believe that human beings have the ability both to understand and to choose the ways they behave.

Along with goals of misbehavior, there are also positive goals that teens (and the rest of us) pursue. As we mentioned, some goals are negative only when they're pursued excessively or at the expense of one's own or another person's well-being. Obviously attention, power, excitement, peer acceptance, and superiority can be positive goals. They can nurture self-esteem while influencing behavior that is socially responsible and personally satisfying. A goal is positive if it fosters self-respect, respect for others, shared responsibility, and cooperation for constructive ends.

Teenagers, like all people, pursue a combination of positive and negative goals. Parents have a responsibility to encourage in their teens behavior that reflects positive goals. The process of encouragement is so important that Chapter 4 is devoted exclusively to this subject. Encouraging cooperation is crucial. By cooperation we mean the willingness to participate in the give-and-take of human relationships—to be as concerned about other people's welfare as one's own. Encouragement increases teenagers' self-esteem and feelings of worth. As these feelings take root and grow, teens naturally become interested in cooperating with their parents and other people. With their parents' help they begin to take responsibility for their own behavior, make decisions wisely, and accept the consequences of their own decisions.

We're not talking magic here—just basic psychology. Teens who act irresponsibly are out to justify their misbehavior—they're afraid to criticize themselves. Healthy teens are more likely to evaluate their behavior and to modify it where it seems to be mistaken. They see the value of cooperating. When teens discover they can gain a sense of belonging through positive behavior, they are less likely to misbehave. They usually won't crave attention because they'll feel assured that their positive actions will be noticed. Teenagers who learn they can be effective through resourceful and responsible action won't feel a need to enter into power struggles with their parents. And as teenagers learn to feel good about themselves, they'll tend to become more respectful of others, including their parents.

## Responding to Misbehavior

Throughout STEP/teen we will present systematic ways to deal with misbehavior: listening skills, communication techniques, methods of discipline, and family meetings. Here, at the beginning of STEP/teen, we want to highlight some of the concepts involved and point you toward some effective strategies.

Misbehaving teens generally do not give up their negative goals and behavior overnight. It takes time and effort on parents' part. Keep in mind that parents can't make teens change; parents can change only themselves and their own behavior. In fact, when parents begin responding differently, teens often increase the amount or intensity of misbehavior. But if parents change, their teenagers will learn in time that old ways and old patterns of behavior simply don't work. It's at that point that teens have an incentive to change. If parents continue to respond to misbehavior in the same old ways, there is no incentive.

The best way to deal with negative, aggressive, or apathetic behavior is to decide how your teenager wants you to respond and then avoid that response. Break the pattern!

> If your fourteen-year-old daughter likes to annoy you by coming to the dinner table dressed up like her favorite rock idol, ignore the clothing and have a discussion about other things that interest her. If you become annoyed, she'll only continue her attention-getting behavior.

The general guideline for responding to attention seeking is to *never give attention on demand—not even for useful behavior.* Parents can instead help teens become self-motivated by *giving attention when it is not expected; they can catch them being "good."*

The major problem most parents have with teenagers is over the issue of power. Parents need to recognize that power struggles are counterproductive because they usually stimulate more teenage rebellion and more parental anger. Remember, too, that teens can fight back with apathy as well as open defiance. When you've got a hoarse voice from giving your child "marching orders," you know you haven't won a struggle.

We suggest that parents *bow out of power struggles.* Let teens experience the consequences of their misbehavior. Win their cooperation by *enlisting their help, opinions, and suggestions.* By abdicating the throne and resigning as decision maker, parents stop giving their children an authority figure worth rebelling against. By not expressing their anger in shouting matches, parents take the wind out of their teens' sails.[5] If there's no wind (anger), teens can't go anywhere. They're stuck until they discover a new, effective way to get going. Through STEP/teen, parents can show them a positive way.

The hurt and anger parents experience when their teens seek revenge can be difficult to overcome. Keep in mind that teens who seek revenge *want* to know they've hurt their parents. In these situations parents need to *consciously avoid feeling hurt.* Instead of seeking revenge in turn, *parents can work to build a relationship based on trust.* Kindness and patience will go a long way toward helping teens shed the desire for revenge.

Giving up on teens who display inadequacy will only allow them to become more discouraged. Showing them pity or disdain will increase their feelings of hopelessness. Encouragement is especially important in dealing with these teens. We suggest that parents *stop criticizing completely* and *encourage any positive efforts their teenagers make.* Discouraged teenagers need to know they can succeed and belong and that they don't have to be perfect.

It isn't appropriate for parents to tell a teen what they think the teen's goal is. This is usually seen as being judgmental.

In the following chapters we will offer numerous examples of ways you can deal with your teenager's irresponsible behavior. We will show how to develop a relationship of mutual respect, how to remove yourself from power struggles, how to decide which problems belong to you and which belong to your teenager, how to encourage your teen, and how to discipline your teen. The key to all of this remains *changing yourself and your typical responses to your teenager's misbehavior.*

# References

1. Rudolf Dreikurs and Vicki Soltz, *Children: The Challenge* (New York: Hawthorn, 1964).
2. Francis X. Walton, *Winning Teenagers over in Home and School* (Columbia, S.C.: Adlerian Child Care Books, 1980).
3. Dreikurs and Soltz, 1964.
4. Eugene Kelly and Thomas Sweeney, "Typical Faulty Goals of Adolescents: A Base for Counseling." *The School Counselor* (March 1979).
5. Dreikurs and Soltz, 1964.

# Questions

1. What are some ways parents pamper teens? How, specifically, can you avoid pampering?
2. The authors discuss equality and mutual respect. How does this apply to your relationship with your teen?
3. What are the challenges you find in balancing teenage independence and responsibility?
4. How might lessening your control reduce power struggles between you and your teenager?
5. What are some ways in which your teen seeks significance and belonging?
6. What are the four basic goals of misbehavior? What additional goals may motivate misbehavior in teenagers?
7. What are the two steps parents can use to identify the goal of teenage misbehavior? How can parents know if a teen is seeking attention? power? revenge? to display inadequacy?
8. In general, what do the authors suggest parents do in response to a teen's bid for attention? power? revenge? display of inadequacy? How can these responses help teens move toward more positive goals?

# Activity for the Week

Analyze your teen's misbehavior in order to identify one of the four basic goals described in this chapter: attention, power, revenge, or display of inadequacy. You might also look for evidence of one of the additional goals: excitement, peer acceptance, or superiority. Use the following steps:

1. Describe what your teen did.
2. Describe your feelings and exactly how you reacted.
3. Describe how the teen responded to your reaction.
4. Considering your feelings and your teen's response to your reaction, decide what you think must have been the goal of the misbehavior.

Look also for positive goals and think about ways you can encourage them.

# Personal Development Exercise

## Parenting Styles

Parenting styles can be permissive, autocratic, or democratic. Your style often relates to a specific area of your teen's life. Identify your typical behavior (how you feel and what you do) and parenting style for the following areas in your teen's life:

| | **My typical behavior** | **My parenting style** |
|---|---|---|
| Teen's homework and schoolwork | _____ | _____ |
| Teen's friends of same sex | _____ | _____ |
| Teen's friends of opposite sex | _____ | _____ |
| Teen's chores around home | _____ | _____ |
| Teen's acceptance of family values and goals | _____ | _____ |

1. Are you consistent, or do your response styles vary? If they vary, can you think of reasons why? _____

_____

_____

_____

_____

2. What has the exercise helped you learn about yourself? _____

_____

_____

_____

_____

_____

3. What would you like to change about your responses? _____

_____

_____

_____

_____

_____

4. How will you begin to change? _____

_____

_____

# The Goals of Teen Misbehavior
## The Basic Four Goals

| Teen's Faulty Belief | Goal | Example* | Parent's Feelings and Reactions | Teen's Response to Parent's Reaction |
|---|---|---|---|---|
| *...elong only when:* | | | | |
| ...m being noticed ...served. | **Attention** | Active: Clowning, minor mischief, unique dress.<br>Passive: Forgetting, neglecting chores. | Annoyed.<br><br>Remind, coax. | Temporarily stops behavior. Later repeats behavior or does something else to attract attention. |
| ...m in control or ...oving no one ...n control me. | **Power** | Active: Aggressiveness, defiance, disobedience, hostility.<br>Passive: Stubbornness, resistance. | Angry, provoked.<br><br>Fight power with power or give in. | If parent fights, teen intensifies or submits with "defiant compliance."**<br>If parent gives in, teen stops. |
| ...hurt others as I ...el hurt. I don't ...el loved or ...vable. | **Revenge** | Active: Hurtfulness, rudeness, violence, destructiveness.<br>Passive: Staring hurtfully at others. | Deeply hurt.<br><br>Retaliate. | Seeks further revenge by intensifying attack or choosing another weapon. |
| ...convince others ...t to expect any-...ing from me. I ...n unable and ...lpless. | **Display of inadequacy** | Passive only: Quitting easily, avoiding trying. Being truant or dropping out of school. Escaping through alcohol or other drugs. | Despairing, hopeless, discouraged.<br><br>Agree with teen that nothing can be done. Give up. (With drug abuse, may take teen for help.) | |

## Additional Goals***

| | | | | |
|---|---|---|---|---|
| ...reate ...citement. | **Excitement** | Avoiding routine. Showing interrest in alcohol, other drugs, promiscuous sex, daredevil sports, exciting events and activities. | Nervous, angry, hurt. What will happen next?<br><br>Is on guard. May share excitement about positive endeavors. | Resists or continues exciting misbehavior. (May become power contest.) |
| ...have wide-...read peer ...ceptance. | **Peer acceptance** | Constantly attempting to obtain widespread peer acceptance. | Approval (if parent agrees with choice of friends)<br>Worried, anxious (if disapproves of friends).<br><br>Try to get teen to seek new friends. | Resists or continues to see friends. (May become power contest.) |
| ...am the best at ...erything (or at ...ast better than ...ost). | **Superiority** | Striving for best grades, most honors. Putting down parents and others. Using superior talents against others. | Approval, inadequacy.<br><br>Praise. Attempt to put teen in his or her place. | Continues striving. Continues putting down others to defend own self-image. |

*...ost examples of misbehavior given in this column may also be used for the other goals. The only way you know the goal of your teen's misbehavior is to examine the consequences: ...how you feel when the teen misbehaves, and (2) what happens when you attempt to correct your teen.

**...een complies only enough to get by, but not to parent's satisfaction.

***These goals can exist outside or inside the parent-teen relationship. Active behavior is usually used to pursue the goals. Although excitement, peer acceptance, and superiority can be ...rsued as positive goals, examples here present ways in which they serve as negative, irresponsible goals.

# The Goals of Positive Behavior

| Teen's Belief | Goal | Behavior | How to Encourage Positive Goals |
|---|---|---|---|
| I belong and get acceptance by contributing to the group. | **Attention*** <br><br>**Involvement** <br><br>**Acceptance** | Helps. <br><br>Volunteers. <br><br>Cooperates. | Share individual and family goals in family meetings. <br><br>Recognize and let teen know you appreciate assistance and cooperation. |
| I am able to make my own decisions and be responsible for my behavior. | **Power** <br><br>**Autonomy** <br><br>**Independence** | Makes own decisions. <br><br>Works without being prodded. <br><br>Is resourceful. | Encourage decision making. <br><br>Express confidence. |
| I want to be cooperative and equal. | **Respect** <br><br>**Equal treatment of self and others** | Seeks own rights responsibly. <br><br>Treats others with respect. | Treat teen as an equal. <br><br>Respect others so teen has model of respectfulness. |
| I can decide to withdraw from conflict and settle things respectfully. | **Withdrawal from conflict** <br><br>**Positive resolution of conflict** <br><br>**Refusal to initiate unproductive conflict** <br><br>**Acceptance of others' opinions** | Ignores provocation. <br><br>Withdraws from power contest. | Avoid power clashes. <br><br>Recognize and encourage teen's maturity in resolving conflict. |

*The attention received in this case is really a by-product of the teen's desire to be involved. Helping solely for attention constitutes negative behavior.

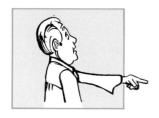

# Points to Remember

**1.** Avoid pampering. Do nothing regularly for teens that they can do for themselves.

**2.** Recognize that parents and teens are of equal human worth. Remember that mutual respect and mutual trust are the basis for an equal relationship.

**3.** Recognize that only by changing themselves can parents have the capacity to create change in relationships with teens.

**4.** Help teens to understand that independence and responsibility go together.

**5.** Stop attempting to control—stay out of power struggles. Remember that parental force invites resistance.

**6.** Develop realistic expectations that permit teens to establish their own standards.

**7.** Learn to recognize the goals of attention, power, revenge, display of inadequacy, excitement, superiority, and peer acceptance.

**8.** Keep in mind these general guidelines for responding to the four basic goals of misbehavior:

**Attention.** Never give attention on demand—not even for useful behavior.

**Power.** Bow out of power struggles. Let the teen experience the consequences of the misbehavior. Seek to win your teen's cooperation by enlisting your teen's help, opinions, and suggestions.

**Revenge.** Avoid feeling hurt. Instead of seeking revenge in turn, work to build a relationship based on trust.

**Display of inadequacy.** Stop criticizing. Encourage any positive efforts the teen makes.

**9.** Seek to create a relationship in which teens are stimulated to pursue the positive goals of cooperation, involvement, self-reliance, and responsibility.

# My Plan for Improving Relationships
(An opportunity to assess progress each week)

My specific concern:

_____

_____

My usual response:

☐ talking, lecturing      ☐ punishing, shaming

☐ complaining, nagging      ☐ giving up, forgetting because discouraged

☐ becoming angry, screaming      ☐ exerting power by removing privilege

☐ being sarcastic, attacking      ☐ other _____

My progress this week:

| | I am doing this more | I need to do this more | I am about the same | | I am doing this more | I need to do this more | I am about the same |
|---|---|---|---|---|---|---|---|
| Understanding the purpose of behavior . . . . | ☐ | ☐ | ☐ | Communicating love, positive feelings . . . . . . | ☐ | ☐ | ☐ |
| Working on developing an equal relationship based on mutual respect . . . . . . | ☐ | ☐ | ☐ | Withdrawing from conflict . . . . . . . . | ☐ | ☐ | ☐ |
| Responding to emotions more effectively . . . . . . | ☐ | ☐ | ☐ | Preventing discipline problems by giving choices . . . | ☐ | ☐ | ☐ |
| Encouraging . . . . . . . . | ☐ | ☐ | ☐ | Correcting discipline problems appropriately . . . . . | ☐ | ☐ | ☐ |
| Appreciating and giving responsibility . . . . . . . . | ☐ | ☐ | ☐ | Arranging democratic family meetings . . . . . . | ☐ | ☐ | ☐ |
| Listening . . . . . . . . . | ☐ | ☐ | ☐ | Being firm and kind . . . . | ☐ | ☐ | ☐ |
| Revealing my feelings without blaming or accusing . . . . . . . . . . . | ☐ | ☐ | ☐ | Staying out of problems that are not my problems . | ☐ | ☐ | ☐ |

I learned:

_____

_____

_____

I plan to change my behavior by:

_____

_____

_____

# CHAPTER 2

•

# *Personality Development*

Adolescence is a time when behavior and attitudes change. Outgoing, sociable teens may become silent and withdrawn. Quiet teenagers may begin to open up, and some may become very aggressive. Acting hostile or defiant can be a teenager's way of demonstrating independence and developing a distinct identity. This was the case for fourteen-year-old Alex:

> As a child Alex had been quiet and courteous—very involved in his schoolwork. He had had only a couple of friends but had gotten along well with them, and his family had considered him dependable and cooperative. Then, as a high school freshman, Alex seemed to change. Instead of being quiet and agreeable, he often argued with his parents and withdrew from family activities. Alex's parents felt he was becoming overly influenced by his friends, and they worried they were "losing" him. Alex was changing, but his parents didn't know why.

If Alex's parents had looked for the goal of his behavior, they would probably have seen that he was better rewarded for being with his peers than with his family. Alex's goal was peer acceptance. In addition, he might have felt that his parents and brother treated him like a child, not like the adult he was becoming. Alex's anger and aggressiveness may have been a result of his feeling babied. By involving his fam-

ily in power contests, Alex may have thought he could force them to recognize that he was growing up.

Understanding your relationship with your teenager can be a challenge. The fact that adolescence is a time of change makes it all the more so! It's important for parents to treat their teens not as children but as emerging adults. Doing so has a far-reaching effect on parent-teen relationships. Think for a moment about your relationships with other adults. Your closest friends probably have personality traits you wish were different. You may wish that a friend were more cooperative, less stubborn, or a better listener. But even though you feel as you do, chances are you wouldn't attempt to change your friend's behavior. After all, any attempt you make could cause ill will, and it probably wouldn't be effective anyway. Parent-teen relationships can be surprisingly similar to the relationships you have with your friends. It is just as ineffective to force a personality change on your teen as it is to force one on a friend.

If parents recognize their teenagers as persons of equal worth, they will feel less inclined to force them into "acceptable" molds. Parents, of course, will continue to guide and influence teens toward a happy, productive adult life. But guiding and influencing are not the same as molding or rejecting a teen's basic personality. Guidance encourages cooperation; rejection encourages rebellion.

I REMEMBER WHEN HE USED TO **DISAPPEAR** AT THE SIGHT OF A COMB.

Adolescence is a time of change.

Personality is the way that an individual perceives and organizes the world. It makes each person unique, different from all others. Personality consists of beliefs, goals, emotions, and attitudes that influence the way each of us behaves. Although personality makes each person one of a kind, all people behave in certain ways for certain purposes, and each person's behavior *can* be understood. A teenager's personality is not always *easily* understood, though. Traits and actions can be confusing and sometimes contradictory! For example, your daughter may be very angry if a friend cancels a date or fails to show up when expected. And yet you may notice that she often does the same thing, canceling social events without reason. This seems to make no sense at all. But what about the *goal* of her behavior? If your daughter believes it's important to be in control of her relationships or that it's important to be special, then both of her actions make sense to her.

To understand your teen's behavior, look closely at the goals your teen is pursuing.

You may need to ask yourself some simple questions to understand behavior that seems to be inconsistent: What is the purpose of the behavior? How does that behavior make sense from my teenager's point of view?

# Lifestyle: A Blueprint for Life[1]

In early childhood, humans use their creativity to develop beliefs to live by. The psychiatrist Alfred Adler called this plan a *lifestyle*. Lifestyle unifies the various aspects of an individual's personality. Each person's lifestyle is unique and includes convictions or beliefs about oneself, others, and the world. It also includes long-range goals that are chosen and in line with the person's beliefs.

Lifestyle beliefs are powerful forces in our lives, even though we may not be aware of all or any of them. Formed from limited experience in early childhood, many lifestyle beliefs contain overgeneralizations and mistaken convictions:

• I *must* be first!
• *All* people are untrustworthy.
• Life is *always* dangerous.

Obviously, these convictions are too exaggerated to be true. While such beliefs may logically be formed by young children, they aren't appropriate for adults. And yet, such biased opinions and convictions often guide the lives of adults, who live according to mistaken notions that may never have been questioned or even clearly identified. These beliefs generally don't change, unless a person has some kind of therapeutic experience, such as a traumatic event, a religious conversion, successful psychological counseling, or self-help.

Each lifestyle is a blueprint, based on a set of beliefs, that an individual *carries out* or *expresses* through actions and behaviors. A lifestyle contains both assets and liabilities. For example, people who believe "I *must* be first" may know how to win. On the other hand, the same people may hamper themselves by withdrawing or giving up, refusing to attempt anything in which they see no chance of being the best. Furthermore, such people may violate the rights of others while striving to get to the top. It's also true that some superstrivers benefit society by becoming fine surgeons or designing the best automobiles. Others may seek to bring harm to society, by committing the perfect crime or plotting the most destructive deed.

## What Influences Lifestyle?

A person's lifestyle is influenced by the following factors. Awareness of these factors can help you recognize the part you've played and continue to play in the development of your teen's lifestyle.

**Heredity.** For some time psychologists and other scientists have debated the influence of heredity and environment on personality. Is one factor more important than the other?

It is impossible to assess exactly what effect heredity has on lifestyle. Cultural perceptions play a big part in this drama. People who believe they are too short may feel inferior or may try to make up for their size. Those who have an athletic build may feel sure of themselves, while those who are overweight may doubt their value and acceptance, even though they can improve their condition. People who feel they're attractive will often have a lot of self-confidence. If, however, people consider themselves unattractive, they may tend to withdraw from their peers. Outstanding talents or abilities can also set people apart. It isn't always easy for a teenage girl to be known as a mathematical genius, or for a male ballet dancer to find acceptance wherever he goes. The extent to which any of these factors influences an emerging lifestyle will vary.

In many instances there is little a person can do about hereditary characteristics; but people can decide what they *believe* about them. Not all short people, for example, view themselves as inferior. Not all "uncoordinated" teens consider themselves unfortunate. Some who do may decide to improve their physical coordination. And some teens may actually use their limitations as a springboard for developing new strengths. For example, a teen with limited physical coordination may become an outstanding coach or sports commentator.

It is important for parents to know what to do about a limiting or exceptional trait so they can encourage teens to accept themselves as they are and move forward. One way parents can do this is by focusing on their teen's assets and strengths and minimizing liabilities.

Of course, sometimes we talk about teenage traits as if they are inherited, when in truth they aren't. Often in a household we may focus on a certain trait, such as temper, and talk about it as if it were something the teen had been born with. Have you ever said, "You're just like your mother" or "He's just like his father"?

**Family atmosphere and values.** The family atmosphere—all of the relationships between and among parents and children—provides young family members with a model of human relationships. Family atmosphere may account for some similarities in the personality characteristics of children in a family. Each child, however, responds to this atmosphere according to individual perceptions. Each person is unique!

The family atmosphere may be chaotic or orderly, rigid or flexible, competitive or cooperative, inconsistent or consistent. Family relationships—including the relationship between the parents—may be equal or unequal. Reasonable or unreasonable standards may be set by parents for their children. All of these elements influence the lifestyle development of the children in the family. Take a few minutes to study Chart 2A. It illustrates the differences between encouraging and discouraging family atmospheres and shows some of the probable results for teenagers.

Family values also have a profound effect on a child's lifestyle. A family value is anything that is important to either parent, regardless of whether both are in agreement on the issue.

There are two basic types of family values—values that family members are conscious of, and those that are outside their level of awareness. Family members are usually aware of values related to education, religion, and money. Winning and being in control are examples of values that are often less clearly defined. Even though parents or teens may not consciously know they hold certain values, these values can still powerfully influence the personalities and lifestyles of family members.

The teen years mark a point where children begin to examine family values. Often teens reject many family values outright, either temporarily or permanently. When this happens, conflict between parents and teens may be strong. Attendance at religious services, choice of dating partners, decisions about continuing education—all of these can become very sensitive areas.

MARSHA, HOW COULD YOU? YOU KNOW THAT GOING TO COLLEGE IS A FAMILY TRADITION.

But do they have to? Parents must recognize that there is no guarantee teenagers will accept all of their parents' values. In order for teenagers to develop values of their own, they must have the opportunity to examine family values for themselves. This means they have to look at what their parents believe, explore the pros and cons related to the issue, and then take, modify, or reject that value according to their *own* beliefs. These are decisions that all people have to make for themselves.

There are many areas in which parents and their teens may hold different values. For example:

Josh's parents may believe that only blue-collar work is worthwhile; Josh and his friends may believe exactly the opposite. Theresa's friends may be from racial, ethnic, or religious groups her parents don't approve of. Dad may believe that Ed's dating should be closely supervised; but Ed may have a totally different idea. Laurel's parents, who believe in the importance of physical conditioning and nutrition, may be distressed when Laurel shows little or no apparent concern for

personal health care. And it isn't easy for parents to see their daughter smoking or to worry about the physical relationship between their son and his girlfriend.

But what can parents do about differences in values that distinguish them from their teen's peers? Recognizing that teens will make their own value decisions, parents have to decide what they themselves want to accomplish as parents. If teens are to become independent and responsible, then they must learn to make decisions for themselves and accept the responsibility for those decisions. The challenge for parents is to give teenagers this responsibility. If, for example, Bertha decides to quit the swim team, she'll have to give up the benefits she's obtained through that experience. If Clem has a weight problem but insists on stuffing himself with doughnuts and potato chips, he'll have to live with the results. By making decisions and experiencing the consequences, teenagers can develop strong values for themselves.

Does this mean you can have no influence on your teen's emerging values? We think not. It's our belief—based on experience—that you can clearly communicate to your teenager what you believe and why you believe it. If this communication is to have any positive effect at all, it needs to be done in a friendly, nondominating way. Once you've stated your opinion, encourage a two-way conversation. And listen to what your teen has to say. Although you may not agree with your teen, you can show that you understand the values she or he is expressing. You can help your teen consider what might be the possible results of a decision. Through open discussion, you and your teen may reach some common ground. You, at least, will have a better idea of the decisions that are being made. And by opening up a dialogue, you may also gain a clearer understanding of your own values. (In Chapters 5 and 6 we discuss listening and problem-solving skills that can help in these discussions.)

It's important that you consider yourself a person who is available to *explore* values, not to enforce them. Unfortunately, many of us seem to live with the hope that it may be possible to impose our will on our teens. We think that if we just shout a little louder or reveal a little more of our anger or disappointment, our teens might do as we say. What actually happens is that we drive our teenagers away from any open, honest contact with us. We close down the channels of communication.

Thus, state your beliefs clearly; don't impose them. At the same time, be cautious when talking about the things your teen values. Attacking values or personalities will get you nowhere fast—in fact, a challenged teen will hold more strongly to a value. For instance, if you demand that your daughter attend religious services, you'll likely find her more determined than ever *not* to attend. If you insist there be no drinking until graduation from high school, your son will probably find drinking much more attractive. Instead, tell him why you think drinking is unwise. What you say—and the example you set—may not change your son's mind about drinking. But it *will* stay in his mind and may help him make decisions about whether to drink, when, and how much. In all cases your best approach to teens is to *trust* them and communicate that you *expect* they will make responsible decisions.

It's worth noting that one of the things we see frequently in teenagers is their sensitivity to the inconsistencies of their parents. For example, some parents who are vehemently against smoking marijuana may use or abuse alcohol. Teenagers usually

know when their parents drink to excess. What the parents seem to be saying is, "Our drug is better than your drug." Recently teens seem to be increasing their use of alcohol. They feel they're hassled less when they indulge in their parents' addiction than when they use other drugs, such as marijuana.

Just as teens must establish their own identities separate from their parents', parents must wean themselves from the feeling that they are important only if their children need them. Often parents tend to borrow significance from their teen's accomplishments. For example, a parent may say, "Maya was on the honor role" instead of saying, "Maya's really interested in school"; or "Dave scored seventeen points in the basketball game" rather than, "Dave is enjoying the basketball season." Naturally, parents are proud of their teen's accomplishments. But parents can't measure their own significance in terms of their teenager's success.

It's okay for you to be needed by your teen—the challenge is to learn *when* you're needed. Instead of dictating values, goals, and ideals, listen to your teen's goals and aspirations. Help make available opportunities for reaching the goals, and provide support where you can. Never suggest you'll be disappointed if your teen doesn't reach a goal. Above all, be available! There are many times when teens may want to talk, to get help with a problem, or to ask for advice. If you establish an open relationship, your teenager will come to you. There's a world of difference between an atmosphere in which a teen feels free to call on parents and one in which parents are constantly looking over their teen's shoulder.

Remember these key concepts:

• Communicate your values clearly.
• Act in accordance with what you say. If you believe in something, your teenager will expect to see you practice it.
• Recognize and accept the fact that teenagers will make their own value decisions.

**Role models.** By watching their parents and other significant women and men, children form ideas about the roles of adults. Teens observe how adults behave, their attitudes, and the kinds of behavior that seem to be effective in various situations. One sibling in a family may decide to model the mother, while another may choose to model the father. Some children select what they think are the best qualities of both parents. Parents have asked us, "Why does my teenager choose to pick up my negative traits and not my positive ones?" If you've wondered the same thing, ask yourself, "Is it possible my teen sees my negative traits as more effective than my positive ones?" For example, if you frequently use anger to get what you want, and your son sees how well this works, he may choose to act the same way. It's important that you be keenly aware of the behaviors and attitudes you are modeling.

**Methods of child training.** The methods of child training used by your parents influenced you as you matured. So too does the way you've raised your children affect their lifestyles and personalities. If parents are highly autocratic, a teen may be compulsive, submissive, or rebellious. In the same way, permissive parents may influence children to feel insecure or to be tremendously demanding. If in the preteen years a child has experienced methods similar to those we are recommending—for example, those taught in the STEP program—then the parent-teen relationship will be smoother. But it's never too late for parents to change their approach!

**Family constellation.** It's simply not true that parents are directly responsible for the total personality development of the child. The most significant factor in the development of any child's lifestyle is the personal meaning the child derives from her or his position in the family constellation.[2]

The family constellation refers to the psychological position of each child in a family in relation to sisters and brothers. Each child in a family is born into a different set of circumstances. Families change! The firstborn is an only child for a certain period of time until a second child is born. The second child and any children born thereafter have to deal with a more advanced sibling, unless the sibling is physically or mentally handicapped.

Siblings often feel they must compete for a place in the family.

Siblings often feel they must compete for a place in the family, and each may choose arenas in which they can be successful. For example:

> If Janella, a first child, does extremely well in school, her sister Rosa, the second child, may decide not to challenge Janella's academic supremacy. Instead, Rosa may look for recognition in some other activity, such as athletics or dramatics. In one family the first child, Michael, pushed himself to do more and become more. Adam, the second child, responded by doing less and less.

Janella, Rosa, Michael, and Adam have all become "special" by their approach to achievement.

Where family atmosphere and values may account for personality similarities among siblings, the family constellation accounts for many of the differences. The most influ-

ential person in an individual's development is the sister or brother most different from that person. This sibling, who is usually the one closest in age, becomes a major competitor. Regardless of the size of the family, the greatest competition usually occurs between the psychologically *first* and *second* children. These two, at least for a period of time, are the only children who have to establish their place in the family, and intense competition is often the result.

Competition between siblings may be expressed directly, as, for example, when two siblings vie to be the top violinist, best volleyball player, or most-favored child. Children can also compete indirectly by deciding not to choose the other's area, electing instead to develop different skills.

Some parents may unintentionally reinforce competition by praising the qualities of the child who models their values and ignoring or criticizing the child who doesn't. If parents become aware of this and stop criticizing the "different" child, that child may become more cooperative and more willing to try difficult endeavors. Building on strengths is crucial to promoting healthy development of children.

When a third child is born into a family, the second child becomes a *middle* child. Middle children often feel "squeezed out"—they haven't the special rights that go with being eldest, and they haven't the attention and privileges of the baby, either.

The *youngest* child may learn to take advantage of being the baby of the family. This child may seek a place by being charming or awkward, rebellious or agreeable, bossy or helpless—all positions from which to demand service.

The *only* child spends the formative years in a world of adults and may develop a distinctive style—perhaps bright and verbal, or quiet and serious. Living in an adult world may influence the only child to grow up prematurely. Or an only child may choose instead to stay a baby, never really "growing up."

Twins have an interesting place in the family constellation. Many parents treat twins not as two distinct individuals, but as one unit—"the twins." When this happens, each twin is likely to strive for a separate identity. Twins are usually aware of who was actually born first, and so they often form a first-child/second-child relationship.

These, then, are the five basic psychological positions in the family constellation: only, first, second, middle, and youngest. Other birth-order positions reflect one of the typical five psychological positions. The third child in a family of four may be in a dual position, such as the youngest of three and the eldest of two. When this happens, the child will exhibit complementary characteristics of both positions.

The meaning your teenager gives to her or his position in the family constellation determines what influence the constellation will have on your teen's life. There are, however, some typical characteristics of each family position, which are shown in Chart 2B. Remember that no two families are alike. Cultural expectations affect the family constellation. Sex differences too can influence perception. If in a family one sex is valued over the other, teens may respond by conforming to the expected role or by rebelling. Age differences can also affect the way children perceive their positions in the family. Because lifestyle is formed between the ages of four and six, a five-year age difference between siblings can be used as a rule of thumb to determine whether a child is in competition with an older or younger sibling, or is psychologically an only child.

In some cases an individual's psychological position will not be that child's actual position, and a switch in roles of siblings may occur. Some firstborn children cannot hold off the challenge to the position they occupy. Some lastborn children refuse to be the baby.

In a large family there may be several constellations. For example, Vernon (18), Janet (16), and Andy (15) might be one constellation. Elliot (10) and Claire (6) might make up another constellation.

In blended families, more than one child may occupy the same position.

> For example, Dad may have two children, ages fourteen and nine. Mom may have a thirteen-year-old and a fifteen-year-old. This family has two firstborns, a second, and a youngest child.

The constellation of a blended family can present special challenges to parents. In Chapter 10 we discuss ways to relate to stepchildren and new families.

It's likely that the position in the family constellation has had a significant influence on your teen's personality development. But, with so many variables, what is the point of knowing the typical characteristics of different positions? The point is that once you are aware of these characteristics and the factors that may affect them, you are in a position to make some guesses about your teen's basic outlook on life—to see the world from your teen's point of view. Understanding the family constellation will help fill in another piece of the puzzle that is your teenager.

## The Development of Self-Concept

As teenagers mature they may adopt new beliefs, establish new values, and change the way they perceive themselves. The basic structure of a person's self-concept, however, tends to remain much the same throughout adolescence. Self-concept *can* change if there is a great difference between the real and the ideal self. The ideal self is the way teens wish to be: smarter, faster, more talented, better looking, and so on. The real self is what teens believe themselves to be: "I am weak and I should be strong."

Adolescence may be a time of crisis, especially for older or highly intelligent teens. Crises often focus on the teen's role in the world of work, in social relationships, in school, and with members of the opposite sex. Sexual development and body image influence a teen's self-perception. For example, an early-developing teenage girl may feel embarrassed next to her more childish-looking friends; a late-developing boy may feel less adequate than his peers. Above all, adolescence is a time when children are discovering what it means to be an adult.

## The Relationship Between Lifestyle and Immediate Goals

Lifestyle includes long-range goals that determine how people live their lives. These goals are based on decisions made early in life. The goal of belonging—the sense of being accepted—is the basic goal of all human beings. When this goal can be achieved through useful behavior, there's no need to misbehave. But when teens think it can't be, they will seek acceptance through misbehavior. The seven goals of misbehavior—attention, power, revenge, display of inadequacy, excitement, peer acceptance, and superiority—can all come into play in this shortcut to the long-range goal of belonging.

When teens become discouraged about any long-range goal, they may decide they can't achieve their ends through useful behavior and may then opt to pursue them through misbehavior. Let's look at an example: Janice's long-range goal is to be in control, but Janice feels she can't do this through useful contributions at home or in school. She may decide to seek control over her parents and peers by misbehaving: perhaps by gaining attention, by attempting revenge when power plays fail, or by displaying inadequacy and thereby convincing others to leave her alone. She may "flirt with danger"—create excitement by trying to keep potentially dangerous things, such as sexual activity or shoplifting, under control. And she may seek peer acceptance or superiority by becoming an expert on how to cheat on an exam, how to obtain liquor, and so forth.

Teenagers who pursue such negative immediate goals do so out of a deep sense of discouragement. Teens who pursue positive immediate goals generally feel more secure in their lives—they feel their long-range goals are within reach.

## Lifestyle and the Challenges of Living

As teenagers move toward adulthood, they meet challenges that will be with them for the rest of their lives. They're faced with important decisions about sexuality, love, school, work, family, and friends.

**Sex and love.** It's important for teens to feel loved and to have the opportunity to give love. Yet many young people feel uncomfortable about expressing their love to parents and siblings. We can't overestimate the importance of creating an atmosphere in which it's natural and safe for family members to express love and to experience being loved. Such an atmosphere evolves as teens observe parents expressing love to each other, as they receive affection from their parents, and as they learn to express love back to them.

During adolescence many teens shift their emotional investment from their parents to someone of the opposite sex or to a close friend of the same sex. This is a difficult time for parents, who may feel rejected by their children. And it's a difficult time for teens. They may feel alienated from their families or immature in expressing affection. It's likely that they'll feel vulnerable in new relationships—at risk of being hurt or rejected.

Dating is one of the ways teenagers learn about love relationships and sexuality. And dating contributes to the development of personality and lifestyle. It helps teens discover not only what personal qualities they like and dislike in their companions, but also what they like and dislike in themselves. In the early phases of dating, physical characteristics and other superficial qualities are often very important to teens. But as they grow older and become more mature, most teenagers begin to look beneath the surface and to see people more completely. They pay attention to a date's values because they've learned more about their own values. In other words, dating can help teens learn about themselves as well as about the people they go out with.

The level of emotional and sexual involvement in a dating relationship is an issue for parents, their teenager, and their teen's peers. It can cause conflict between dating partners, between parents and teens, and among peers. Obviously, emotional and sexual intimacy are important matters that parents and teens need to discuss. No "expert" can tell you what to say to your teenager. We hope you started talking with your children about sex when they were young, and that you've continued to discuss the subject with them in greater depth as they have matured. Most teens respect the values of people who are honest with them and who treat them as mature individuals. Lecturing and moralizing will not be effective. If anything, they might serve to make emotional and sexual intimacy appealing—and for all the wrong reasons. It *is* effective for parents to state their beliefs and values firmly, clearly, and respectfully, and to help their teen think through the values they've presented.

**School.** School is another major factor in the ongoing development of lifestyle. At school, teenagers can learn how to set goals, how to apply themselves to tasks, and how to achieve their goals. They can learn how to become more independent and more responsible for their own work. Although teens may complain a lot about school, many enjoy their classmates, the extracurricular activities, and the stimulating classes too.

Studies have consistently shown that self-image and academic performance go hand in hand. One reinforces the other. Adolescents who come from families that emphasize the importance of education will probably have high aspirations and expectations for themselves, unless, of course, they are in rebellion against their family standards.

What's the role of parents in the education of their teenager? We believe that school is the teen's job, not the parents'. Parents may buy school materials, provide educational opportunities, and offer an attentive ear. But it's best that they not supervise homework, pry into their teenager's life at school, or set up a system of reward and punishment for grades. All of these actions will backfire sooner or later. Why? Because

through them teens learn how to please or disappoint their parents, not themselves.

**Work.** Work is an extremely important part of adult life. Adolescence can be a time for exploring the world of work. Parents can introduce their teens to a variety of occupations and encourage work opportunities. The type of work a person chooses is directly related to lifestyle. It's important, therefore, that teens be encouraged to understand their personal values and interests. Exploring interests, talents, and opportunities can lead to a satisfactory career choice. Contributing to the family by working around the home builds responsible behavior necessary for successful work performance.

**Family.** During the teenage years children become more and more emotionally independent from parents and other adults. Teens want very much to be respected and treated as equals. They're looking for people who will accept their ideas as having merit—for people who'll take them seriously! If your daughter or son wants respect and responsibility, be thankful your teen is maturing.

In the teen years children are increasingly interested in peer acceptance—even at the risk of their parents' disapproval. This shift from parents to peers is to be expected—it's a normal part of growing up.

Teens want to control their own actions. Don't we adults want to do the same for ourselves? Differences of opinion are bound to arise about such issues as borrowing the family car, household tasks, or weekend plans. But differences don't have to lead to a breakdown in communication, or hurt feelings.

## Promoting a Positive Personality in Your Teen

Some of the topics we've discussed in this chapter show that parents can influence the development of negative personality traits in their children. Since none of us wants to do that, we'll close with a list of guidelines for encouraging positive personality traits.

1. Live together in mutual respect, treating each other as equal human beings with equal rights. As you develop mutual respect, you and your teen will be more trusting and less interested in denying each other's rights.
2. Focus on positive behavior. Notice efforts, contributions, and any movement toward cooperation. Minimize mistakes.
3. Accept your teen as is, apart from your expectations. Acceptance helps teenagers feel good about themselves and accomplish goals.
4. Help your teen become responsible by giving responsibility and expecting responsible behavior.
5. Let your teen learn from the logical consequences of living. Avoid a relationship based on reward and punishment.
6. Have the courage to be imperfect.[3] Recognize your own limitations and don't place unreasonable demands on yourself. In the same way, encourage your teen to have the courage to be imperfect and to live with limitations.
7. Develop reasonable standards and expectations. More important, serve as a model by living up to them yourself as consistently as possible. Teens learn more from parents' actions than from their words.
8. Listen carefully to what your teen has to say. Make the attempt to understand your teen's feelings.
9. Take your teen seriously. Care about things that are important to your teen: clothes, social relationships, sports, art, music, school activities, books, movies, and so on.
10. Understand and appreciate the wonderful way in which your teen is developing.

## References

1. Much of the material regarding lifestyle is taken from Don Dinkmeyer, Gary D. McKay, and Don Dinkmeyer, Jr., *Parent Education Leader's Manual* (Coral Springs, Fla.: CMTI Press, 1978).
2. Walter Toman, *Family Constellation* (New York: Springer, 1961).
3. Janet Terner and W. L. Pew, *The Courage to Be Imperfect* (New York: Hawthorn, 1978).

## Questions

1. Why is it important to treat teenagers as emerging adults?

2. How can identifying the goal of misbehavior help parents understand the misbehavior?

3. What is lifestyle? How does it influence behavior and misbehavior?

4. What are the five major influences on lifestyle?

5. What is family atmosphere? How do family atmosphere and values influence lifestyle?

6. What are some specific ways you might deal with differences in values between yourself and your teen?

7. What is the family constellation? How can understanding the family constellation help you in your relationship with your teen?

8. The authors state that when the long-range goal of belonging can't be achieved through useful behavior, teens may seek significance through one of the seven immediate goals. Explain what this means.

9. "School is the teen's job, not the parents'." What does this mean? How do you feel about it?

## Activity for the Week

1. Study Chart 2B. Compare the characteristics for each position in the family constellation with those of your children. How is each child like and unlike the typical child in the same situation?

2. Plan specific ways you can begin to encourage the positive traits in your teen and other children.

# Personal Development Exercise

## Family Dynamics Survey

You have been reading about the effect family atmosphere and the family constellation have on the formation of your teen's lifestyle. This exercise is designed to help you discover the influence patterns in your family and find ways to encourage positive personality development.

First describe the personality traits of yourself and your spouse. (If you are divorced, describe the traits of your ex-spouse. If you are remarried, describe your children's natural parent.) Describe both negative and positive traits.

**My Spouse**                                           **Me**

_____          _____

_____          _____

_____          _____

_____          _____

Now, list each one of your children from oldest to youngest. Choose adjectives that describe their personality traits.

Name: _____ _____ _____ _____

Personality
    traits: _____ _____ _____ _____

_____ _____ _____ _____

_____ _____ _____ _____

_____ _____ _____ _____

_____ _____ _____ _____

Now answer the following questions. Review the concepts in Chapter 2.

1. How are you and your spouse alike? (Again, consider your children's natural parent.)_____

_____

_____

_____

_____

2. How are you and your spouse different? _____

_____

_____

_____

_____

*Continued on next page.*

3. How are your children alike?*  _____

_____

_____

_____

_____

4. How are your children different? _____

_____

_____

_____

5. Considering the characteristics you, your spouse, and your children have in common, what do you think some of your family values might be? _____

_____

_____

_____

6. The differences in the personalities of your children show the areas of competition between them. How do you unintentionally reinforce this competition? _____

_____

_____

_____

7. How will you recognize each child as a unique individual? Make a specific commitment. _____

_____

_____

_____

_____

*If you have an only child, or psychologically only children, answer questions 3-6 in this way: Consider the child in relationship to you and your spouse. Which parent is the child most like? How is the child different from each parent? Consider the child's friends. How is the child like and different from them? How do you unintentionally reinforce competition between your child, yourself, and your spouse?

# Some Discouraging and Encouraging Family Atmospheres

| Discouraging Family Atmospheres | Probable Results for Teen | Encouraging Family Atmospheres | Probable Results for Teen |
|---|---|---|---|
| Overprotection | Relies on others rather than self. | Independence | Becomes self-reliant. |
| Overindulgence | Becomes irresponsible. | Respect | Becomes responsible. |
| Rejection | Feels discouraged about self-worth. | Acceptance | Develops positive self-worth. |
| Authoritarian | Depends on power and works to defeat authority, or becomes dependent. | Equality | Appreciates self and others. Believes all people are worthwhile. |
| Permissive | Is unconcerned about others' rights. | | |
| Excessive standards | Is discouraged about own ability; lacks self-confidence. | Realistic standards | Sets realistic, attainable goals. Believes in own ability. |
| Pity | Feels sorry for self. | Confidence | Believes in own power to handle life. |
| Inconsistent discipline | Feels a lack of trust; believes life is unfair. | Consistent discipline | Trusts life and self. |
| Discouragement | Becomes cynical, pessimistic. | Encouragement | Becomes optimistic about possibilities in life. |
| Denial of feelings | Learns to cover up or avoid feelings. | Expression of feelings | Is not afraid of own or others' feelings. |
| Competition | Becomes anxious, strives to be the most or become the "best worst." Is afraid to try unless success guaranteed. | Cooperation | Develops social interest. Can participate in give-and-take of life. Will attempt new experiences, and accept consequences. |

# Typical Characteristics of Different Positions in the Family Constellation*

The following characteristics will not apply to *all* children in *every* family. *Typical* characteristics, however, can be identified.

| Only Child | First Child | Second Child | Middle Child of Three[1] | Youngest Child |
|---|---|---|---|---|
| Pampered and spoiled. | Is only child for period of time; used to being center of attention. | Never has parents' undivided attention. | Has neither rights of oldest nor privileges of youngest. Feels life is unfair. | Behaves like only child. Feels everyone bigger and more capable. Expects others to do things, make decisions, take responsibility. |
| Feels incompetent because adults are more capable. | Believes must gain and hold superiority over other children. Being right, controlling often important. | Always has sibling ahead who's more advanced. | Feels unloved, left out, "squeezed." | |
| Is center of attention; often enjoys position. May feel special. | | Acts as if in race, trying to catch up or overtake first child. If first child is "good," second may become "bad." Develops abilities first child doesn't exhibit. If first child successful, may feel uncertain of self and abilities. | Feels doesn't have place in family. | Feels smallest and weakest. May not be taken seriously. |
| Self-centered. | May respond to birth of second child by feeling unloved and neglected. Strives to keep or regain parents' attention through conformity. If this fails, chooses to misbehave. | | Becomes discouraged and "problem child" or elevates self by pushing down other siblings. | Becomes boss of family in getting service and own way. |
| Relies on service from others rather than own efforts. | | | Is adaptable. Learns to deal with both oldest and youngest sibling. | Develops feelings of inferiority or becomes "speeder" and overtakes older siblings. |
| Feels unfairly treated when doesn't get own way. May refuse to cooperate. | | May be rebel. Often doesn't like position. | | Remains "The Baby." Places others in service. |
| Plays "divide and conquer" to get own way. | May develop competent, responsible behavior or become very discouraged. | Feels "squeezed" if third child is born. May push down other siblings. | | If youngest of three, often allies with oldest child against middle child. |
| May have poor peer relations as child but better relations as adult.[2] | Sometimes strives to protect and help others. | | | |
| Pleases others only when wants to. | Strives to please. | | | |
| Creative.[3] | | | | |
| May have striving characteristics of oldest and inadequacy feelings and demands of youngest. | | | | |

NOTES: 1. The middle child of three is usually different from the middle child of a large family. The middle children of large families are often less competitive, as parents don't have as much time to give each child and so the children learn to cooperate to get what they want. 2. Only children usually want to be adults, and so don't relate to peers very well. When they become adults, they often believe they've finally "made it" and can now relate better to adults as peers. 3. During their formative years, only children live primarily in the world of adults. They must learn how to operate in the big people's world as well as how to entertain themselves. Thus they often become very creative in their endeavors.

*Adapted from Don Dinkmeyer, Gary D. McKay, and Don Dinkmeyer, Jr., *Parent Education Leader's Manual* (Coral Springs, Fla.: CMTI Press, 1978).

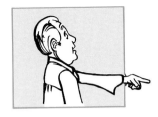

# Points to Remember

**1.** Personality is the unique way each person perceives and organizes the world.

**2.** Lifestyle is the unifying aspect of personality.

**3.** Lifestyle is a "blueprint," or plan for living, that is formed early in life.

**4.** Lifestyle contains convictions about self, others, and the world, as well as long-range goals based upon these convictions.

**5.** Lifestyle contains both assets and liabilities.

**6.** The following factors influence lifestyle:

• heredity
• family atmosphere and values
• role models
• methods of child training
• family constellation

**7.** Teens will decide whether to accept or reject family values.

**8.** Value differences are best handled by open discussions in which parents communicate their values and listen seriously to their teen's point of view.

**9.** The family constellation refers to the psychological position of each child in the family in relation to the siblings. One's position does not cause certain traits, but provides an influence.

**10.** Competition among siblings for a place in the family influences personality traits.

**11.** A teen may choose to express long-range or life goals through any of the immediate goals: attention, power, revenge, display of inadequacy, excitement, peer acceptance, and superiority.

**12.** As teens move toward adulthood, they meet challenges in the areas of sex and love, school, work, and family and peer acceptance.

**13.** Parents can follow these guidelines to encourage their teen's positive personality traits:

• Live together in mutual respect.
• Focus on the positive.
• Accept your teen as is.
• Give responsibility and expect responsible behavior.
• Let your teen learn from the logical consequences of living.
• Have and communicate the courage to be imperfect.
• Develop reasonable standards and expectations.
• Listen carefully.
• Care about things that are important to your teen.
• Appreciate the wonderful way in which your teen is developing.

# My Plan for Improving Relationships
(An opportunity to assess progress each week)

My specific concern:

_____

_____

My usual response:

- ☐ talking, lecturing
- ☐ complaining, nagging
- ☐ becoming angry, screaming
- ☐ being sarcastic, attacking

- ☐ punishing, shaming
- ☐ giving up, forgetting because discouraged
- ☐ exerting power by removing privilege
- ☐ other _____

My progress this week:

| | I am doing this more | I need to do this more | I am about the same | | I am doing this more | I need to do this more | I am about the same |
|---|---|---|---|---|---|---|---|
| Understanding the purpose of behavior | ☐ | ☐ | ☐ | Communicating love, positive feelings | ☐ | ☐ | ☐ |
| Working on developing an equal relationship based on mutual respect | ☐ | ☐ | ☐ | Withdrawing from conflict | ☐ | ☐ | ☐ |
| Responding to emotions more effectively | ☐ | ☐ | ☐ | Preventing discipline problems by giving choices | ☐ | ☐ | ☐ |
| Encouraging | ☐ | ☐ | ☐ | Correcting discipline problems appropriately | ☐ | ☐ | ☐ |
| Appreciating and giving responsibility | ☐ | ☐ | ☐ | Arranging democratic family meetings | ☐ | ☐ | ☐ |
| Listening | ☐ | ☐ | ☐ | Being firm and kind | ☐ | ☐ | ☐ |
| Revealing my feelings without blaming or accusing | ☐ | ☐ | ☐ | Staying out of problems that are not my problems | ☐ | ☐ | ☐ |

I learned:

_____

_____

_____

I plan to change my behavior by:

_____

_____

_____

# CHAPTER 3

●

# *Emotions: A Source of Support or Frustration?*

A major principle of STEP/teen is that people *choose* how they behave. Parents and teens alike decide for themselves what they will do. By now you've discovered that behavior serves a purpose. We set for ourselves long-range and short-range goals that we believe will gain us a place in the world. But what about emotions, those feelings like love, anger, fear, and contentment, that seem to descend upon us from some outside force or to well up from the depths of our soul? Are we responsible for our feelings too? Do we really decide how we feel? To answer, carry out the following exercise. Before beginning, read through directions 1-4.

1. Lie down, or relax in a comfortable chair.
2. Close your eyes and visualize a pleasant scene from your past. Let yourself actually be part of the scene: notice how you and others look, hear what is being said, and look at facial expressions. Be aware of how you're feeling. Stay with your pleasant scene for a while, experiencing those feelings.
3. After about a minute or so, still with your eyes closed, leave your pleasant scene and switch to an unpleasant scene from your past. As before, let yourself fully experience this new scene. Hear what is being said, and note facial expressions and body language. How do you feel? Stay with your unpleasant scene for a while and note the feelings it evokes.

4. After about a minute or so, keeping your eyes closed, return to your pleasant scene and relish those feelings again for a short while.[1]

What did you discover about controlling your own emotions? Did you have difficulty moving from one scene to another? Some people have problems leaving the pleasant scene and moving to the unpleasant one. Others find it hard to leave the unpleasant scene. Some have little difficulty moving back and forth. What you experienced depends on how you look at life.

Through this exercise you can see that people *do* create their own emotions, just by what they tell themselves about their experiences. Your beliefs determine how you feel. In the first scene, you told yourself you were having a pleasant time, and so you experienced pleasant feelings. In the second scene, you told yourself the scene was unpleasant, so you experienced unpleasant feelings. Later in the chapter we'll examine exactly how we talk ourselves into unpleasant feelings and how we can talk ourselves out of them. Right now, though, we want to explore emotions as they affect your relationship with your teen.

## Taking Responsibility for Your Emotions

People, regardless of age, do all kinds of things to avoid taking responsibility for their behavior or their feelings. At some time we've all said, "That makes me feel . . ." Whatever "that" refers to, a statement like this puts us in a passive role, as if we have no control over ourselves. All we can do is respond. Likewise, we've all been known to say, "I lost my temper." Is temper something we carry around in our pockets—something that can get lost like a set of keys? Rudolf Dreikurs, a noted Adlerian psychiatrist, pointed out that we don't lose our tempers, "we throw them away." How right this is!

When you catch yourself using a passive phrase, take responsibility. For example:

> Instead of saying, "That made me feel angry," say "I felt angry," "I *chose* to feel angry," or "I *decided* to get angry." When you hear your teenager use passive phrases, don't accept them. Say, "You know, when you say, 'Alan made me feel sad,' you're giving him power over your feelings. Do you really want to do that?" Teens need to understand that people are responsible for their own feelings.

Emotions, like behavior, serve a purpose. In general, emotions give us the energy to act on our beliefs and goals.[2] For instance, if we believe that people can be trusted and are mostly friendly, we will create positive emotions to provide the "fuel" to move us close to people. If, however, we believe people can't be trusted and are only looking out for themselves, we'll create negative feelings so that we can keep some distance from them. We may generate feelings of anger, coolness, or hostility just to keep people at a "safe" distance.

We use emotions to give meaning to life. If there were no love, no caring, and no warmth in the world, what a miserable place it would be! But what about negative emotions? Do we also need them? Mild, unpleasant feelings like frustration or low-level anxiety can spur us on to action—they can help us take care of discomfort or dissatisfaction. But deep, powerful emotions, like anger, guilt, hurt, self-pity, and high-level anxiety, are self-defeating. They can actually block personal growth and harm people and relationships. For example, suppose you get angry when your daughter stays on the telephone too long. You really blow your top! She gets angry in return and insults you. Both of you end up using anger to control and punish each other, thus preventing any cooperation and damaging your relationship. We think there's a better way to deal with anger and other negative feelings—better for you and for your teenager.

## Avoiding Emotional Traps

When teens become discouraged, they may misbehave by using their emotions to trap parents into certain kinds of responses. Take crying for example—tears are powerful! There is, of course, crying that is not manipulative, as in grief or hurt. Emotions aren't always used to trap other people. But most crying is "water power" because children, teens, and adults can use tears to gain control.[3] A teen's angry crying may invite parents to back off, give in, or charge into battle. Each of these reactions is self-defeating because the parents have *thrown away* their power. Frustrated or sad crying can invite parents to feel sorry for their teen, or to feel guilty or discouraged.

Emotional traps can take many forms, but here we will focus on those that correspond to the seven goals of misbehavior. For example, teenagers may cry and pout to get attention, cry and shout to fuel a power contest, cry and attack to get revenge, cry and mope to display inadequacy, cry to stir up excitement, cry to get the support of peers, or cry to prove a point (to gain superiority).

The most effective way to avoid emotional traps is to let teens be responsible for their own feelings. Learn *not* to respond in the usual ways. There will be times, of course, when parents have to listen, understand, and help their teenagers work through difficult problems. Remember, children don't always use their emotions to lay traps. (Chapters 5 and 6 will deal with these situations.) But even when parents and teen work together to resolve the teenager's hurt, anxious, or angry feelings, the responsibility for those feelings rests with the teen.

While encouraging teens to be responsible for their feelings, parents need to keep an eye on their own behavior. It takes at least two to tangle! Just as your teen can invite you to feel angry or annoyed, you also can invite your teen to feel a certain way. You can contribute to your child's feelings—both positive and negative—even though, in the final analysis, you are each responsible for your own feelings.

## Typical Negative Emotions of Teenagers

Study Chart 3A to discover the purpose of each emotion listed and the steps you can take to avoid emotional traps. In later chapters we'll present some ideas for dealing with these emotions in situations where teens are not using them to manipulate.

**Anger.** When people are angry, it's hard to talk to them because they have little or no interest in cooperating. They're busy putting their energy into getting what they want. This is why we suggest (unless your relationship with your teen is mostly positive) that you back out of power contests. Save your words for a quieter time when the two of you aren't in conflict.

**Apathy.** Teens who use apathy to defeat adults need a lot of encouragement. Their "I don't care" attitude says they don't believe they're in control of their lives. Getting teens involved in decision making and family life can show them that they do count. Teenagers can make their own decisions about such things as clothing, electives to take in school, and career planning. They can participate in family decisions concerning chores, outings, major purchases, and vacations. Parents can ask their teenagers to do things for the family, such as shopping or researching an appliance the family is thinking of buying. They can discuss current political and social issues and ask their teen's opinion.[4] While contributing and participating are important for *all* teens, they're especially important for teens who use apathy to gain power.

**Boredom.** "I'm bored." "There's never anything to do around here!" "School is so boring." What parent hasn't heard words like these from a teenage son or daughter? Boredom happens a lot, with teens, younger children, and even adults. We believe the parent's role is to provide guidance while a teenager explores ways to make life more interesting. By guidance we don't mean

that parents tell their teen what to do. Teenagers, like their parents, have the responsibility for making their own lives interesting and fulfilling. A parent might simply say, "There are lots of things you could do that you'd find interesting. Why don't you think about it for a while? I'm sure you'll come up with something."

Depression isn't a very effective way to cope, but it does give a person some time out from life.

**Sadness and depression.** When life doesn't go the way we want it to, we can choose to become sad or depressed. Depression isn't a very effective way to cope, but it does give a person some "time out" from life. Depression can best be understood as anger that people turn inward on themselves. Dreikurs referred to some types of depression as "silent temper tantrums." When parents refuse to be manipulated by their teenager's sadness or depression, the depression often loses its value. The teen sees that it isn't an effective way to behave.

We must point out, however, that persistent depression should not be treated in the same way as the occasional kind just described. Some forms of depression are actually brought on by physical illness. The use of drugs can induce depression. And deep depression, whatever its cause, will not go away by itself. Teenage suicide is increasing at an alarming rate, and parents need to know how to tell when their teen is deeply depressed. Psychiatrist Mary Giffin, founder of the Adolescent Suicide Project in the Chicago area, describes eight warning signals of depression in her *Depression Alert List:*[5]

1. *Declining school performance, coupled with expressions of apathy and helplessness.* This might include a sudden loss of interest in those areas—sports, hobbies, organizations—that had previously been a source of much enthusiasm and pleasure for the person.
2. *The recent loss of a loved one, particularly someone in the family.*
3. *An abrupt change in behavior, ranging from some degree of hyperactivity to social isolation.* This might include a teenager's sudden reckless driving or repeated attempts to run away.
4. *A marked change in sleeping or eating habits,* such as excessive sleepiness, loss of appetite.
5. *Familial disruptions,* such as divorce, or other traumatic changes within the home, such as a life-threatening illness of a family member, a move to a new location, loss of employment by one or both parents, and so forth.
6. *Evidence that the teenager is being disparaged in the home.* Friends and teachers should take note when it becomes apparent that a teenager is not communicating with the family, that he or she is feeling alienated.
7. *An absence of normal social contacts.* This might include the teenager's desire to spend excessive amounts of time alone; a noticeable withdrawal from family and close friends.
8. *Impulsiveness.* Erratic behavior not appropriate to a given situation nor characteristic of the teenager.

In addition to these signals, Giffin points out that teens who give away cherished belongings may be planning suicide. If they seem to be obsessed with death and dying, this too could be a warning signal. For example, a person who constantly listens to sad music or to the same sad tune may be deeply depressed.

It is a popular myth that if people talk about committing suicide, they aren't likely to do so. This isn't necessarily true. Most people who have committed suicide talked about doing so beforehand.

What can parents do if they suspect their teen is deeply depressed and possibly contemplating suicide? Of course, seek professional help. Many parents are reluctant to seek psychological counseling because they believe it's their fault that their teen is depressed or because they worry about what other people might think. At a time like this it's important to focus on the essential—your teen needs help! A professional counselor usually involves the whole family in the process. That's a positive sign because deeply depressed teens need family support. A school counselor, member of the clergy, hospital, or local referral service can help guide parents to a professional counselor. In an emergency or crisis situation, check the local phone directory under *crisis intervention* or *suicide prevention,* or call the police emergency number.

In addition to seeking professional guidance, here are some things Giffin suggests parents can do to help a depressed teen.[6]

- Discuss suicide. If there's been a suicide in the news, neighborhood, or family, discuss it frankly and openly.
- Recognize that an unsuccessful attempt at suicide does *not* mean that there won't be other attempts.
- Listen.

- Show love and give encouragement.
- Keep communication lines open. If you don't communicate well with your teen, find someone who does. Perhaps it's another member of the immediate family—the teen's brother or sister, for example—an uncle or an aunt, or an adult the teen is close to. That person needs to give the teen a chance to discuss the troubled feelings.
- Realize that a suicidal teen feels worthless. The teen needs to feel worthwhile and loved. Look for ways to demonstrate this. (Chapter 4 discusses encouragement and gives specific ways to show teens they are worthwhile.)

**Guilt.** Guilt feelings serve a special purpose. Society teaches us that if we do wrong, we should feel guilty—that guilt is necessary to make us change our ways. Actually, the opposite is true. When we feel guilty we usually don't change. The real purpose of guilt is to allow us to evade responsibility for changing. By choosing to feel guilty, we've paid the price for our "crime." Again we turn to the words of Rudolf Dreikurs to summarize the meaning of guilt feelings: "Guilt feelings are good intentions we really don't have!" Those words may surprise some parents, but our own experience has proved them true.

Since guilt is a negative emotion that doesn't promote change, it's important to try *not* to induce guilt feelings in your teenager. Equally important is to avoid regularly accepting your teen's good intentions or apologies, when these are offered without a willingness to change. Apologies are often expressions of guilt feelings. Our tendency to accept the words "I'm sorry" lets a person off the hook. When teens apologize, parents can respectfully ask what they're willing to do to avoid the same problem in the future. When *you* make a mistake, you can model responsible apologies by follow-

ing University of Oregon professor Ray Lowe's advice: Say, "I'm sorry I _____ and I'm *working* on _____" or, "From now on I'll _____."

Fearful or anxious teens lack self-confidence.

**Fear and anxiety.** Fearful or anxious teens lack self-confidence. Self-confidence doesn't grow overnight, but parents can help teens develop confidence and courage. One way to do this is by reminding teens of times when they handled a similar situation successfully. Parents might also ask them to remember a time when they felt self-confident and to recall that memory each time they feel anxious. Discussing the possibility of failure, and exploring what failure might mean in a particular instance, will serve to help teens put their anxiety into perspective. Parents might also help teens examine alternative opportunities to succeed.

**Stress.** Stress, like emotions, is not something imposed from the environment. Many people lead busy lives without experiencing stress. That's because stress comes from our response to situations. If we tell ourselves that life is too much for us, our bodies will find ways to prove us right—

perhaps through stomach problems, headaches, high blood pressure, or nervous tics.

Stress involves emotions such as anger and anxiety. If parents and teens learn to deal with those emotions, then they should be able to avoid suffering from stress. It's important for you to help your teen set priorities, and, above all, learn to relax.

# Your Beliefs Influence Your Emotions

Whether they're your own feelings or your teen's, negative emotions are tough to deal with. In Chapter 1 you learned that to stop reinforcing your teen's goal of attention, power, revenge, or display of inadequacy, you need to change the way you respond to the misbehavior. You must change your emotional response of annoyance, anger, hurt, or despair because these emotions fan the flames of teenage misbehavior. Teenagers expect parents to respond in these ways, and parents' typical responses let teens know their purpose has been achieved.

The question that parents must ask themselves is this: Just how can I stop my negative emotions? To discover this, we need to examine how people create these emotions. Then we can look at ways to stop creating them. Notice that we said *stop,* not repress or control. Trying to swallow, repress, deny, or control a negative emotion like anger does not work. You end up fighting with yourself, a battle usually lost. *Stopping* an emotion is a very different process, which we want to describe in detail.

Albert Ellis and Robert A. Harper have offered a clear explanation of how we talk ourselves into negative feelings.[7] They discuss the process by using the letters **A, B,** and **C. A** is the *activating* event—something that happens in our lives. **B** is our *belief* about **A. C** is the emotional *consequence* of our belief about the activating event.

Most people think that **A** causes **C**; that an event causes a specific emotional response. For example, let's suppose that your teenage son tells you he can't stand listening to you and thinks your advice is lousy. He rejects you and you feel sorry for yourself. Did the *activating* event (being rejected) actually cause the emotional *consequence* (your self-pity)? We know that we create our own emotions, so we can't conclude that you feel sorry for yourself because your teen rejected you. Remember, he can't *make* you feel that way. We need to look instead at **B**, your *belief* about **A**. Very probably you told yourself something like this when your son rejected you: "It's *terrible* to be rejected! I *can't stand* being rejected! I *should* be loved! I'm *worthless* because my son doesn't love me!"

Naturally, if you told yourself these things, you'd feel sorry for yourself and perhaps depressed! Feeling this way would prevent you from relating well with your son, and it might leave you vulnerable to manipulation.

He'd know that whenever he rejected you, he could count on your feeling sorry for yourself and giving in to his wishes. Even if you decided to fight back, he'd get what he was after: a negative response from you.

Suppose you told yourself something different when your teenage son rejected you? How would you feel if you told yourself: "Being rejected is very *frustrating* and *unfortunate*, but it's *not* terrible! I *can stand* it even though I *don't like* it. I really *want* to be loved, but I'm still a worthwhile person even if my son rejects me. Besides, I know he's acting out of *his own discouragement*. I *won't help* him or me by feeling sorry for myself, so instead I'll *remain firm and kind*."

If you told yourself these other things, you'd probably feel disappointed about being rejected, perhaps frustrated, but not sorry for yourself or depressed. In addition you'd allow yourself to sense your teen's discouragement and to decide how you'd like to act. Backed by these beliefs, you wouldn't be in a position to be manipulated.

Ellis explains that we cause problems for ourselves by holding irrational beliefs about unpleasant things that occur in our lives. We make ourselves upset because we mistakenly think of preferences as needs; we strongly *prefer* something to happen (or not happen), and therefore we think it *should* (or should not) happen. In all, Ellis lists four elements of an irrational belief.[8] We call them the four Cs: *catastrophizing, can't-stand-it-itis, commanding,* and *condemning.*

Using the example of your son rejecting you, we can map the four Cs as follows:

*Catastrophizing:* It's *terrible* to be rejected!

*Can't-stand-it-itis:* I *can't stand* being rejected!

*Commanding:* I *should* be loved!

*Condemning:* I'm *worthless* because my son doesn't love me!

**Catastrophizing.** By viewing the world with irrational beliefs, we actually make ourselves unhappy and often ineffective in getting along with others. We're going to be upset when things don't go the way we think they should, and we're bound to see disappointments as *catastrophes,* instead of seeing them simply as frustrating, unfortunate, or inconvenient events.

**Can't-stand-it-itis.** If we believe we have a catastrophe on our hands, we're likely to tell ourselves that we *can't stand* it. But by saying this, we're proclaiming ourselves to be weak, powerless to handle a disappointment.

**Commanding.** When absolute words such as *should, ought, must,* need, have to, always,* and *never* appear in our conversations or thoughts, we are translating our preferences into requirements. To believe things *should* or *must* turn out to our liking is to make unreasonable demands on life—we're *commanding* reality to be as we want it, rather than recognizing that reality does not conform to our wishes.

**Condemning.** When problems in our relationships with our teens have us overwrought, we can easily slip into condemning. "I'm *worthless* because my son

---

*The "conditional must" is an exception to this statement. For example, the parent who says "*If* I'm going to improve my relationship with my daughter, I *must* work to see things from her point of view" is not stating an absolute. The word *if* tells that this parent does not see improving the relationship as absolutely necessary. There is, however, no "conditional should." Even when used with a qualifier, *should* denotes a moral standard and invites feelings of guilt and denotes failure.

doesn't love me." "He's *horrible* and *ungrateful*." By looking at disappointments as disappointments and not as catastrophes, we'll be able to see that we, and our teens as well, are not worthless or bad. We can learn to evaluate people's *behavior,* and not the people themselves.

There are numerous irrational beliefs and numerous problem situations between parents and teens. There are, however, some common irrationalities about parenting. As you read through this short list, ask yourself if you hold any of these beliefs:

- To be a good parent I *must* (should) have the approval of everyone in the community.
- I *should* (must) be competent in all aspects of parenting.
- Things *should* turn out the way I want them to.
- People are victims of circumstances and *should not* try to change what can't be changed.
- I *should* take the responsibility for my teenager's behavior. If I were a more effective parent, my teen would *always* be well behaved.

No one needs to go through life at the mercy of irrational beliefs. Rational beliefs exist—they are alive and well in STEP/teen! How can you go about developing rational beliefs? First, reevaluate your view of the activating event (**A**), by concentrating on changing your belief (**B**). Recognize that disappointments in your relationship with your teen are simply that—disappointments. They aren't catastrophes, but frustrating, unfortunate, or inconvenient problems. Realize that you *do* have the power to handle such problems. Ellis calls this "I'll-never-like-it-but-I-can-stand-it-itis"! Admit to yourself that just because you really want things to go well, there's no reason why they should or must.

Taking our example again, we can show how the four Cs are countered:

*Anti-catastrophizing:* It's *frustrating, unfortunate,* and *inconvenient* to be rejected, but it's *not terrible.*

*Anti-can't-stand-it-itis:* I *can stand* it, even though I *don't like* it.

*Anti-commanding:* I *really want* to be loved. (*translating a command into a preference*)

*Anti-condemning:* But I'm still a *worthwhile* person if you don't love me.

Beyond countering the four Cs, we can work to create positive emotions, such as empathy and determination:

*Understanding and action statements:* I know you're *discouraged* and I'd like *to help.* I'll remain *firm and kind.*

By using and believing phrases such as "If I could choose," "I'd prefer," "I want," and "It would be better if," we can express preferences rather than commands. More important, we can think more rationally.

## Your Emotions and Your Teen's Goals of Misbehavior

Chart 3B illustrates both irrational and rational responses to the goals of attention, power, revenge, and display of inadequacy. (Responses to the goals of excitement, peer acceptance, and superiority are not given because teens usually use these goals to achieve the four others. Parents' responses to these goals will be similar to their responses to the four basic goals.) The chart includes examples of irrational and rational beliefs, purposes generated by the beliefs, and emotional and behavioral consequences of the beliefs and purposes.[9] Take time to study the chart and the following comments.

**Responding to the goal of attention.**
Suppose your daughter is trying to get your attention by distracting you. An irrational belief about attention getting—"She *should* stop distracting me!"—is strong enough to produce annoyance, but it doesn't lead to catastrophizing, can't-stand-it-itis, or condemning. If you command your daughter to stop distracting you, you become annoyed. The annoyance motivates you to step forward and demand that she stop misbehaving. But take a closer look at this process. Why *should* your daughter stop what she's doing? After all, the behavior works—you're providing the sought-after attention!

A more rational belief about attention getting—"I *wish* she'd stop distracting me"—eliminates your annoyance and your tendency to remind and coax. If you *prefer* rather than *require* that your daughter stop distracting you, your own behavior will have a new purpose: helping her become self-reliant. With a new sense of determination you'll be able to choose new ways of be-having that won't reinforce the same old patterns of attention getting.

**Responding to the goal of power.** When teens display power, we often feel angry because we believe their behavior is a challenge to our position and authority. If we choose to show who's boss, the purpose of our anger is to gain control. If we decide to give in, we use anger to get even for losing the battle. Using the four Cs of irrational thinking, let's examine a parent's irrational belief about a teen's bid for power:

*Catastrophizing:* It's *awful* when you try to take control!

*Can't-stand-it-itis:* I just *can't stand* it!

*Commanding:* I *have* to be in control and you must obey me . . .

*Condemning:* or I'm a *bad* parent and a *worthless* person!

What will happen when the parent changes to a rational belief about power? The parent will win the teen's cooperation! Rational thinking doesn't lead to fighting *or* giving in. Instead of giving control, it gives determination. And it allows parents to empathize with teens who are making themselves unhappy by struggling for power. Let's see how rational thinking works:

*Anti-catastrophizing:* While it's *frustrating* when you challenge me, it's *not awful* . . .

*Anti-can't-stand-it-itis:* And I *can stand* it.

*Anti-commanding:* I'd *really like* to control you, but I can't and it's *discouraging* to both of us.

*Anti-condemning:* I'm still a *worthwhile* parent and person.

*Understanding and action statements:* I'm going to *stop fighting* or *giving in* and will establish *mutual respect.* I'm *sorry* you've decided that power is the only way to feel important, and I'll *help* you change your belief.

**Responding to the goal of revenge.**
Many people have trouble understanding how they create their own hurt. Aren't other people responsible? We believe not. Hurt, like other emotions, is a person's own responsibility. Actually, hurt gives parents permission to get back at revengeful teens.

Hurt stems from an irrational belief in which one first condemns oneself for being attacked—"I *must* be *totally worthless* or you wouldn't attack me!"—and then immediately covers up the hurt, replacing it with anger, and condemns the teen—"How *awful* for you to attack me! You're *horrible!*" Why does the parent carry out a counterattack? Because even though anger is uncomfortable, for many people it's still more comfortable to condemn someone else than to engage in self-condemnation.[10] Here is how an irrational belief influences a parent's response to revenge-seeking behavior:

*Catastrophizing:* You attacked me and it's *terrible!*

*Condemning:* I *must* be *totally worthless* or you wouldn't attack me!

*Catastrophizing:* Hey, wait a minute—why am I blaming myself? I've been fair to you. How *awful* for you to attack me!

*Can't-stand-it-itis:* I *can't stand* it!

*Commanding:* You *must not* treat me that way!

*Condemning:* You're *horrible!* I'll fix you!

To leave behind irrational responses to revengeful behavior, we must realize that we don't necessarily deserve the attack. A revenge-seeking teen is operating out of his or her own mistaken beliefs. When we understand this, we free ourselves to feel regret, empathy, and determination to look for ways to help. A rational response to revengeful behavior looks like this:

*Anti-catastrophizing:* Although you treated me *unfairly,* it's *not the end of our relationship.*

*Anti-can't-stand-it-itis:* I *can take* it.

*Anti-commanding:* I *really don't like* it . . .

*Anti-condemning:* but I'm still *okay.*

*Anti-catastrophizing:* Your behavior is *frustrating* and *unfortunate* . . .

*Anti-condemning:* because I *do love* you and want to get along with you. I know you're *not* a *horrible* person, only *very discouraged.*

*Understanding and action statements:* You're *unhappy* and I know how *tough* this must be for you. I'm going to *help* you feel better about yourself and our relationship.

**Responding to the goal of display of in-adequacy.** A parent whose teen displays inadequacy will feel despair *if that parent has an irrational belief about inadequacy.* Despair gives parents permission to give up on their teens. Parents think they can't help, and so they view *themselves* as inadequate. But then, to cover up feelings of inadequacy, parents begin viewing the *teen* as inadequate. This allows parents to get off the hook. Let's look at the elements of this irrational belief:

*Catastrophizing:* How *horrible!* I've failed to help you!

*Can't-stand-it-itis:* I *can't bear* to fail!

*Commanding:* A good parent *should* be able to help . . .

*Condemning:* so I'm an *inadequate* person!

*Condemning:* Actually, *you are unable* to be helped. *You are* the one that's *incapable . . .*

*Catastrophizing:* and that's really *awful!*

If parents can realize that neither they nor the teen is inadequate, they'll be taking the first step toward developing faith and confidence in themselves and their teenager. Parents can then make a decision to help their teen. As the chart shows, this rational approach involves the following steps:

*Anti-catastrophizing:* It's *very difficult* to help you and so far I've failed. That's *frustrating* and *unfortunate,* but it's *not horrible.*

*Anti-can't-stand-it-itis:* I *can accept* it.

*Anti-condemning:* I'm still a *competent* parent and person . . .

*Anti-commanding:* who *can decide* to help you.

*Understanding and action statements:* I know it's going to be rough. I'll be *tempted* to give up at times because you are so *discouraged* and will *try* to get me *to give up.* I'll do *my best* to *show* you . . .

*Anti-condemning:* that *you are capable.* I know *you can handle* the *challenges* of life.

# Strategies for Changing Irrational Responses

The following strategies will help you combat irrational responses. Use them in combination and discover what works best for you. These strategies are intended to keep you from engaging in unproductive conflict. They're not recommended for emergencies or when your teen really needs your help.

**Admit your feelings, accept yourself, and make a commitment to change.** If you're truly angry, admit it. Realize that at times you *do* feel hostile. Don't give yourself a hard time about it! Determine whether these feelings are helping you improve your relationship with your teenager.

Make a decision. Do you want to change? If so, make a commitment to experiment with some of these strategies for at least a week. At the end of the week, look at the progress you've made and decide whether to continue or to experiment with other strategies.

**Identify the purpose of your negative emotions.** Study the text or Chart 3B to help you determine the purpose of your negative emotional responses to your teen's misbehavior.

**Watch your tone of voice.** Your tone of voice is one of the clearest signs of your true attitude. Concentrate on talking in a firm but friendly manner. Your feelings and beliefs can be changed as you practice being firm and friendly and experience the results of your new approach.

**Watch your nonverbal behavior.** Your facial expressions, your body posture, and your gestures all indicate how you feel. Practice using firm but friendly gestures and facial expressions in front of a mirror.

Distracting yourself is one way to stop negative emotions.

**Distract yourself.** There are times when talking isn't appropriate. Many parents, however, have a hard time keeping silent, let alone stopping negative emotions. If you can leave the room, this might be the best thing to do. If not, force yourself to think of something that has nothing to do with what your teen is doing: perhaps a pleasant scene, a television program, or an activity you plan to do. Get your mind off the problem. If something is bothering you and you want to get it out of your mind, talk out loud to yourself about something that's totally unrelated. "Well, let's see, what do I need from the store?" "Tomorrow I'm going to mow the lawn." If you can, keep moving.

**Avoid your first impulse and do the unexpected.**[11] Whenever you act on your first impulse, you do exactly what your teen ex-

pects. This reaction reinforces your teen's misbehavior. If you do the unexpected, you thwart your teen's attempts to achieve his or her goal. For example, if you're trying to discuss something with your teenage son and he's being rude and flippant, don't rise to the bait! Instead, remain silent, withdraw, walk around, or use the distraction tactics mentioned above. Do anything that he doesn't expect. In fact, talking to your teen when he is misbehaving is often the most ineffective thing you can do because this is probably what he expects from you.

Whenever you act on your first impulse, you do exactly what your teen expects.

**Learn to relax.** Get away from the stress of being a parent by experimenting with the following:

• Take some time for yourself—everyone needs some time alone! Tell your family that at a certain time each day you want to be alone to do something strictly for yourself. Encourage them to do the same.

• When you feel tense, say calming things aloud to yourself: "Calm yourself." "Relax." "Take it easy." "Things will work out." Take deep breaths as you talk to yourself.

**Use your sense of humor.** Psychologist Walter O'Connell has said, "Life is too important to take seriously." Can you laugh at yourself and see humor even in discouraging situations? You might collect cartoons that show your own eccentricities (we all have them) and place them where you'll see them frequently. You could post comical reminders to yourself on the refrigerator or bulletin board: "Don't blow your top, volcanoes can be dangerous!"

Admit that you're imperfect by laughing at your own errors in front of your teen. This gives your teen the freedom to make mistakes.

**Work directly on changing your irrational beliefs.** If the strategies listed above don't work as well as you'd like, you may need to concentrate more deliberately on your beliefs. Here are two methods you might try:

• *Challenging:* Mistakes in parenting can discourage the most responsible of parents. Sometimes parents' discouragement prevents them from taking future risks. If you feel discouraged, ask yourself what the consequences of your feelings and irrational belief might be. By avoiding risks, you may destroy your chances for success.

Ask yourself if this is what you want to do. How long do you want to feel discouraged and keep yourself from growing? Make a decision. Then make some positive plans.

• *Taking charge:*[12] When you're feeling very upset, search for the four Cs—your commanding, catastrophizing, can't-stand-it-itis, and condemning statements. Tell yourself, "Stop!" Do this until you've successfully removed your irrational belief. Then replace the belief with a rational belief. Keep repeating your rational belief until you feel more rational feelings about the activating event.[13]

# References

1. Harold H. Mosak and Rudolf Dreikurs, "Adlerian Psychotherapy," in *Current Psychotherapies,* ed. Raymond Corsini (Itasca, Ill.: F. E. Peacock, 1973) and Don Dinkmeyer, Gary D. McKay, and Don Dinkmeyer, Jr., *Teacher's Handbook: Systematic Training for Effective Teaching* (Circle Pines, Minn.: American Guidance Service, 1980).

2. Rudolf Dreikurs, *Psychodynamics, Psychotherapy, and Counseling: Collected Papers* (Chicago: Alfred Adler Institute, 1967).

3. Rudolf Dreikurs and Vicki Soltz, *Children: The Challenge* (New York: Hawthorn, 1964).

4. Francis X. Walton, *Winning Teenagers over in Home and School* (Columbia, S.C.: Adlerian Child Care Books, 1980).

5. Mary Giffin, "Cries for Help," *Guideposts* (July 1980): 35. Excerpt reprinted by permission from *Guideposts Magazine.* Copyright ©1980 by Guideposts Associates, Inc., Carmel, New York 10512.

6. Ibid., pp. 32-35.

7. Albert Ellis and Robert A. Harper, *A New Guide to Rational Living* (Englewood Cliffs, N.J.: Prentice Hall, 1975).

8. Albert Ellis, *How to Live With and Without Anger* (New York: Reader's Digest Press, 1977).

9. Gary D. McKay and Oscar C. Christensen, "Helping Adults Change Disjunctive Emotional Responses to Children's Misbehavior," *Journal of Individual Psychology* 34 (1978): 70-84.

10. Albert Ellis, "Techniques of Handling Anger in Marriage," *Journal of Marriage and Family Counseling* 2 (October 1976): 305-315.

11. Dreikurs and Soltz, 1964.

12. J. A. Schmidt, "Cognitive Restructuring: The Art of Talking to Yourself," *Personnel and Guidance Journal* 55 (1976): 71-74.

13. More strategies for changing irrational beliefs can be found in Ellis and Harper, 1975.

# Questions

1. How do beliefs influence emotions?
2. What are some specific ways your teenager misuses his or her negative emotions? What can you do about this?
3. How can parents tell that a teen may be deeply depressed or contemplating suicide? In addition to seeking professional help, what can parents do to help a discouraged teen?
4. Using the **A, B, C** model, explain how people create their own emotions.
5. What are irrational beliefs? How do your irrational beliefs interfere in your relationship with your teen?
6. Using the four Cs of irrational thinking, give an example of how an irrational belief is created.
7. Rephrase your response to Question 6 to create an example of rational thinking.
8. What strategies can parents use to change their irrational responses to their teen's misbehavior?

# Activity for the Week

Using the "Strategies for Changing Irrational Responses" explained in the chapter, practice changing your typical emotional responses to your teen's misbehavior.

# Personal Development Exercise

## Exploring My Shoulds

1. Write out a "should" about your role as a parent or about how you think your teen should behave. This is your command. When searching for an irrational belief, first look for your command—it is the root of irrational thinking.

2. Locate the other three Cs and record them.

3. Identify how you feel when each of your "shoulds" is violated.

4. Reevaluate the situation and rephrase your beliefs so that they are rational beliefs.

5. Identify how you will feel if you concentrate on these new beliefs.

**Example:**

1. As a parent I *should* set a good example.

2. *Catastrophizing:*          How *awful,* I set a poor example!
   *Can't-stand-it-itis:*      I *can't handle* setting poor examples!
   *Commanding:*               I *should* set a good example!
   *Condemning:*               I'm a *bad* parent for not setting a good example!

3. I feel depressed.

4. As a parent I *strongly prefer* setting a good example, but there's no objective reason why I *should.*

*Anti-catastrophizing:*        It's *unfortunate* and *frustrating* that I set a poor example.
*Anti-can't-stand-it-itis:*    But I *can handle* it.
*Anti-commanding:*             I *strongly prefer* setting a good example but there is no objective reason why I *should.*
*Anti-condemning:*             I'm *still okay* as a *parent* even though I goofed.
*Understanding and action statements:*   I'm *entitled* to a mistake. I'll do *my best* to set good examples in the future, but if I slip, I'm *still okay.*

5. I now feel frustrated and disappointed but not depressed.

# Purposes of Emotional Misbehavior

| Emotion | Possible Purpose(s) | Steps for Redirecting Teen's Emotional Misbehavior |
|---|---|---|
| Anger | To win; to control; to get even | Refuse to be intimidated. Don't fight or give in. Offer to discuss problem later, in calmer atmosphere. If parent-teen relationship basically good, reflect teen's feeling and negotiate mutually acceptable solution. |
| Apathy | To demonstrate power ("I have no say in things that affect me, so I'll do only what it takes to get by, nothing more!")* | Invite teen's participation in decision making. Demonstrate that teen's ideas, opinions, and contributions are respected and needed in the family. Ask teen to perform a responsibility usually handled by you. Show interest in teen's interests. |
| Boredom | To avoid participating in life or getting involved with others** | Invite teen to explore ways to make life more interesting. If teen's behavior indicates teen wants to stay bored, respect that decision. Let teen work it out for self. |
| Sadness and depression | To control others; to avoid responsibility; to gain pity; to get revenge | Show teen you understand feelings and invite teen to explore ways to solve the problem. If teen wants to remain sad, respect that decision. Let teen work it out for self. Avoid pity. Avoid taking over teen's responsibilities. Avoid feeling guilty. Avoid trying to cheer up teen. If persistent, seek professional help. |
| Guilt | To control others; to demonstrate "goodness"; to punish self; to gain pity; to prove "good intentions"* | Avoid being impressed by guilt feelings. Avoid letting teen evade responsibility for actions. Show teen you understand feelings; respectfully ask what teen intends to do to remedy situation. |
| Fear and anxiety | To protect self from perceived danger (threat to self-esteem) | Show understanding of teen's feelings; invite discussion of ways to handle perceived problem. Express confidence in teen's ability to handle situation. |
| Stress | To convince self of inability to handle responsibilities ("It's too much for me") | Help teen see what's contributing to stress. Usually disorganization, taking on too much, not taking time for self. Help teen arrange priorities and learn to relax and pace self. |

*Francis X. Walton, *Winning Teenagers over in Home and School* (Columbia, S.C.: Adlerian Child Care Books, 1980).
**Shirley Gould, *Teenagers: The Continuing Challenge* (New York: Hawthorn, 1977).

# Some Irrational and Rational Parent Responses to Teen's Misbehavior*

## Irrational Responses

| Teen's Goal | Belief | Purpose | Emotion | Behavior |
|---|---|---|---|---|
| **Attention** | You *should* stop distracting me! | To stop distraction | Annoyance | Reminding and coaxing |
| **Power** | It's *awful* when you try to take control! I just *can't stand* it! I *have* to be in control and you *must* obey me, or I'm a *bad* parent and a *worthless* person! | To take control; to get even | Anger | Fighting or giving in |
| **Revenge** | You attacked me and it's *terrible!* I must be *totally worthless* or you wouldn't attack me! Hey, wait a minute—why am I blaming myself? I've been fair to you. How *awful* for you to attack me! I *can't stand* it! You *must not* treat me that way! You're horrible! I'll fix you! | To give parent permission to get even; to get even | Hurt, then anger | Retaliating |
| **Display of Inadequacy** | How *horrible!* I've failed to help you! I *can't bear* to fail! A good parent *should* be able to help, so I'm an *inadequate* person! Actually, *you are unable* to be helped. *You are* the one who's *incapable,* and that's really *awful!* | To give parent permission to give up | Despair | Tending to agree with teen that nothing can be done ("If you don't try, neither will I") |

---

*Adapted from Gary D. McKay and Oscar C. Christensen, "Helping Adults Change Disjunctive Emotional Responses to Children's Misbehavior," *Journal of Individual Psychology* 34 (1978): 70-84

# Rational Responses

| Teen's Goal | Belief | Purpose | Emotion | Behavior |
|---|---|---|---|---|
| **Attention** | I *wish* you'd stop distracting me. But you're after attention because you think this is the only way you can belong. *I'll help* you change your discouraged outlook by *not reinforcing* your bid for attention and *focusing* instead on your contributions. | To stimulate self-reliance | Determination | Not giving attention on demand; ignoring inappropriate bids for attention; doing the unexpected by "catching" teen being "good" |
| **Power** | While it's *frustrating* when you challenge me, it's *not awful,* and I *can stand* it. I'd *really like* to control you, but I can't and it's *discouraging* to both of us. I'm still a *worthwhile* parent and person. I'm going to *stop fighting* or *giving in* and will establish *mutual respect.* I'm *sorry* you've decided that power is the only way to feel important, and I'll *help* you change your belief. | To win cooperation | Determination; regret for teen's suffering | Withdrawing from conflict and letting teen learn from consequences; helping teen use power constructively by enlisting teen's help |
| **Revenge** | Although you treated me unfairly, it's *not the end of our relationship.* I *can take* it. I *really don't like* it, but I'm still *okay.* Your behavior is *frustrating* and *unfortunate,* because I *do love* you and want to get along with you. I know you're *not* a *horrible* person, only *very discouraged.* You're *unhappy* and I know how *tough* this must be for you. I'm going to *help* you feel better about yourself and our relationship. | To show compassion | Regret and empathy; determination | Avoiding being hooked into hurt feelings and revenge; building a trusting relationship through understanding and acceptance |
| **Display of Inadequacy** | It's *very difficult* to help you and so far I've failed. That's *frustrating* and *unfortunate,* but it's *not horrible.* I *can accept* it. I'm still a *competent* parent and person who *can decide* to help you. I know it's going to be rough. I'll be *tempted* to give up at times because you are so *discouraged* and will try to get me *to give up.* I'll do *my best* to *show* you that *you are capable.* I know *you can handle* the *challenges* of life. | To show confidence | Faith; determination | Avoiding criticism, pity; encouraging positive efforts; arranging success experiences |

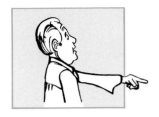

# Points to Remember

**1.** Emotions serve a purpose. They provide the energy for us to act.

**2.** Take responsibility for your own emotions and encourage your teen to do the same.

**3.** Typical negative emotions of teenagers include:

• anger
• apathy
• boredom
• sadness and depression
• guilt
• fear and anxiety
• stress

**4.** You can help your teen handle negative emotions through listening, encouragement, and involving the teen in constructive family responsibilities.

**5.** To redirect our teens' misbehavior we must change not only how we respond, but what we feel as well.

**6.** We create our own emotions by holding certain beliefs about things that happen in our lives.

**7.** We catastrophize by translating our preferences into needs.

**8.** When we make demands on life, we are involved in irrational thinking.

**9.** Some typical irrational beliefs of parents regarding teens are:

• To be a good parent I *must* (should) have the approval of everyone in the community.
• I *should* (must) be competent in all aspects of parenting.
• Things *should* turn out the way I want them to.
• People are victims of circumstances and *should not* try to change what can't be changed.
• I *should* take the responsibility for my teenager's behavior. If I were a more effective parent, my teen would *always* be well behaved.

**10.** Your responses to your teen's misbehavior are created by what you tell yourself about the misbehavior. You can change your responses by changing your thinking (your belief).

**11.** Irrational responses can be changed by using the following strategies:

• Admit your feelings, accept yourself, and make a commitment to change.
• Identify the purpose of your negative emotions.
• Watch your tone of voice.
• Watch your nonverbal behavior.
• Distract yourself.
• Avoid your first impulse and do the unexpected.
• Learn to relax.
• Use your sense of humor.
• Work directly on changing your irrational beliefs.

# My Plan for Improving Relationships
(An opportunity to assess progress each week)

My specific concern:

_____

_____

My usual response:

- ☐ talking, lecturing
- ☐ complaining, nagging
- ☐ becoming angry, screaming
- ☐ being sarcastic, attacking

- ☐ punishing, shaming
- ☐ giving up, forgetting because discouraged
- ☐ exerting power by removing privilege
- ☐ other _____

My progress this week:

| | I am doing this more | I need to do this more | I am about the same | | I am doing this more | I need to do this more | I am about the same |
|---|:---:|:---:|:---:|---|:---:|:---:|:---:|
| Understanding the purpose of behavior . . . . | ☐ | ☐ | ☐ | Communicating love, positive feelings . . . . . . | ☐ | ☐ | ☐ |
| Working on developing an equal relationship based on mutual respect . . . . . . . | ☐ | ☐ | ☐ | Withdrawing from conflict . . . . . . . . | ☐ | ☐ | ☐ |
| Responding to emotions more effectively . . . . . . | ☐ | ☐ | ☐ | Preventing discipline problems by giving choices . . . | ☐ | ☐ | ☐ |
| Encouraging . . . . . . . . | ☐ | ☐ | ☐ | Correcting discipline problems appropriately . . . . . | ☐ | ☐ | ☐ |
| Appreciating and giving responsibility . . . . . . . . | ☐ | ☐ | ☐ | Arranging democratic family meetings . . . . . . | ☐ | ☐ | ☐ |
| Listening . . . . . . . . . . | ☐ | ☐ | ☐ | Being firm and kind . . . . | ☐ | ☐ | ☐ |
| Revealing my feelings without blaming or accusing . . . . . . . . . . . | ☐ | ☐ | ☐ | Staying out of problems that are not my problems . | ☐ | ☐ | ☐ |

I learned:

_____

_____

_____

I plan to change my behavior by:

_____

_____

_____

# CHAPTER 4

•

# *Encouragement: Building Your Teen's Self-Esteem*

Consider the following situation:

> Sixteen-year-old Jason is tenth person on the junior-varsity basketball team and seldom plays in games. His last report card showed four Cs and two Ds. Both on the basketball court and in the classroom, Jason feels discouraged. His coaches think he's lost his enthusiasm for basketball, and most of his teachers have given up on him. Jason's parents too have a feeling of despair and are beginning to doubt they can do anything to help him start trying.

There are lots of teenagers like Jason in our society—girls or boys who have considerable potential but who are discouraged about their talents and capabilities. When teens lose interest in extracurricular activities or schoolwork, they aren't necessarily going through a phase or experiencing a case of the "blahs." *They are discouraged.*

Discouraged teens believe they have no chance to succeed or make progress. They lack confidence, have a low opinion of their own worth, and doubt that they can cope with the challenges of living. Such teens appear to have given up. Even more important, discouraged teens convince *others* that they've given up and can't succeed. As a result, their discouragement spreads to parents, teachers, and friends who may want to encourage them.

At this point you may be saying to yourself, "You're talking about my teenager." If so, we have suggestions that can help you understand and help your discouraged teen. The first step is to understand discouragement; from there you can go on to learn how to become an effective encourager.

## What Is Discouragement?

Discouragement is the reason for most teenagers' failure to function effectively. Discouragement occurs when teens assume they're inadequate or feel they've failed to meet standards they or others have set. Some teens feel that parents, teachers, coaches, and other authority figures don't value them. When this happens, teens often decide to reject those people's standards. They quit trying to be successful in areas where they think they can't succeed.

The meaning teens give to all of their life experiences influences their actions. Jason, for example, sees the coach putting other players into the ball game and concludes, "I'm not as good as the other guys—and never will be." If Jason competes with a sister, brother, or peer who does very well in school, he may decide he can't keep up with that person.

SO THAT'S YOUR BIRDHOUSE...
YES, IT'S CERTAINLY FOR
THE BIRDS!

Sarcasm can be very discouraging.

Some discouraged teens seek recognition and significance in areas where they're more certain of being accepted. Visit almost any high school and you'll find some students who are seeking significance in negative ways—by fighting, by drinking or using other drugs, by throwing food or destroying property, by being vulgar or sullen or "cutting up" in class, by being sexually promiscuous, or by withdrawing from teachers and peers. For other teens, discouragement can lead to frustrated desires and ineffective efforts:

Louisa, who has strong musical ability, had been the French horn section leader in her hometown school. When her family moved and she entered a different school, she was placed in the second-horn section. The new band director, who had expected Louisa to lead the second horns, was surprised to see that she was withdrawn and didn't play at the level expected. Louisa's parents observed that their daughter was practicing less and less. The more they reminded her that she wasn't living up to her potential, the less she seemed to care about using and building her special talent.

It's important for parents to recognize that in our society, underachievement seems to be linked only with children and teenagers, who are supposed to meet the expectations their parents have set for them. But we all have weaknesses and strengths, and most of us prefer to display the strengths. We like competition when we're sure we can excel; but when we feel we can't, we'll most likely decide not to compete. An adult who has an advanced degree but goes to work as a storekeeper is seen to be executing a choice. On the other hand, a teen who has academic ability is expected to use it. If not, the teen is an "underachiever." If Louisa's parents continue to nag about her potential, they'll be feeding competition and she'll likely grow more discouraged. Why not encourage her instead—by helping her see the value of her place in the band and the contribution she can make by cooperating and practicing?

Some parents spend a lot of time trying to get teens to be more successful and productive. We all want the best for our children! But while the intentions may be good, the methods often provoke resistance or foster discouragement. Badgering, threatening, and even begging a teen to do his work or "make something of herself" are all ineffective means toward a desirable end. Power and getting one's way seem to be at the heart of many clashes between parents and teenagers. To break power deadlocks, parents have to become aware of their *own* stubbornness. They need to recognize that they may be as unyielding in their opinions as their teens are in theirs. Remember, it takes two to tangle. Once parents see clearly how they themselves contribute to power struggles, they're ready to reduce their teen's stubbornness. They're ready to encourage.

## Some Ways Parents Discourage Teens

Nothing can discourage a young person faster than a parent's concern with status and prestige. Is high achievement an important expectation in your family? Do you emphasize the value of making the varsity, getting lead parts, having the "right" friends, being on the honor roll, or pursuing a prestigious career? If so, what happens if your teen doesn't live up to these expectations? How does your teen feel valued?

Overambitious parents always communicate to teens that the teens should do more and be more. Faced with a report card of three Bs and three As, overambitious parents focus on the three Bs. They talk about how, with a little more effort, the report card could have been perfect. Their intentions may be good, but the result is usually less productivity. Overambitious parents who insist on the pursuit of excellence often influence their teens to avoid activities and interests in which they may not be outstanding.

In your relationship with your teen, you can be an intimidator or an encourager.

Negative expectations are communicated in words and gestures. If parents believe teens will fail at difficult tasks, they'll communicate that belief in one way or another. This leads teens to doubt their own ability, and consequently they often *do* fail—or fail to try—just as the parents expected.

In your relationship with your teenager you can choose your own style. You can be an *intimidator* or an *encourager*.[1] If winning is your main goal, then you'll be involved in continual power struggles, and your child will probably behave the same way—intimidation usually inspires rebellion. Take a look at the difference between an intimidator and an encourager, and you'll be able to tell which type of relationship you're fostering with your teen. Intimidators put an emphasis on competition, on winning, on getting their way, and on power. Encouragers put an emphasis on working together, cooperating, and making decisions jointly. Encouragers believe that sharing is the basis for the most productive type of relationship.

## What Is Encouragement?

Encouragement is a process of focusing on a person's resources and giving positive recognition in order to build that person's self-esteem, self-concept, and feelings of self-worth. Parents can encourage their teen by recognizing any ability the teen may have and fully accepting that ability.

## Ways to Encourage

Some of the ways parents can encourage their teens are fairly simple. When applied consistently, they're almost certain to bring about a new parent-teen relationship. In your relationship with your teen, focus on the positive. Positive expectations and encouragement go hand in hand. Encouraging parents value teens as they are. They don't burden teenagers with negative expectations or demand that they improve. Some of the methods that encouragers use include showing faith, building self-respect, recognizing effort and improvement, and focusing on strengths and assets.

**Showing faith.** Encouragers have confidence in their teens. These parents believe in teens without requiring teens to prove that the faith is deserved. Parents who constantly supervise their teens by checking on where they're going, what time they get there, and when they return are not encouraging teens to take responsibility for themselves. Of course, this does not mean that parents don't set limits and restrictions—teens need guidance. It does mean that once guidelines have been established, parents consistently indicate to teens that they expect the guidelines to be followed, and that they *believe* they will be. If parents discover their faith isn't warranted, they need to renegotiate the guidelines. (Methods for doing this are discussed in Chapters 7 and 8.)

**Building self-respect.** Encouragers avoid comparing teens with their sisters, brothers, or peers. Comparisons are often a slap in the face. Why mention how well another teenager is doing, or point out that someone is more assertive, more outgoing, more industrious, more helpful, or more *anything?* Comparison reduces self-respect by devaluating a teen's efforts. Encouragers recognize and value their teen's goals, efforts, and endeavors on their own merits.

By the same token, encouraging parents are accepting of individual differences. Teenagers may want to live differently from their parents, and they may have different ideas and beliefs. Marsha, for example,

may want to go to school to become a teacher. Her parents may value the world of business and wish that she'd work toward a more high-paying job with room for advancement. Unless Marsha's parents accept her right to make a decision for herself, there may be family conflict.

Encouragers also look for ways to be enthusiastic about their teen's interests. Encouragement isn't a way to get teens to do only what parents want—it's a way to help teens reach their goals and fulfill their potential. Though you may want to, you can't force your values on your teen. Teenagers are independent, thinking people who will, regardless of parents' wishes, make their own choices. Giving them the freedom to make these choices in an atmosphere that is open and accepting will allow teens to grow in confidence and self-respect.

**Recognizing effort and improvement.** It's easy to give recognition for completed tasks such as earning a merit badge, winning a contest, or getting a part-time job. But no one achieves such things every day! If parents restrict their encouragement to completed efforts, they'll have far fewer opportunities to encourage. By systematically encouraging their teen's *efforts,* rather than just achievements, parents can help the teen find value in work and improvement as well as in final accomplishments.

Encouragers look at what their teen is engaged in and find ways to encourage that. Their first step is to guide the teenager to develop realistic goals. These goals may be improving a grade, making a team, playing a musical instrument, fixing a car—anything positive the teen seeks to accomplish. Encouragers then accept their teen's level of accomplishment without pressuring the teen to do more. That's a difficult challenge for many parents! It might help to keep in mind that by applying pressure—openly or

SAY, YOU'RE MAKING PROGRESS. YESTERDAY YOU COULDN'T LIFT IT OFF THE FLOOR!

subtly—for more success, parents are essentially saying, "You are not enough. You don't live up to my expectations." This rejection is guaranteed to produce rebellion or apathy in teens. Just as applying pressure to an infected wound is sure to create soreness, applying pressure to a teen to be more or to do better is sure to discourage any further effort on the part of the teen.

**Focusing on strengths and assets.** We live in a society that puts a great deal of emphasis on mistakes. Fault finding rivals football as the national pastime! But instead of nagging and pointing out mistakes, encouraging parents look for their teen's assets and comment on them. Encouragers are talent scouts, busy searching for positive behavior in their teen. They encourage all sorts of strengths and assets to help their teen become a responsible adult: helpfulness around the house, interest in a family outing, ability to get along well with friends, consideration of other people's needs.

Sometimes in their effort to encourage, parents need to actively search for a teen's strengths and resources when these re-

sources are not things the parents most wish to see. For example, seventeen-year-old Roderick is very outgoing and assertive. His parents would prefer that he were more quiet and reserved. But instead of criticizing, they decide to accept Roderick as he is, and to recognize the value in his sociability and directness. They point out actions they see as positive in his relationship with others. In response to this positive attitude, Roderick is becoming more cooperative— both at home and with his peers.

Even when a teenager has a strong trait that seems a liability, a parent can creatively consider how that trait might be used as an asset. For example, fifteen-year-old Peter is extremely stubborn. Rebellious, he wants to go his own way, and his relationship with his mother is stormy. If Peter's mother learns to view this stubbornness as a move toward independence and self-determination, she can find ways to encourage independent behavior that can help Peter achieve positive goals. By helping Peter see the usefulness of his self-reliance and determination, she will give him an opportunity to channel his energies into pursuing a job or campaigning for a school office. His mother's changed attitude can allow Peter to reduce his resistance, thus widening Peter's opportunities and improving family relations. To be effective encouragers, parents must learn to use positive methods to counter negative situations.

Do you ever focus on your teen's weaknesses and liabilities? If so, ask yourself why. Are you trying to compete with your teen? Are you trying to establish that you're superior in certain situations? Perhaps you're fearful for your teen, or afraid your teen's failures will reflect on you as a parent. If you remind yourself that we *all* have weaknesses, you'll be able to put those of your teen into perspective. Why harp on negative traits when you could be building on positive ones? By focusing on the strengths your teen possesses, you'll be able to provide support and encouragement to face the challenges of living.

These four ways of encouraging teens serve as the foundation of a parent-teen relationship based on equality and mutual respect. They are tried-and-true methods that build self-esteem. Parents who learn to use them can help teenagers discover their own personal worth and meaning—their own sense of significance.

As you work at becoming an encourager, keep your sense of humor. It's important to see the funny side of family relationships and to sense the absurdity of some of the expectations we have for ourselves and our teens: "I must decide everything." Who appointed you to be in charge of everybody's decisions? "My teen must never get in trouble." Do you really expect that your teen will never make a mistake? Get to the point where you can laugh at your own mistakes—we all make them! When you recognize the humor in your mistakes, you'll be able to see how faulty beliefs get in the way of effective parenting.

## The Difference Between Praise and Encouragement

To improve your relationship with your teen, you may decide to change the way you've been communicating—to try a more positive approach to your teen. We support such a decision—it will help you reap the rewards of parenting. As you proceed, however, be sure that you use encouragement, and not praise, to guide your teen. We've observed that parents sometimes confuse these two approaches. Because praise will bring out decidedly different results from

encouragement, it's important to be aware of the distinction.

Praise is a reward given for a completed achievement. It emphasizes personal gain, and it's usually given by people in authority (parents or teachers, for example) who are pleased that teens have achieved a goal that's been set for them. Praise is acquired through success—no one receives it unless it's earned. In contrast, encouragement can be given when someone is *not* successful: for effort, improvement, and even interest. Encouragement shows appreciation of a teen's assets, personal resources, and contributions, as well as achievements. It doesn't *reward;* it *acknowledges* and *recognizes.* Encouragement is a gift that can be given freely, because everyone deserves to receive it!

Praise and encouragement send two very different messages. When parents praise, they're saying that their teen is worthwhile when the teen does what *parents* want. The focus is on pleasing *parents* and meeting *parents'* expectations. Faced with such demands and expectations, many teens feel smothered. Encouragement, however, sends the teenager a different message: "The most important thing is how you feel about yourself and your efforts." Encouragement helps teens set realistic goals for themselves and manage their own lives.

The probable results of the two approaches are quite different. With praise, teens learn to measure their worth by their ability to conform. Fearing disapproval, they learn to please. One of the dangers is that teens may connect praise with their own personal worth; this invites failure. They may develop unrealistic standards and measure their worth by their closeness to perfection. Who's perfect? Teens may believe they aren't okay unless they're praised. If their focus is on pleasing others, they may make choices that aren't in their best interests.

Praise, though warmly intended, is really a cold value judgment on the teen as a person: "Marcus, you're such a good boy!" This isn't an easy expectation for Marcus to live up to. When Marcus isn't being "good," is he "bad"? "I'm so proud of you, Elsie." What this really means is, "You make me look so good, Elsie." Such praise is patronizing as well. Its message is that the parent speaks from a position of superiority. With encouragement, parents and teens interact as equals.

Encouragement focuses on strengths, so teens can recognize their own abilities and feel confident and useful. And encouraged teens develop the courage to be imperfect.[2] They learn to make an effort even though perfection is impossible, and to minimize mistakes and liabilities. They take responsibility for their behavior; they evaluate their own progress and decision-making ability.

# The Language of Encouragement

At times, encouragement has its own language, which you'll find used throughout STEP/teen. This way of talking avoids value judgments by eliminating words like *good, great,* and *terrific.* Instead, it helps teens believe in themselves.

Phrases that demonstrate acceptance:

• I like the way you handled that.
• How do you feel about this?
• I'm glad you enjoyed yourself.
• Since you're not satisfied, what do you think you can do so you *will* be pleased with it?

Phrases that show confidence:

• You'll make it!
• You're making progress.

• I believe you'll handle it.
• I have confidence in your judgment.

Phrases that recognize effort and improvement:

• I can see you put a lot of effort into that.
• I can see a lot of progress.
• You're improving in _____. (Be specific.)
• Looks like you're moving along.
• You may not feel you've reached your goal, but look how far you've come!

Phrases that focus on strengths, contributions, and appreciation:

• Thanks for helping—it took a load off me.
• You have a talent for _____. (Be specific.)
• Would you help me with this?
• I really appreciated your help on _____.

When using the language of encouragement, don't tag on a discouraging comment at the end of your statement. When you say, "Willa, I can see you worked hard on that," don't add, "but you still could have done a neater job," or "so why don't you do that all the time?" or "Keep up the good work!" These added comments imply that you are looking for perfection and make the encouragement meaningless—they're like giving with one hand and taking away with the other.

## Self-Encouragement

Learn to encourage yourself as well as your teen. You need to value yourself as a person, not only as a parent; if you don't, you may not be able to recognize all of your strengths. You don't need your teen's successes to make you feel worthwhile. Whether your daughter or son excels in some area or dates someone who's considered a real "catch" may please you, but it isn't a measure of your worth as a person. Avoid placing expectations and demands on your teen in order to make yourself feel successful. Instead, become a self-encourager. Look inside yourself to see what gives you satisfaction. Recognize where you feel respected and valued: in your friendships, your career, your marriage, family life, or your involvement in civic or religious activities. Learn to take responsibility for your success.

If you encourage yourself, you'll be more satisfied with your life. As you begin to recognize and value your own strengths and resources, you'll start to give yourself more and more positive messages. Rational beliefs will take the place of irrational ones. As you become more satisfied with yourself, you won't feel a need to compare yourself with other people. Instead, you'll note your own progress and set your own standards. You'll feel like working with people, not against them.

Equally important, the model you set will help your teen become more self-confident and more able to set realistic expectations. Remember, self-confidence is more often *caught* from a parent than *taught*. Your example will have more effect than dozens of lectures.

## Ten Strategies for Encouraging Teens

Do you usually communicate faith and trust in your teen? Do you provide support and confidence? Do you restrain yourself from making negative comments? Does your teen feel free to take a risk and learn from it? If your answer to any of these questions is no, or if you don't understand why they're important, chances are you need to learn more about encouragement. Here are ten strategies, with examples, to help you encourage your teenager.

**Give responsibility.** Take the attitude that your teen is a responsible person. Expect that your teen will take responsibility for her or his actions. For example:

> When fourteen-year-old Carmela stopped practicing her guitar, her mother didn't want to nag. But she was concerned, and she didn't want to keep paying for the lessons if Carmela wasn't going to practice. She decided that Carmela had to accept the consequences of her decision not to practice. She told her daughter that if she didn't practice, she'd have to pay for her own lessons.

Carmela's mother used a method of discipline that we call logical consequences. (You'll read more about logical consequences in Chapter 7.) She assumed that her daughter was responsible. The giving of responsibility is a gift to be valued and prized. It says to the teen, "I respect you and trust you, and I believe you can succeed and be responsible for yourself."

**Show appreciation for contributions at home.** When your teen is willing to take the car and run errands, to help make dinner, or to become a contributing member of the family in other ways, be sure to recognize this. Show that you appreciate positive efforts. For example:

> After fifteen-year-old Steve biked to the corner store for some hamburger buns, his grandfather turned to him and said quietly, "Thanks for getting those, Steve. It saved me a trip."

Steve's grandfather doesn't hesitate to say things like this in front of his own friends or Steve's. He doesn't say them when the other children in the family are around, however. He's noticed that doing so stimulates competition and rivalry among them—something he doesn't want to do.

**Ask your teen for opinions and suggestions.** Your daughter or son probably knows things that you don't—things about automobiles, fashion, art, computers, music, politics, sports, or other topics. Find out what your teen has to offer. For example:

> Hal Jacobi was struggling to install an electrical outlet in the basement. While fumbling with the instructions, he remembered that his sixteen-year-old daughter, Pat, had worked with electricity in her shop class. He asked Pat for help, and got the job done faster because she knew what to suggest.

Hal wasn't the only one who benefited from this experience. Pat too felt valued because she knew her father was really open to her suggestions.

**Encourage participation in decision making.** Show respect for your teen's opinions by getting her or him involved in making decisions about such things as plans after high school, subjects in school, careers, family vacations and outings, household chores, and allowance. For example:

> When her son Mario turned thirteen, Ruth Black told him that she would be giving him a clothing allowance. She explained that the money was his to spend as he saw fit, but that she wouldn't be buying any more clothes for him. She told her son she believed he could handle the responsibility. Mario made a few purchases he wasn't happy with, and he spent some of the money unwisely at first. But in time, Mario learned to make careful decisions before buying.

**Accept mistakes.** Without mistakes, there would be no learning. Mistakes can occur at home, in school, with friends, on the job—anywhere. Don't catastrophize over mistakes—your own or your teen's. Use your own mistakes as an opportunity to reveal your humanity to your teen. We suggest that you create an atmosphere in which it's safe to make a mistake, to discuss it, and to learn from it. For example:

After receiving a D on an important French test, sixteen-year-old Sarah went to her parents and cried. She felt terrible about the grade and told her parents she hadn't wanted to tell them about it. Sarah's parents reassured their daughter that they weren't angry with her. Then they told her that they could see she didn't like to get low grades and asked her how she could avoid another one. Sarah soon stopped catastrophizing over the grade and started thinking about why she had done poorly and how she could improve her performance on the next test.

Sarah's parents didn't punish their daughter for her "mistake"; they didn't insist she improve. Instead, they reassured her of their love and then helped her deal with her problem. They encouraged Sarah by allowing her to find her own solution.

**Emphasize the process, not just the product.** Your task as an encourager is to focus on the *process* (the effort, progress, or movement), not merely to comment on the *product* (the goal, achievement, or accomplishment). Remember that it takes time to accomplish any kind of change or to reach any goal. By encouraging efforts and progress, you can help increase your teen's self-confidence. For example:

Anne Schramski arrived home from work to find her two teenage sons hard at it—rebuilding the engine of an old car they'd just purchased. She stopped, noticed how interested they were in their work, and commented, "That engine sounds even better today than yesterday—I can see you guys are really enjoying what you're doing."

Anne chose to comment on her boys' project as it was, not as it would or might be. She recognized the process of their efforts, not the product. She chose *not* to say something like, "Sounds good—it'll sound even better when you're finished." And she chose not to find fault or to "inspect" their work.

**Turn liabilities into assets.** Become an expert at scouting for positive potential. As the song says, accentuate the positive! For example:

Si Marcotte felt that his daughter, Mali, became upset too readily. She was easily hurt and often came home crying about things that had happened in her relations with other people. Si decided to try to help Mali use her sensitivity to "tune in" to the feelings of her friends. Mali learned that she was able to empathize with the problems of others, and this trait helped her build close, trusting relationships.

Si recognized that Mali's sensitivity was a problem, but he chose to help her use this trait to the benefit of herself and others.

Taking a positive point of view, he opened up communication and was able to work constructively with his daughter.

**Show confidence in your teen's judgment.** How can you expect your teenager to make good judgments unless you have confidence in her or his ability to do so? You can show confidence by accepting your teen's decisions about clothing, friends, future plans, and use of leisure time. You can consult your teenager about plans or purchases that are important to the whole family. For example:

> Les and Jeanne Brisman decided that they wanted to add a microwave oven to their kitchen. Since their teenage children, Andrea and Saul, were interested in the purchase, Les and Jeanne gave them the responsibility of recommending two or three models that would be appropriate. Saul and Andrea researched various brands and made their recommendations. Their parents were able to use the information to make their selection.

By showing confidence in their teenagers' judgment, the Brismans helped them increase their self-esteem. And the family bought the right appliance too!

**Have positive expectations.** If you expect the worst from your teen, chances are you'll get it. The opposite of expecting the worst is not, however, expecting the best. Parents who demand perfection are bound to be disappointed, and their teens are bound to have doubts and nagging fears about their abilities. Instead, expect positive things from your teen. For example:

> Fifteen-year-old Susan told her mother that she was afraid to give a speech to her entire tenth-grade class. Susan's mother sat down and listened, acknowledged that Susan was anxious, and then reassured her by saying, "I know you're nervous about your speech, but I have confidence in you."

Susan's mother didn't tell her daughter not to be nervous, nor did she toss out a glib "You'll be great!" She took time to show that she understood the circumstances and had faith in Susan's ability.

**Develop alternative ways of viewing situations.** Use your creativity to discover different ways to see the same situation. When your teen comes to you with a discouraging problem, ask yourself what is *encouraging* about the situation. For example:

> Seventeen-year-old Mike Burke was turned down for a part-time job he had applied for. He had wanted the job badly and was angry and hurt about not getting it. He told his mother, "It isn't fair—it just isn't right they didn't hire me." Without trying to deny how bad he felt, Mike's mother suggested he look at what he'd accomplished by applying for the job:

he'd learned how to send a job-application letter, how to interview, and so on. She helped Mike learn from the experience by showing him how to view it from several angles.

## The Encouragement Habit

It takes time and effort to become an effective encourager, and you won't necessarily awake one morning to discover you've become one. Because encouragement is a learned skill, it improves with practice. We suggest you begin to think of your spouse, your friends, *and* your teen as people who have been placed before you to receive encouragement. Their ideas, attitudes, feelings, problems, and talents exist so that you may encourage.

Don't forget about yourself, either. Self-encouragement leads naturally to the encouragement of others. As you identify and acknowledge your own strengths and resources, you'll begin to see those of your teenager more clearly. You'll feel free to use the language of encouragement to inspire your teen's self-confidence and self-esteem.

## References

1. Don Dinkmeyer and Lewis E. Losoncy, *The Encouragement Book: Becoming a Positive Person* (Englewood Cliffs, N.J.: Prentice Hall, 1980).
2. Janet Terner and W. L. Pew, *The Courage to Be Imperfect* (New York: Hawthorn, 1978).

## Questions

1. What does discouragement mean to you?
2. What are some evidences of discouragement you have observed in your teen?
3. What are some ways you might be encouraging your teen?
4. What are some ways you encourage your teen?
5. Consider one of your teen's negative traits. How might you view the trait as an asset?
6. What are some differences between praise and encouragement?
7. In what ways can the results of encouragement and praise differ?
8. What are some specific phrases you can use to provide encouragement?
9. To encourage your teen, what strategies do you think will be most effective?

## Activity for the Week

Consider what is discouraging your teen, and find specific ways to provide encouragement. In each instance, notice how you encouraged your teenager and how your teen responded.

# Personal Development Exercise

## Encouragement

1. Take an inventory of your assets: what are the things you like about the way you relate with your teen? (Recognize any positive aspects of the relationship, including effort and improvement.) List at least five things.

_____

_____

_____

_____

_____

2. How can you use these assets more and to better advantage in relating with your teen? _____

_____

_____

_____

_____

_____

_____

3. What are the things you like about your teen? (Recognize any positive traits, including effort and improvement. Consider the alternatives to what may appear to be negative traits.) List at least five things.

_____

_____

_____

_____

_____

4. How can you focus on these assets and become a more encouraging parent? Make some specific plans:_____

_____

_____

_____

_____

_____

_____

_____

Chart 4

# Some Encouragement Skills

| Skill | Situation | Discouraging Response | Encouraging Response |
|---|---|---|---|
| **To be accepting and empathic** | Teen practiced hard but did not place in piano contest. | Don't give up—just work harder! That's what *I* do. | I know you've worked hard. |
| | Teen backed into car in parking lot. Other driver was very angry. | That's really stupid to back into someone like that! Didn't you look? | We all make mistakes. What can you do to avoid another accident like this in the future? |
| **To focus on strengths and contributions; to show appreciation** | Teen does better at tennis practice than in preceding match. | I told you you weren't ready for the match, but you never listen. | I noticed your game was faster and stronger today than it was last time I saw you play. |
| | Teen admits mistake and corrects it. | You never think before you act! | I'm glad to see you taking responsibility for your mistakes. |
| **To look for the positive; to develop alternative ways of viewing a situation** | Against own better judgment, teen goes to drinking party. Party is raided by police. | *Now* do you see why I've never approved of that crowd? I sure would've thought you knew better. | I think you've learned something here about following the crowd. |
| | Teen is unhappy to be spending summer at home while friends are all going on vacation. | Are you ever spoiled! When I was your age, I worked all summer. | It's not often you get three months to use any way you'd like—let's think of some things you could do here at home. |
| **To focus on effort and improvement** | Teen has been trying to improve overall academic performance; report card is not as good as expected. | I thought you said you were going to *work* this quarter— look at that algebra grade! | You've improved in English and history. It looks like you're sticking to your goal. |
| | Teen is having difficulty memorizing lines for a play. | Maybe you should drop out. Some people aren't very good at memory work. | You may not have all your lines memorized yet, but every time you read them you seem to put more expression into your part. |

# Points to Remember

**1.** Discouragement is the basis for most failure.

**2.** One of the major roles of a parent is to be an encourager.

**3.** Encouragement is the process of focusing on an individual's resources in order to build self-esteem.

**4.** Learn to recognize some positive aspect in every trait.

**5.** Encourage teens to pursue their own goals, provided the goals are socially acceptable.

**6.** Methods of encouragement:

• showing faith
• building self-respect
• recognizing effort and improvement
• focusing on strengths and assets

**7.** Praise is a reward given for an achievement. It fosters competition and fear of failure. Encouragement is given for effort and improvement. It fosters cooperation and self-esteem. It inspires confidence and acceptance.

**8.** Recognize your own strengths by valuing yourself as a person, not only as a parent.

**9.** Strategies for encouraging teens:

• Give responsibility.
• Show appreciation for contributions at home.
• Ask your teen for opinions and suggestions.
• Encourage participation in decision making.
• Accept mistakes.
• Emphasize the process, not just the product.
• Turn liabilities into assets.
• Show confidence in your teen's judgment.
• Have positive expectations.
• Develop alternative ways of viewing situations.

# My Plan for Improving Relationships
(An opportunity to assess progress each week)

My specific concern:

_____

_____

My usual response:

- ☐ talking, lecturing
- ☐ complaining, nagging
- ☐ becoming angry, screaming
- ☐ being sarcastic, attacking

- ☐ punishing, shaming
- ☐ giving up, forgetting because discouraged
- ☐ exerting power by removing privilege
- ☐ other_____

My progress this week:

| | I am doing this more | I need to do this more | I am about the same | | I am doing this more | I need to do this more | I am about the same |
|---|---|---|---|---|---|---|---|
| Understanding the purpose of behavior | ☐ | ☐ | ☐ | Communicating love, positive feelings | ☐ | ☐ | ☐ |
| Working on developing an equal relationship based on mutual respect | ☐ | ☐ | ☐ | Withdrawing from conflict | ☐ | ☐ | ☐ |
| Responding to emotions more effectively | ☐ | ☐ | ☐ | Preventing discipline problems by giving choices | ☐ | ☐ | ☐ |
| Encouraging | ☐ | ☐ | ☐ | Correcting discipline problems appropriately | ☐ | ☐ | ☐ |
| Appreciating and giving responsibility | ☐ | ☐ | ☐ | Arranging democratic family meetings | ☐ | ☐ | ☐ |
| Listening | ☐ | ☐ | ☐ | Being firm and kind | ☐ | ☐ | ☐ |
| Revealing my feelings without blaming or accusing | ☐ | ☐ | ☐ | Staying out of problems that are not my problems | ☐ | ☐ | ☐ |

I learned:

_____

_____

_____

I plan to change my behavior by:

_____

_____

_____

# CHAPTER 5

•

# *Communication: Listening*

When most people hear the word communication, they think of talking. But talking is actually only part of communication. In fact, it's the least important part when two people are establishing a relationship. A case in point: Say that you went to a party where you met George. Later you tell your spouse or friend, "George is such a good conversationalist." We'll venture a guess that you mean George is a good *listener!*

Yes, like all people, you like to be listened to. Why? Because it means the listener values you and believes that what you say deserves attention.

Your teenager is no different from you in this respect; teens feel valued and important when their parents listen to them. Of course, expressing feelings and thoughts is also part of communication—you want your teen to understand you. The trick is to determine when it's appropriate to listen and when it's important to communicate your feelings. In any given instance, the most effective way to determine this is to decide who owns the problem—you or your teenager.

## Who Owns the Problem?

Some parents feel they must be involved in all aspects of their teen's life. But some problems actually belong to teens. By insist-

ing on taking charge of a teen's problems, parents may stimulate dependence or rebellion. And they deny their teen the opportunity to develop responsibility to handle personal problems.[1]

It's important that parents let teens learn to handle their own problems—this is training for life! Certainly parents don't need to stop caring and loving in order to show faith in their teens' ability to cope. Parents can, of course, provide guidance and a ready ear. But by permitting teens to cope with.problems on their own, parents are giving the gift of self-reliance. How else are teenagers to become self-confident, responsible adults?

Quite simply, we suggest that if it's not your problem, don't get involved. How do you decide who owns a problem? Ask yourself these questions: "Does this problem interfere with my rights and responsibilities? Does it involve the safety of my teen, or others?" If the answer is no, it's not your problem. "Who is experiencing a problem with whom?" If your teen is in conflict with a teacher, your spouse, a friend, or a sibling, the problem is between the teen and the other person.

Consider these two situations:

Sixteen-year-old Ted is very upset because he just broke up with his girlfriend, Karen. His mother listens and shows him she understands his pain, but how can she solve this problem? She certainly won't help her son learn how to handle relationships if she calls Karen and tries to patch things up. This is something Ted must deal with, and it doesn't affect his mother's rights. It's clear that Ted owns this problem.

KAREN, WHAT HAPPENED BETWEEN YOU AND TED? HE'S SO UNHAPPY.

Eighteen-year-old Carla used the family car last night. Her father, Dirk, has an early morning appointment, but when he jumps in the car he finds the gas tank empty. Dirk may be late to his appointment, and he's inconvenienced—things that interfere with his rights. In this case, Dirk owns the problem!

In the following list of typical parent-teen problems, decide who owns the problem— the parents or the teen. Then read on to compare your conclusions with ours.

## Problems

1. Joe has a science report due tomorrow. It's 9:00 P.M., and he has not yet started it.
2. Carol has left her coat in the middle of the kitchen table.
3. Román stays up late on school nights.
4. Youngeui backs the car out of the driveway too fast.
5. Tom is always late for dinner for no legitimate reason.
6. Marcella has taken up smoking cigarettes.

## Conclusions

1. This is Joe's problem because it doesn't interfere with his parents' rights. He will have to face the consequences at school. If Joe's parents get involved, they may spark rebellion and rob him of the opportunity to learn from the consequences.
2. This is the parents' problem. The table is unsightly and it can't be set with a coat in the middle of it.
3. Román may be tired in the morning and late to school. He has to face the consequences. This is his problem.
4. Since Youngeui may be jeopardizing the safety of herself, others, and the car, this is the parents' problem.
5. If Tom misses dinner, it's his problem. If his parents save dinner and clean up after him, it's their problem.
6. If Marcella smokes in bed, or if someone in the home is bothered by the smoke, then this is the parents' problem. But if she is careful of where and how she uses cigarettes and doesn't smoke around people who are bothered by the smoke, it's her problem. (Chapter 8 addresses in greater detail the issue of cigarette smoking.)

Whenever you encounter a problem involving your teen, do two things: First, consider the goal of the misbehavior. Then consider who owns the problem. Both of these considerations will help you decide what approach to take. When your teen owns the problem, you may decide to ignore the situation and let your teen work it out.

You may decide to provide encouragement. Perhaps you will want to permit your teen to experience the consequences of what has happened. Or you might sense that this is a time to listen. In this chapter we'll focus on listening as an approach to teen-owned problems. Discussion of other approaches and of parent-owned problems will come in later chapters.

# Barriers to Communication

Stop and think about the conversations you have with your teenager. They're probably not much different from those that take place in most families:

*When will you be home?* Midnight.
*Did you empty the trash?* Not yet, I will.
*Don't forget to feed the dog.* Okay, okay!
*Do you have to work tonight?* Yes.
*Do the dishes.* Why me all the time?

We call this "business" conversation because it deals with the everyday affairs of the family. It's necessary to talk about these things, of course. But if positive relationships are to develop between parents and teens, conversations must go further. Feelings, beliefs, and opinions need to be shared; closeness and mutual respect need to be developed. Learning to listen to your teen is a vital step in building such a positive relationship. Listening shows your teen that you care.

Many teens, however, won't share their feelings with their parents because they're not used to doing so or because they've tried and haven't liked the way their parents have responded. Let's face it, some parents respond in ways that discourage sharing. Suppose you've just had a conflict with your supervisor at work. You're fuming! You want to talk about it, so you approach a friend, saying, "I'm sick and tired of the way he treats me! Do you know what happened today?" How would you feel if your friend responded in any of the following ways?

Take it easy, you're going to raise your blood pressure!
You shouldn't let him get you so upset.
Why don't you just tell him where to go!
Getting upset about it isn't going to solve anything.
The two of you act like a couple of kids!
The trouble is, you let him walk all over you.
You'll feel better after you've had a chance to relax.

How would you feel if you received one of these replies? Angry? Frustrated? Discouraged? Would you feel your friend understood you? Would you want to open up and talk about your problem with this person? Now ask yourself what you would want the listener to do instead. Would you want your friend to remain silent and just listen? Perhaps you'd appreciate some type of comment that showed your friend understood.

Many of us aren't very comfortable with another person's upset feelings. As we grew up, we learned it wasn't proper to express feelings like anger or frustration—we were supposed to keep those "bad" feelings to ourselves. Consequently, most of us didn't learn how to respond appropriately to someone else's upset feelings. It's little wonder, then, that when our teenagers share these feelings, we don't know what to do. And though we may have good intentions, too often we end up playing one of the following traditional roles:[2]

**The Commander-in-Chief** orders the upset person to get rid of those negative feelings. The order may be given politely: "Take it easy, you're going to raise your blood pressure!" With teenagers, the Commander-in-Chief can become threatening:

> Don't you dare talk to me like that!
> I told you to stop hanging around with her!
> If you talk like that one more time, I'll . . .

The Commander-in-Chief.

**The Moralist** tells the upset person what he or she "should" or "should not" feel and do. When speaking to teenagers, the Moralist tends to preach and patronize:

> You shouldn't let him get you so upset.
> You should apologize to your teacher for the way you acted.
> You should know better!
> That's not the right way to handle it.

The Moralist.

**The Know-It-All** has all the answers. "Why don't you just tell her where to go?" is this person's perfect solution to someone else's problem. With teens, the Know-It-All lectures, advises, reasons, appeals to logic, and generally acts superior:

> I told you so.
> Think about it for a minute. Use your head!
> When I was a teenager . . .

The Know-It-All.

**The Judge** evaluates and pronounces judgment on other people's feelings. Parents who take the role of Judge are interested in proving themselves right and the teenager wrong:

> Okay, what mess did you get yourself into this time?
> Well, what did you expect? You didn't study for the test!
> I think it was your fault!

The Critic.

The Judge.

**The Critic** has the same motive as the Moralist, the Know-It-All, and the Judge: to be right. But with the Critic, the tactics are different. This person uses ridicule, name-calling, sarcasm, and jokes to respond to teenagers:

> Act your age!
> Don't think you're so grown up!
> The coach can't be *that* bad. Trying to coach a bunch of clowns like you would drive anybody crazy!

**The Consoler** doesn't really want to get involved and thus lightly dismisses the upset person's feelings. This person believes a simple pat on the back, some reassurance, or a cup of chicken soup will take care of anything. The Consoler loves to use clichés with teens:

> You'll feel better after you've had a chance to relax.
> Things always work out for the best.
> It's just a stage you're going through. We all went through it.
> Once you think it over, you'll see.

The Consoler.

**The Amateur Psychologist** questions, analyzes, and diagnoses. The parent who plays this role is out to show that the *teen* is the problem:

> The trouble is, you let him walk all over you.
> Why did you take *that* approach?
> You're too concerned with popularity.

Most parents step into these roles simply because they don't know what else to do. They want to get their teen on the "right track." Unfortunately, methods such as these often send teenagers down the wrong track, or sidetrack them altogether. Clearly, these methods do nothing to encourage open communication and responsible decision making.

The Psychologist.

## Becoming a Better Listener

Teens desperately want to be understood, especially when they're upset. Just like you, they need the acceptance of others. Acceptance doesn't mean that you need to agree with your teen's feelings and opinions. It simply requires that you understand.

For example, imagine that your teenage daughter storms in and says to you, "I've had it with school! I hate it! I'm quitting and getting a job!" What can you say at this point? You probably don't want her to quit, and maybe she doesn't really want to, either. She *is* upset. If you try to have a conversation with her about the benefits of finishing high school, she won't feel you understood her anger and you may lose your influence with her.

What if you begin by showing her you do understand? You might say, "Sounds like you've had a miserable day at school." Here you acknowledge your daughter's feelings. If you continue to do this, giving her a chance to talk and unravel her feelings, she'll gradually calm down and will be ready to look for ways to solve her problem.

When parents understand their teen's feelings, they build a foundation for problem solving. Many parents have good suggestions for teens. But jumping in with these ideas too soon often results in their being rejected without being given any consideration at all. When people are upset, they aren't ready to hear instant solutions. They may want to be left alone for a while or to have someone simply listen and understand.

Let's look more closely at understanding feelings and communicating that understanding. Often, feelings are not clearly demonstrated or stated. To be an effective listener, you need to tune in to what you see and hear.

## Stop, Look, and Listen to What You See

Facial and eye expressions, hand and body gestures, posture, and tone of voice all communicate feelings and meanings. In fact, some people say that the large majority of all messages are communicated nonverbally. If we are to understand how our teens feel, we need to sharpen our observation skills—to look as well as listen.

Consider the range of feelings conveyed by some behaviors. Crying can be used to express sadness, despair, anger, pain (both psychological and physical), frustration—even joy. When we smile, we can communicate happiness, anxiety, or even contempt. If we throw dishes or pound the tabletop we can be expressing anger, frustration, or despair. We may express fear or uncertainty by standing stiffly. Some of us shake our heads for yes and nod our heads for no; others do exactly the opposite. Yawning may mean we're uninterested or simply sleepy. Staring might indicate shock, intense interest, or rudeness. In some cultures eye contact is a sign of disrespect. In others, avoiding eye contact can signify anxiety or lack of interest.[3]

Tone of voice also communicates a lot about a person's feelings. Hesitation, stuttering, and long pauses could mean nervousness or sadness. Rapid speech rates often indicate elation or nervousness. Stressing certain words usually says, "This is the main point of my message."

The range of feelings we've just described shows how the same words or actions can convey very different messages. Each person is unique. The point is that all of us must learn to pay attention if we want to improve our listening skills.

## Hear the Feelings and Meanings Behind the Words

While listening, parents need to watch their own nonverbal behavior. When your teen shares something with you, make eye contact, but don't stare. Avoid interrupting and be attentive. Relax, lean forward, and let your face express your interest. Show you're following by saying things like "I see," "Yes," and "Uh-huh." An occasional nod of the head also communicates attentiveness. All these gestures say, "I care and I'm listening." Don't move around, fidget, turn your back, or get involved with something else. These actions tell your teen that you're not really interested. Be careful too to avoid saying you know or understand how your teen feels. This usually turns people off, and it's not completely true. You can't really *know* how another person feels; you can only *guess*.[4]

While silence and recognition statements are important, you can really help your teen feel understood by learning and using the important skill of reflective listening.

# Reflective Listening

Reflective listening is a way to show teens that their message has been fully understood. As a reflective listener, the parent becomes a mirror to help teens "see" themselves and their feelings more clearly. Let's see an example of how this works. Ann tried out for the basketball team but didn't make it. Looking dejected, she told her mother what had happened:

**Ann:** I didn't make the team. There were just too many girls better than me.
**Mother:** You feel pretty depressed because you were cut.

Ann's mother reflected her daughter's hurt feelings: "You feel pretty depressed . . ." Then she reflected the circumstances that led to the feeling: ". . . because you were cut." Notice that her mother didn't simply repeat what Ann said. This would have been parroting, and Ann would probably have thought she was talking to a tape recorder. Instead, her mother restated Ann's message, picking up the feelings she saw and heard. She added nothing to what Ann said but merely gave words to what Ann was trying to say—Ann could have said the same words herself.

When people express their feelings, they usually don't use *feeling words*. One reason for this is that most of us have been discouraged from directly expressing negative feelings. Another reason is that when we're upset, we often don't think clearly. A great advantage of reflective listening is that parents can help teens see a problem from a more rational perspective. By labeling emotions, parents help teens understand them.

At times teens *will* use feeling words. Parents can still reflect the feeling by simply repeating the word or by choosing a synonym. What's important is to catch the meaning behind the teen's message and reflect—not interpret—that meaning. There's a difference between reflecting and interpreting:

**Eli:** (Sadly) Betsy said she'd meet me at the party, but she never showed up! I was the only one there without a date.

**Dad:** You feel hurt and embarrassed because she didn't come? (*Reflective response*)
**Dad:** You were afraid the others would think you weren't able to get a date. (*Interpretive response. While it may be true, this is not what Eli said. He may feel he's being analyzed instead of understood.*)

# How to Phrase a Reflective Listening Response

You can learn to make an effective response by watching body language and listening to tone of voice as well as to the words themselves. When your teen gives you a feeling message, wait about ten seconds before responding, to give yourself time to think. Use this time to ask yourself two questions: *What is my teen feeling?* and *What brought on this feeling?*[5]

Fine, you may be thinking, I know *what* my teen is feeling and *why*. Now, what do I say? There are several ways to phrase a reflective listening response. The most important thing to remember is to respond to your teen tentatively, not in a know-it-all manner. You can't read your teen's mind, so don't try to *tell* your teen how he or she feels. Indicate by your choice of words, tone of voice, and body language that you're checking out a hunch. Your teen will then feel free to tell you whether your hunch is correct.

When they begin reflective listening, some parents feel comfortable using a simple format. One such format runs, "You feel _____ because _____."[6] Of course, the format can be varied. "You feel" can become "You're feeling," "Seems like you feel," "You sound," or "You seem." And "because" might be replaced with "about," "with," "at," or "by." You can start off your response with any of the following phrases: "I'm sensing," "Could it be that," "I wonder if," "Is it possible that," "Do you feel," "Correct me if I'm wrong, but," "I get the impression (feeling) that," or "Is this the way you feel (see it)?"[7]

EVEN THE GARBAGE GETS TAKEN OUT ONCE A WEEK.

YOU FEEL HURT BECAUSE YOU WEREN'T ASKED OUT.

We suggest you avoid a flat statement like, "You feel that _____." This reflects an opinion, not a feeling. If you're discussing opinions about an issue, this response is appropriate. You might say, for example, "You feel that you should be allowed to stay out as late as you want to?" But if you're reflecting feelings, don't use this format.

To help you see how reflective listening works, here are some exchanges between parents and teens:

**Rod:** I don't see why I can't go. All the other guys get to!

**Parent:** You feel I'm being unfair because none of your friends has to live by this rule?

**Shalayna:** Every time I'm in that class I almost fall asleep. I mean, the subject's so dull.

**Parent:** You sound bored because the class isn't interesting to you.

Sometimes a teen's message contains two feelings. In these cases, reflect both feelings. You could say, "You feel (sound, seem) both _____ and _____ because _____."[8] Here are some examples:

**Bridget:** I don't know what to do. If I go to the party with Tony, I know I'll have fun with him. But his friends Al and Eric will be there, and I just can't stand them! But if I turn Tony down, I might hurt his feelings—and he's such a nice guy.

**Parent:** You feel both confused and worried because you want to be with Tony but you don't want to be around Al and Eric.

**Dee-Dee:** I can't make any friends at that school. They're all in their own little groups, and most of them won't even talk to me.

**Parent:** You seem to feel left out and lonely because it's so hard to make friends in your new school.

Sometimes teens have mixed feelings about an event. Study the following examples for possible ways to respond.

**Robert:** I want to join the navy after graduation. They offer some great opportunities in electronics, and the travel would be great too. But I have to join for four years, and that's a long time!

**Parent:** You sound both excited and uncertain because the navy has what you want but plans to keep you longer than you want to stay.

**Trinh:** This guy kept getting on my nerves, so today I told him off. The only thing is, he's got some tough friends and I don't know what'll happen tomorrow.

**Parent:** Sounds like you have mixed feelings about what you did. You're glad you told him how you felt, but you're worried about what his friends might do.

# Open vs. Closed Responses

Parents want teenagers to keep sharing their feelings so they can help teens handle the turbulent emotions they sometimes have. By making open responses, not closed ones, parents can encourage this sharing of feelings.

Closed responses often pass judgment.

An open response neither adds to nor subtracts from your teen's message; it's interchangeable with the teen's message. When you use an open response, you show that you understand what your teen is trying to tell you. A closed response, on the other hand, implies you haven't really understood what your teen has said. Closed responses often pass judgment, interpret, or analyze. Let's look at how three different parents responded to a teenager's problem:

**Marcia:** Of all the times to give a test, she had to pick this Monday! Just when I've made plans for the weekend! Now I've got to spend most of it studying.

**1st Parent:** Well, sometimes our plans don't work out, you know.

**2d Parent:** You think the school should operate according to your plans?

**3d Parent:** Sounds like you're pretty frustrated and discouraged because you have to give up your plans.

The first parent ignored Marcia's feelings and took the role of Know-It-All. The second parent made an interpretation that Marcia will probably see as an attack. The third parent heard and understood Marcia's feelings. This parent paved the way for open communication.

Let's take another example. Here's what thirteen-year-old David had to say about his sister: "Will you *please* keep Sarah out of my room! She keeps taking my things!" Which of the following are open responses?

**Responses**

1. She's only a little kid—there's no reason to get upset.
2. Why don't you just lock the door?
3. If you'd stop teasing her, she wouldn't bother you.
4. Okay, I'll tell her.
5. You're angry with Sarah because she doesn't seem to respect your property—is that right?

6. You seem a little disturbed with the way Sarah messes with your things.

**Conclusions**

1. *Closed.* It tells David how to feel.
2. *Closed.* It gives advice and doesn't respect David's feelings.
3. *Closed.* It blames David.
4. *Closed.* It takes away David's responsibility for solving the problem.
5. *Open.* This statement catches David's feelings and the circumstances associated with those feelings.
6. *Closed.* Although this response is in the format of a reflective listening statement, it understates David's feelings. He's angry, not just a little disturbed.

By using reflective listening, you aren't indicating that you agree with your teen's perceptions. You're simply showing that you understand how the teen feels.

# Okay, I'll Listen, but My Teen Won't Talk to Me

Here you are, armed with your new skills and just itching to try them out, but your teen won't open up! What do you do? First, realize that it takes time to change your behavior. You may still be playing the Commander-in-Chief, the Consoler, or some other intimidating role. Your teen may feel it's not safe or satisfying to share feelings. If you think this is the case, you have to take the initiative. Here are three suggestions to get things going. Use any or all of them. Don't *overuse* them, though, because doing so may provoke resistance in your teenager.

**Make a guess about nonverbal messages.** When you see a smile, a frown, or an angry expression, comment on it: "You seem happy about something." "Looks like you're feeling down." "Seems like you're feeling angry."

If you're responding to an unpleasant look, your teen may deny that it was there: "No I'm not down—just thinking." When this happens, accept your teen's reply, and try again later. At other times when you make a guess about an expression or gesture, you'll open Pandora's box:

**Dad:** You seem angry about something, Pam.

**Pam:** You're darn right I'm mad! Whenever Mark and I go out, we always have to go where *he* wants. I've just about had it!

**Ask for comments.** Parents can ask teens to tell them about their day, things that interest them, and what they think about certain issues. You may very well get a response of "Fine," "Okay," or "I don't know." These are all ways to say, "I'd rather not talk." Don't pry. Respect your teen's decision, and continue to indicate interest at other times. Sometimes a simple question will start a real conversation:

**Mom:** How's the job going?

**Jeremy:** Not so good. The boss is really tough. It seems there's no pleasing her.

**Mom:** Sounds like you're discouraged because she expects a lot.

**Jeremy:** I do my best, but it's never good enough! I just don't know what to do!

**Mom:** You're confused about how to do what she wants?

**Jeremy:** Yeah, and if I lose my job, there goes the car!

A conversation like this creates an opportunity for a parent and teen to discover ways to solve a problem. In Chapter 6 we'll encounter this situation again and show how

Jeremy's mother could help him explore alternatives.

**Be a model.** Share your feelings about things that happen to you—don't expect your teen to do all the sharing. Limit your comments to areas that aren't a source of conflict between the two of you. You might talk about your job, your friends, sports, books, and so forth. "I had a rough day today." "I feel really concerned about what's happening with the school board election." Your model will demonstrate it's okay to share feelings.

# Dos and Don'ts

To become a reflective listener, keep in mind the following suggestions.

**Do experiment with reflective listening.** Until you're used to giving them, reflective listening responses may seem awkward. But remember that any new skill seems strange at first. An improved relationship with your teen will be worth some initial awkwardness.

If "You feel" or "Sounds like" are simply not comfortable, try using phrases that are. For example, if your daughter says to you, "It's really hard to spend time alone with Susan—Peggy's always butting in!" you might choose to reply in one of the following ways:

> It really bugs you to have Peggy around all the time.
> Peggy's interference is really getting to you.
> Peggy is hard for you to take.
> You wish Peggy would butt out.
> Peggy can be a real pain?

It might help to write a few of your own responses, in your own style of speaking, to some of the examples in this chapter. Then compare them to the ones provided to see if you're picking up the same feelings and meanings.

Some parents complain that they don't like to stop and think before they talk. They prefer to respond "naturally" to their children. We think this is unfortunate—impulsive responses reinforce a teenager's mistaken goals and prevent cooperation. It *does* pay to stop and think!

There are also parents who are afraid they won't understand their teen's feelings. If you don't understand, simply make a guess: "I wonder if . . . ," "Could it be . . . ," or "Is it possible? . . ." You might also simply remain silent, letting your teen continue talking until you get a clue. Then you could say, "Let me see if I understand what you're saying," or "I really want to understand. Could you tell me again how you're feeling?"[9]

**Don't try to force your teen to share feelings.** Open, reflective responses are probably as new to your teen as they are to you. It may take time before your teen is willing to open up. Your son or daughter

At times, it's best to respect your teen's decision not to talk.

may decide to share, to clam up, to simply agree and walk away, or to deny what you've said. Whatever your teen's response, respect it! You'll have many opportunities to show your willingness to help.

Some teens may never share their feelings. Their own individual way of looking at life prevents them from doing so. When this happens, it doesn't mean that the parent has failed. It simply means the teen has made a decision that needs to be respected. Most teens, however, *will* share—once they feel they'll be accepted. Both you and your teen may have to create or renew a sense of mutual trust. Gentle encouragement will usually pay off, so keep trying!

**Do respond as accurately as you can.**
Sometimes, in their attempt to understand, parents may miss the target by over- or understating their teen's feelings. While it is best to choose the most appropriate feeling word, overstating the feeling is safer than understating it. If parents understate the feeling, a teen may think they really don't care enough to understand:

**Bill:** Ellen *never* trusts me!
**Dad:** You're disappointed in her?

Bill is angry, not disappointed. Dad's reply will likely leave him feeling misunderstood. When parents overstate, teenagers usually sense their attempt to understand and simply correct them: "No, I'm not hurt, just a little disappointed."

Sometimes teens will give incomplete messages that leave parents in the dark. For example, your teenage daughter may say, "I can't stand her!" You know your daughter's angry, but you don't know the reason for the anger. You could say, "You seem very angry with her," and let your teen fill in the details if she wants to. You might also

ask for more information: "Can you tell me more about this?"

It's important to match the intensity of your teen's feeling. Using adverbs helps do this: being *very* disturbed is stronger than feeling just plain disturbed. The careful use of such adverbs as *very, pretty,* and *really* can help convey understanding.

Sometimes parents use accurate feeling words that teens just won't accept. For instance, you may sense that your son is afraid. But if you say, "You're afraid" or "You're scared," he may deny it. He might, however, accept words like *worried, anxious,* or *nervous.* You know your teenager— choose words that he or she is likely to accept and relate to.

**Don't ask too many questions.** Some parents turn reflective listening into the "third degree." Please don't! Some questions are necessary: "How did you feel then?" "What happened next?" "Want to tell me about it?" Yet, if sharing is to take place, even these questions need to be used sparingly. If you have enough information to make a statement, there's no need to ask a question. To keep your response open and tentative, say,

"You feel _____?" rather than "How do you feel?"

**Do take time to listen.** A positive relationship takes time to build. When your teen wants to share, do your best to find the time to listen. If you just can't stop to listen at a particular moment, show that you want to, say why you can't, and set a definite time to talk: "It seems you're worried about this. The problem is, I have an appointment. I really want to listen—how about talking as soon as I get back?"

A good way to make time to talk is to do something together—go shopping, take in a movie, or do anything else you both enjoy. Time to and from the event can be used to talk. By the way, your conversation doesn't necessarily have to be about problems. It can be about anything of mutual interest.

Listen for questions indicating hidden feelings that call for a reflective response. For example, a sixteen-year-old may ask her mother, "If I don't get a certain number of A's, does that mean I can't get into a good college?" This type of question indicates anxiety and needs a reflective response. Her mother could reply, "You seem worried about whether your grades will get you into a good school," and then talk about the admissions criteria of various colleges.

**Don't expect to be a perfect reflective listener.** Mistakes are to be expected. If you show you really want to understand but miss the feeling your teen is trying to express, your teen will probably sense your sincerity and simply correct you. At any rate, don't be afraid to take another stab at it.

Some parents worry if their teen remains silent after they reflect a feeling. The teen may simply be thinking about what the parents have said—digesting it. Resist the urge to fill the void. Wait and see what your teen does. If the silence continues, venture a guess about why your son or daughter isn't responding: "You seem upset about what I said."

**Do reflect pleasant feelings.** Most of our examples of reflective listening have focused on troubled feelings. But it's also important to show that you understand and care when your teen is feeling good. Be sensitive to pleasant feelings by noting, "You're feeling really good about that," "You're really excited," or "You seem proud of what you did."

**Don't overuse reflective listening.** When some parents first learn reflective listening, they start responding to their teen's every word and look. This can drive teenagers batty! And, more seriously, it can drive them away. Be sparing in your use of reflective listening. Save your comments for what seems to be important. If your son asks, "What time's dinner?" don't jump in with, "You seem hungry." That's going too far!

Parents can misuse reflective listening and actually reinforce a teenager's mistaken goal. For example:

> Fourteen-year-old Kirk constantly complains to his parents about how unfairly his math teacher treats him. They've listened and tried to understand, but Kirk hasn't made any attempt to remedy the situation. In this case it's quite possible that Kirk is using his problem to gain his parents' attention (and sympathy). It's not helpful to keep reinforcing these negative bids for attention. Kirk won't learn to solve his problems if he's rewarded for having them.

If you suspect your teen is sharing problems with you simply to get your attention, tell your teen, firmly but kindly, that you're not able to help. Express confidence in your child's ability to find a solution to the problem. You might say, "This seems to be a problem you'll need to work out for yourself. I'm sure you'll find a solution." If your teen keeps trying to get you involved, don't be available. Get busy with other things or talk about something else. Your teenager may not like these responses, but he or she will come to understand that you're willing to help when your teen starts making an effort to do something about the problems.

It's important, however, to give your teen attention when it's *not* expected. For example, if you notice improvement in schoolwork, appearance, or responsibility, make a positive reflective response: "It looks like you've really been working in English class."

A teen may also use problems to defeat parents, proving "You can't help me!" If you find yourself feeling angry when your teen keeps bringing you problems, that may be a sign you need to withdraw.

Sometimes teens express anger toward their parents in order to involve them in power contests or to get even with them. At such a time, reflective listening may reinforce the misbehavior and thus escalate the conflict. Sometimes, though, reflective listening can end power contests and move parents and teens toward cooperation. Only *you* know your teen and your limits. You'll have to decide whether to listen at a given moment or to withdraw and discuss the problem at a calmer time. If you decide to withdraw, you could say, "It seems you're really angry with me, but if we talk about it now, I feel things will only get worse. So I'm choosing to talk about it later when we're both calm." This procedure is not meant to be used as a way to anger or punish a teenager. It isn't intended to provide a way to avoid dealing with conflict. With-

drawal is a means to prevent unproductive conflict that could harm your relationship with your teen, and it should be used in a spirit of mutual respect.

When used thoughtfully and carefully, reflective listening is a very useful skill. With practice, you can become a proficient listener and establish a more open, effective relationship with your teen.

# References

1. Thomas Gordon, *Parent Effectiveness Training* (New York: Peter H. Wyden, 1970).
2. Don Dinkmeyer, Gary D. McKay, and Don Dinkmeyer, Jr., *Teacher's Handbook: Systematic Training for Effective Teaching* (Circle Pines, Minn.: American Guidance Service, 1980).
3. Peter H. Buntman and Eleanor M. Saris, *How to Live with Your Teenager: A Survivor's Handbook for Parents* (Pasadena, Calif.: Birch Tree Press, 1979).
4. Robert H. Bolton, *People Skills* (Englewood Cliffs, N.J.: Prentice Hall, 1979).
5. Dinkmeyer, McKay, and Dinkmeyer, 1980.
6. Robert R. Carkhuff, David H. Berenson, and Richard M. Pierce, *The Skills of Teaching: Interpersonal Skills* (Amherst, Mass.: Human Resource Development Press, 1977).
7. George M. Gazda et al., *Human Relations Development: A Manual for Educators,* 2d ed. (Boston: Allyn & Bacon, 1977).
8. Gerard Egan, *Exercises in Helping Skills: A Training Manual to Accompany the Skilled Helper* (Monterey, Calif.: Brooks/Cole, 1975).
9. Dinkmeyer, McKay, and Dinkmeyer, 1980.

## Questions

1. Why is it important to determine who owns the problem? What are some examples of teen-owned problems? of parent-owned problems?

2. What are some of the traditional roles parents play when responding to their teen's feelings? How can these responses discourage teens?

3. In listening and responding to teens, how can nonverbal language and silence be as important as words?

4. What is reflective listening? In what sense is reflective listening different from telling teens you know how they feel? How is it different from parroting?

5. What is the value of reflective listening? Why is it important to reflect both the feeling and the circumstances that led to the feeling?

6. What are some ways to phrase reflective listening responses? Think of as many as you can.

7. What is the difference between an open response and a closed response? Give some examples of both, other than those found in the chapter.

8. What are some ways parents can encourage teens to share feelings?

9. What cautions need to be kept in mind about reflective listening?

10. What are some specific situations with your teen where you think reflective listening would be useful?

## Activity for the Week

Practice using reflective listening with your teenager.

# Personal Development Exercise

## Developing a Feeling-Word Vocabulary

Below are words describing both unpleasant and pleasant feelings. Your teen may respond more easily to some words than to others. For each word, list as many synonyms as you can. Use the expanded lists to add variety and accuracy to your responses to your teen.

**\*Words for unpleasant feelings**

afraid _____
angry _____
annoyed _____
bad _____
bored _____
confused _____
defeated _____
disappointed _____
discouraged _____
disgusted _____
embarrassed _____
frustrated _____
guilty _____
hurt _____
indifferent _____
insignificant _____
irritated _____
put down _____
rejected _____
sad _____
shocked _____
uncertain _____
uncomfortable _____
unfairly treated _____
unloved _____
others _____

_____
_____
_____
_____

**Words for pleasant feelings**

accepted _____
appreciated _____
brave _____
capable _____
comfortable _____
compassionate _____
determined _____
encouraged _____
excited _____
glad _____
good _____
grateful _____
important _____
interested _____
loved _____
pleased _____
proud _____
relaxed _____
relieved _____
satisfied _____
sure of yourself _____
surprised _____
sympathetic _____
trusted _____
wonderful _____
others _____

_____
_____
_____
_____

---

\*Avoid overusing the word *upset*. This is a very general word; it's usually more effective to be specific.

Chart 5

# Reflective Listening

Reflective listening involves hearing teen's feelings and meanings and stating them so teen feels understood. It provides a mirror for teen to see self more clearly.

**Open Responses:** Demonstrate that listener accepts what teen says and feels; acknowledge teen's right to feelings. Open responses are interchangeable with teen's comments.

**Closed Responses:** Block communication by showing little or no understanding of teen's feelings.

| Teen's Comment | Closed Response | Open Response |
|---|---|---|
| (Crying) Bill and I just broke up. | You'll find another boyfriend. Don't worry. | Sounds like you're very sad. |
| I finally did it! I got an A! | I told you you could if you applied yourself. | You're really happy about getting that A. |
| You expect me to be perfect—everybody makes mistakes. | Well, you can certainly do a lot better than you're doing! | As I hear it, you're angry because you think I expect too much. |
| The teacher yelled at me in front of the whole class, and everybody laughed. She's always doing that to people! | Well, what did you do to upset the teacher? | You feel both angry and embarrassed because the teacher chewed you out in public. |
| I think I've got a good chance to pass the college entrance exam—I've really studied. But they only take fifty freshmen. | I know you've studied hard and I'm sure you'll make it. | You're feeling both confident and worried because you're well prepared, but it's tough to get into that school? |

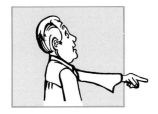

# Points to Remember

**1.** To determine how to respond to your teen, first consider the teen's goal and then decide who owns the problem.

**2.** To determine who owns the problem, ask: "Does this problem interfere with my rights and responsibilities? Does it involve the safety of my teen or others?" If the answer is no, it's not your problem.

**3.** Listening is one approach to help teens cope with teen-owned problems. It shows teens that parents care and helps teens clarify feelings and meanings.

**4.** To listen effectively, avoid nagging, criticizing, threatening, lecturing, prying, ridiculing, or reassuring.

**5.** An effective listener needs to "hear" both nonverbal and verbal messages.

**6.** Make sure your nonverbal behavior communicates interest and understanding. Be relaxed and show concern.

**7.** Reflective listening involves being a mirror— reflecting your teen's feelings and the circumstances of those feelings.

**8.** Be tentative in your response.

**9.** Open responses encourage further communication. They accurately reflect feelings and the circumstances of those feelings: they are interchangeable with the teen's message.

**10.** Closed responses shut off communication. They add interpretations and judgments or miss the feelings being expressed.

**11.** To encourage your teen to share feelings:

• Make a guess about nonverbal messages.
• Ask for comments.
• Be a model.

**12.** Follow these dos and don'ts of reflective listening:

• Do experiment with reflective listening.
• Don't try to force your teen to share feelings.
• Do respond as accurately as you can.
• Don't ask too many questions.
• Do take time to listen.
• Don't expect to be a perfect reflective listener.
• Do reflect pleasant feelings.
• Don't overuse reflective listening.

# My Plan for Improving Relationships

(An opportunity to assess progress each week)

My specific concern:

_____

_____

My usual response:

☐ talking, lecturing                   ☐ punishing, shaming

☐ complaining, nagging              ☐ giving up, forgetting because discouraged

☐ becoming angry, screaming      ☐ exerting power by removing privilege

☐ being sarcastic, attacking        ☐ other _____

My progress this week:

| | I am doing this more | I need to do this more | I am about the same | | I am doing this more | I need to do this more | I am about the same |
|---|---|---|---|---|---|---|---|
| Understanding the purpose of behavior | ☐ | ☐ | ☐ | Communicating love, positive feelings | ☐ | ☐ | ☐ |
| Working on developing an equal relationship based on mutual respect | ☐ | ☐ | ☐ | Withdrawing from conflict | ☐ | ☐ | ☐ |
| Responding to emotions more effectively | ☐ | ☐ | ☐ | Preventing discipline problems by giving choices | ☐ | ☐ | ☐ |
| Encouraging | ☐ | ☐ | ☐ | Correcting discipline problems appropriately | ☐ | ☐ | ☐ |
| Appreciating and giving responsibility | ☐ | ☐ | ☐ | Arranging democratic family meetings | ☐ | ☐ | ☐ |
| Listening | ☐ | ☐ | ☐ | Being firm and kind | ☐ | ☐ | ☐ |
| Revealing my feelings without blaming or accusing | ☐ | ☐ | ☐ | Staying out of problems that are not my problems | ☐ | ☐ | ☐ |

I learned:

_____

_____

_____

I plan to change my behavior by:

_____

_____

_____

# CHAPTER 6

●

# *Communication: Expressing Your Feelings and Exploring Alternatives*

In the previous chapter we described ways to listen when your teen shares a problem. But what do you do if you're the one with the problem? At times, you might decide to ignore a small irritation. But for many problems you have with your teenager, you need effective problem-solving skills—skills that can help you express your feelings about a situation, negotiate with your teen, or use a disciplinary method called natural and logical consequences.

In this chapter we'll discuss positive ways to communicate your feelings about things your teen does that you find irritating or upsetting. You will learn the process of exploring alternatives, which you can use to help your teen cope with a problem. Exploring alternatives can also aid you in negotiating with your teen to reach mutually agreeable solutions.

## Why Don't Teenagers Listen to Us?

> I've told you five times to wash the windows! Honestly, you're so lazy!
> Quit leaving your coat on the couch! How many times do I have to tell you!
> Turn down that TV! Can't you see I'm on the phone? You're so inconsiderate!

Suppose you were on the receiving end of these messages. How would you feel? Would you want to listen and cooperate?

These messages are all put-downs. They assign blame or name-call. They insult a person's intelligence. And they're ineffective messages because they get us the opposite of what we want. Instead of encouraging cooperation, they invite resistance and rebellion.

In moments of frustration, we've all been known to say these kinds of things. Not knowing what else to do, we lash out. Unfortunately, though, when we show our teens disrespect, they have no reason to respect *us*. Instead of blaming or accusing, what if we decided simply to share how we feel when a teen's behavior interferes with our rights?

Let's use one of the examples shown above. Imagine that you're the teenager. How would you react if your mother said to you, "I've told you five times to wash the windows! Honestly, you're so lazy!" Would you be likely to cooperate? Suppose instead you were told: "When I have to ask so many times to have the windows washed, I feel really frustrated because it seems that what I want doesn't count." What exactly are the differences between the two messages? Before you read on, think about those differences for a few minutes.

In the first message, your mother called you a name (lazy) and blamed you for the way she felt. In the second message, she simply told you how she felt about the

101

problem. She didn't blame you, but took responsibility for her own feelings ("I feel frustrated"). She respected you and trusted you to help her out.

## You-Messages and I-Messages

When our teens don't listen or cooperate, it may be because we send "you-messages" instead of "I-messages."[1] You-messages are statements that put teens down; they blame or criticize. These messages often provoke anger, hurt, embarrassment, and feelings of worthlessness in teens. Teenagers may take statements such as "You're inconsiderate" or "You don't use your head" as testimonies to their lack of personal value. When we parents talk to teens in these ways, we actually try to blame them for our feelings. Unfortunately, many teens have come to expect reminders, criticisms, and accusations. By fulfilling their expectations, we only reinforce their goals of misbehavior.

I-messages are an alternative to you-messages. An I-message simply shares our feelings and concerns and communicates that we trust our teens to respect our feelings. When we use I-messages, we don't criticize or blame. We don't imply that teens "make" us feel angry or hurt or frustrated. By using I-messages we assert that we're responsible for our own emotions—that we're in charge of our feelings. Instead of saying "You make me feel bad," we say "I feel discouraged."

To illustrate the important differences between you-messages and I-messages, let's look at our other earlier examples:

**You-Messages:** Quit leaving your coat on the couch! How many times do I have to tell you!

Turn down that TV! Can't you see I'm on the phone? You're so inconsiderate!

**I-Messages:** When I see a coat on the couch, I feel discouraged because I try hard to keep the living room straightened up.

I feel frustrated when the TV is so loud, because I can't hear what the caller is saying.

Do you sense the respect that I-messages convey? There are no orders or solutions sent in an I-message—your teen will know what needs to be done. When you avoid providing solutions to problems, you appeal to your teen's intelligence, good nature, and desire to cooperate. This is the greatest form of respect.

## How to Formulate an I-Message

I-messages focus on your feelings about your teen's behavior—not on you or your teen as individuals. When expressing feelings to teens it's essential to separate the deed from the doer. To do this, focus on actions, not on people themselves. Using the word *when* conveys that you're upset only with a particular behavior: "When I find the door left unlocked," "When I see the gas tank's empty," or "When you're two hours late" are phrases that refer to specific actions. They point out the behavior you're concerned about without laying blame on anyone.

Next, describe how you feel when you encounter an upsetting deed: "I feel disappointed," "I'm concerned," or "I worry" are phrases that refer to your feelings. Realize that it's not actually the deed that has you upset, but the *consequences* the deed produces for you, for others, or for your teen. If your teenage daughter comes home two hours late on a Friday night, is it actually her lateness that feeds your feeling of

worry, or is it the prospect of what might have happened to her? Your feelings about her staying out late are really a response to the consequences of that behavior: "When you're two hours late, I worry because something might have happened to you."

I-messages have a specific form. To formulate I-messages, follow these three steps:[2]

1. Describe the behavior you find bothersome. Simply describe, don't blame: "When I see the gas tank's empty, . . ."
2. State your feelings about the possible consequences of the behavior: "I feel anxious . . ."
3. State the consequences: "because I have to get gas and I might be late for my appointment."

Simply stated, the format looks like this: "When _____, I feel _____ because _____."

## Examples of I-Messages

Study the following examples of problems and I-messages:

**Problem:** Dad and Inga have planned an activity together. At the last minute, Inga decides to go out with friends instead.
**I-Message:** When we have plans to spend time together and you change your mind, I feel disappointed because I've been looking forward to being with you.

**Problem:** Sixteen-year-old Leo is the last one to leave the house in the morning and neglects to lock the door.
**I-Message:** When I find the door unlocked, I get worried because we might be robbed.

Feel free to vary the "When _____, I feel _____ because _____" format. For example, you might say, "I get worried when I find the door unlocked because we might get robbed." This is still an I-message—it's a nonjudgmental reporting of your feelings, your teen's behavior, and the consequences that influence your feelings.

Remember to keep blame out of your I-messages. One word that often conveys blame is the word *you*. At times you'll have to use this pronoun because you'll be referring directly to your teen, but you can still use it without placing blame. "When you come home two hours late" doesn't place blame, it merely states a fact. Whenever possible, however, avoid the word *you*; talk, instead, about the *situation* that bothers you.

Remember, too, the importance of nonverbal communication. I-messages are a friendly, respectful, and honest way to communicate feelings. But if your tone of voice and body language are out of sync with what you say, your teen will be more influenced by your nonverbal behavior than by your words.

Sometimes an I-message will leave out a feeling and simply state the behavior and the consequences: "I can't talk on the phone when there's so much noise." "I can't set the table when there's a coat in the middle of it."

When communicating your feelings, it's important to choose your words carefully. Instead of saying you feel *upset,* identify your precise feeling: "I feel nervous." "I'm shocked." "I feel disrespected." Words that label or judge may turn I-messages into you-messages:

**You-Messages:** When you're so messy . . .

When you inconvenience us . . .

**I-Messages:** When I find crumbs on the family-room floor . . .

When we make plans and you change your mind at the last minute . . .

I-messages provide a format for expressing feelings and solving problems parents and teens own together. They can occasionally be used to focus on a teen-owned problem as well, if that problem is one about which the parent has serious concern: "When you hang out with John, I really worry because he may decide to break the law while you're with him and you could get in trouble." "When you eat so much junk food, I really get concerned about your health." Although your teen may decide to continue the behavior, you've at least communicated your love, respect, and concern. You can also encourage your teen to be responsible by emphasizing your faith that she or he will make a sensible decision.

# Angry Messages Aren't Effective

An I-message delivered in anger is often a you-message. Why? Because when we show we're angry about something our teens have done, it's very difficult for them to believe we're not blaming them for our anger. Hostile feelings usually put the other person on the defensive. When this happens, both people become more hostile, and a battle may occur. Obviously, shouting angry, hurtful things at each other probably won't solve the problem.

There are exceptions, of course. If you and your teen have an open, honest relationship, *occasional* anger can be effective. But I-messages won't help if they're used to vent hostility. Just because you say "I feel" before you say "angry" doesn't mean your teen won't view your remark as an accusation!

So what do you do with anger and other hostile feelings? You may wish to refer back to Chapter 3, where we suggested some ways to deal with irrational feelings and beliefs. Keep in mind that your anger can reinforce your teen's goal of power or revenge. Anger often occurs with other feelings, such as worry, frustration, concern, disappointment, or fear. If you learn to express *these* feelings instead of the anger, you will be communicating that you really respect and care about your teen. Your teenager in turn will be more interested in cooperating.

Let's look at an example: Suppose your son promised to be home right after school to help you get ready for guests. He hasn't shown up and school has been out for over two hours. How do you feel? You probably feel angry—after all, you're afraid you won't be ready on time. But aren't you also feeling let down, worried, anxious, or rushed? These feelings probably led to your anger. The more worried or rushed you felt, the more anger you probably generated. When your son walks in the door, will you ease the problem by lashing out at him? What if instead you express the feeling that led to your anger? "When you promise to help me and show up two hours late, I feel let down because I need your help to get all this work done." Your son will be more likely to pitch in and help if you do the unexpected and avoid venting your anger.

Of course, there will be times when you will slip and send angry you-messages. When this happens, simply make a responsible apology: "I'm sorry I blew up and I'm working on my temper." And there may be times when you decide it's necessary to express your annoyance, anger, or hurt. If you decide to do this, we suggest writing it down in a note. Notes are often effective because they defuse anger and help you steer clear of confrontations that can lead to more problems. You have time to think carefully about how to express your feelings, and your teen has time to think about the situation and decide what to do. Post the note—after you've calmed down—where your teen will see it. Phrase it as respectfully as you can and offer your teen a chance to talk about the problem. For example:

> When I went into the kitchen this morning to fix breakfast, I found the dirty dishes still in the sink. I felt angry because this has happened several times, even though we made an agreement that you would clean up after dinner on Tuesday and Thursday nights. I'm willing to work out another arrangement, but I feel it's unfair for me to have to clean up every night. We need to talk about this.

## Dos and Don'ts of Using I-Messages

**Do be prepared to listen when you send an I-message.** Your teen may simply say okay and take care of the problem. Or your teen may give you an I-message in return. When this happens, be ready to change directions and use your reflective listening skills:

**Dad:** When I discovered long-distance calls to Anne on our bill, I was surprised because I didn't expect you to make calls without talking to me about it.
**Owen:** You make long-distance calls to your friends—why can't I?
**Dad:** It seems unfair to you that I expect you to check with me first?
**Owen:** Yeah, and besides, I only called her twice. What's the big deal?
**Dad:** You're angry because it seems to you I'm overreacting?
**Owen:** Yeah.
**Dad:** Well, I can understand your anger. But I get worried because long-distance calls add up to expensive phone bills.
**Owen:** Well, I guess I could pay for my calls.

**Dad:** I'm glad we could work this out.

Here the father took a firm stand, but he was also respectful of Owen's feelings. Not all problems are solved this easily. Nevertheless, many potential conflicts can be avoided by combining I-messages with reflective listening.

**Don't overuse I-messages.** I-messages are valuable skills for influencing teens. But if we send an I-message every time teens do something we don't like, we may quickly turn them off. You may decide it's best to ignore some behaviors if you feel your teen expects you to respond.

Like reflective listening, I-messages can sometimes reinforce a teen's misbehavior, leaving parent and teen locked in a power struggle. In these cases, it's best to delay conversation until a time when you and your teen aren't in conflict. Remember, teens expect parents to say something when they misbehave. If you choose another time to send your I-message, you'll be doing the unexpected.

Simple requests are often effective ways to gain cooperation:

> Would you be willing to do the dishes tonight?
> It would really help if you'd take your sister to the library.

Keep in mind that by making a request you're giving your teen the right to say no. We suggest that you offer your teen this right—doing so demonstrates respect and may very well encourage a willingness to help in the future. If your teen says yes but doesn't follow through, use I-messages to gain cooperation.

**Do use I-messages to express positive feelings.** It's important to communicate your good feelings—don't be shy!

> Thanks for cleaning the yard today. It really looks nice!
> I appreciate how you helped Grandpa when I was busy yesterday.

Be generous with your good feelings. Teenagers need to know they can make important contributions to the family.

Sometimes teens will reject the best I-message. When this happens, it's time to explore alternatives for negotiating a mutually acceptable agreement.

# Exploring Alternatives

Effective communication involves more than reflective listening and I-messages. These methods help teens to feel better and to find a rational perspective, but they won't always solve a problem or resolve a conflict. At this point, parents can decide to explore alternatives.

Exploring alternatives has two uses: to help parents assist teens in dealing with challenges they face in their lives, and to help parents negotiate solutions to conflicts with teens. Asking effective, respectful questions is the key to exploring alternatives.

# The Art of Questioning

Questions, like listening responses, can be thought of as closed or open. A closed question usually calls for a yes or no answer and may cut off conversation. Some closed questions ask the listener to agree with you: "Do you think _____?" expects an answer of no; "Don't you think _____?" expects an answer of yes. *Why* questions can also be closed. "Why did you do it?" often calls for a defensive answer or a rationalization; the question seems like an accusation. Other closed questions often begin with a verb, such as *is, are,* or *were.*

Open questions, on the other hand, usually begin with *where, when, what, who, which,* or *how.* They tend to keep conversation going because they ask for information the parent needs in order to help or about feelings that teens can share. "Where will you begin looking for a job?" "What do you like about him?" "How do you feel about this?"

Just because a question begins with *where, when, what, who, which,* or *how* doesn't guarantee it's an open question. Your tone of voice, nonverbal expression, and intention are crucial. "*Who* told you *this* was true?" "*Where* are you going?" "*What* do you like about *him?*" No one being asked these questions is likely to feel like opening up.

Here are some ways you can turn closed questions into open ones:

**Closed:** Are you still having trouble with your term paper?
**Open:** How's the term paper going?

**Closed:** Why don't you _____?
**Open:** Which option appeals to you most?

**Closed:** Why can't you get along with your teacher?
**Open:** What does the teacher do that bothers you?

Of course, asking open questions won't guarantee that sharing will take place. For example, you may ask your teen, "How are things going?" and get a reply of "Fine" or

"Okay." When this happens you could ask, "What's fine (okay) about it?" Your teen's answer will let you know if "fine" or "okay" is really how your daughter or son feels, or if it's just a learned response.[3] *What* questions often work better than *how* questions. For example, instead of asking, "How are things going?" you can ask, "What's happening with _____?"

Closed questions aren't always ineffective; sometimes they're necessary! You need to know if your teen wants to talk about a problem: "Do you want to talk about it?" You need to see if your teen wants to look at alternatives: "Would you like to talk about some possible solutions to this problem?" Commitments and agreements are important: "Are you willing to _____?" "Shall we talk about it again on Friday to see how it's going?" A *why* question can be open when it's used to explore another person's motives: "Have you considered why she does this?"

In problem-solving discussions with your teen, it's important to keep questions to a minimum. Ask only for information you *really* need to understand the problem, and keep most of your questions open. One last guideline: Don't ask a question if you have enough information to make a statement. For example, if your teen looks and sounds sad, don't ask, "How do you feel?" Reflecting the feeling is more likely to open a dialogue: "You seem down tonight."

## Exploring Alternatives When Your Teen Owns the Problem

Exploring alternatives is not a fancy way of giving advice, and it doesn't mean that parents solve problems for teens. Advice is often not taken—teens may see it as an attempt to control them. Also, advice can make teens dependent upon parents for answers. Exploring alternatives *is* a way of helping teens look at options available to solve a problem. There are five steps in the process:[4]

**1. Understand and clarify the problem.** Use your reflective listening skills to help your teen feel understood and accepted. Start to identify the specific things contributing to the problem. Ask open questions. If you need more information, you may have to return to this step several times during your conversation with your teen.

**2. Explore alternatives through brainstorming.** Begin by asking, "Would you like to look at some possible solutions to the problem?" If your teen's answer is no, back up to Step 1. Show that you understand, and offer your help for another time. If the answer is yes, continue by asking if your teen has considered what to do about the problem. Encourage brainstorming—free, creative thinking without evaluation. Seek as many ideas as possible, being careful not to evaluate any individual suggestions until all are out on the table. This process of generating ideas leads to effective problem-solving skills. If your teen's ideas seem like workable options, you're ready for Step 3. If they don't, or if your teen has no ideas, here are some ways you can stimulate thinking:

• Ask your teen to pretend a friend has the problem. Sometimes we're better at finding solutions to other people's problems than to our own. Ask your teen, "What would you tell (Joan) if *she* had this problem?" After some ideas have been proposed, ask, "Do you think any of these ideas will work for *you?*"
• Use role reversal. Have your teen take the role of the person with whom there is a problem; you, in turn, can take the part

of your daughter or son. This gives you an opportunity to show your teen an alternative way to handle the problem. When finished, ask how *your* response differed from your teen's usual approach.
• Make a suggestion. A suggestion is different from advice. Advice tells people what they should do. A suggestion offers a possibility that teens are free to accept or reject. Make your suggestion tentatively, putting it in the form of a question: "Have you considered _____?" "What do you think might happen if _____?"

A suggestion is different from advice.

**3. Evaluate proposed alternatives.** Once all the possibilities have been brainstormed, it's time to evaluate them carefully. One by one, summarize each idea and have your teen evaluate it: "What do you think of this idea?"

**4. Choose a solution.** Ask, "Which idea do you think will work the best for you?" Let your teenager decide. To make sure your teen really understands the problem and why a particular solution will work, use open questions to clarify your teen's reasons for the choice. By doing this, you're modeling a problem-solving process that can be used again and again in various situations.

If you think your teen's solution won't work, help explore possible consequences: "What do you think will happen if you do this?" You may want to offer your opinion: "It seems to me that _____. What do you think?" Then invite your teen to look at the other ideas generated, or to brainstorm some more. But remember, unless a situation is actually dangerous, the choice of an action is up to your daughter or son. Your teen owns the problem—and the consequences.

**5. Obtain a commitment and set a time for evaluation.** There's a big difference between trying and doing. When people say, "I'll try," they often mean they think the idea won't work. Exploring alternatives requires a firm commitment to action. Ask your teen to experiment with the agreed-upon solution for a specific period of time, no matter what happens. Usually a few days or a week is long enough to see if a plan is working. You can ask your teen, "Are you willing to use the plan until _____?"

Next, set a time for evaluation. In this follow-up conversation, you and your teen talk over how the plan is going. If your teen's solution hasn't worked out, don't offer I-told-you-sos. Let your teen decide to keep the plan, modify it, or choose something else. Then the two of you can determine whether another discussion is needed and when it will take place.

If, before the agreed-upon evaluation time, your teen complains that the plan isn't working, you could comment, "I thought we agreed you'd experiment with the plan until _____, but you decide." Many teens—and parents, too—are impatient and have

unrealistic expectations of themselves. Emphasize that changes have to be gradual.

Don't take over the responsibility of tracking down your teen if she or he doesn't talk to you at the time you've set. Sometime later, mention that you didn't talk about the plan at the agreed-upon time, and ask how things are going. You might add, "Do you still want to talk about it?"

## An Example of Exploring Alternatives When Your Teen Owns the Problem

You'll recall that in Chapter 5, Jeremy shared his feelings about his part-time job. Let's continue the conversation between Jeremy and his mother to illustrate the process of exploring alternatives:

**Mom:** How's the job going?
**Jeremy:** Not so good. The boss is really tough. It seems there's no pleasing her.
**Mom:** Sounds like you're discouraged because she expects a lot. (*Step 1: Understanding and clarifying the problem*)
**Jeremy:** I do my best, but it's never good enough! I just don't know what to do!
**Mom:** You're confused about how to do what she wants?
**Jeremy:** Yeah, and if I lose my job, there goes the car!
**Mom:** Would you like to talk about some possible solutions to this problem? (*Step 2: Exploring alternatives through brainstorming*)
**Jeremy:** What solutions?
**Mom:** Well, I don't know yet. But maybe if we talk about it, we can figure something out. What do you think?
**Jeremy:** Maybe.
**Mom:** What options have you thought of?

**Jeremy:** Getting another job, I guess, but I don't know if I can find one.

**Mom:** So getting another job is one idea, but you're uncomfortable with that because you don't know if one's available. (*Step 1*)

**Jeremy:** Yeah.

**Mom:** Okay, that's one possibility. Let's do some brainstorming. We'll see how many we can think of, and I'll write them all down, no matter how strange some may seem. Is that okay with you? (*Step 2*)

**Jeremy:** I guess so.

**Mom:** Okay. Have you thought of any other ideas?

**Jeremy:** Not really.

**Mom:** You said earlier that you don't know what your boss wants. How could you find out?

**Jeremy:** I don't know.

**Mom:** If your friend Linda had this problem, what would you suggest she do?

**Jeremy:** I guess I'd tell her to ask the boss what she wants.

**Mom:** Do you think that could work for you?

**Jeremy:** Maybe. I don't know.

**Mom:** Is it at least a possibility?

**Jeremy:** Yeah.

**Mom:** Okay, so far you've said you can look for another job or ask the boss what she wants. Any other ideas?

**Jeremy:** None that I can think of.

**Mom:** Well, you have two ideas. Let's look at each one. What about looking for another job? (*Step 3: Evaluating proposed alternatives*)

**Jeremy:** It's probably impossible to find one.

**Mom:** So, that's not something you want to do. What about asking her what she wants? (*Step 4: Choosing a solution*)

**Jeremy:** I suppose I could do that.

**Mom:** How could you go about it? (*Step 5: Obtaining a commitment*)

**Jeremy:** Maybe I could get an appointment with her and go over everything I'm supposed to do at work.

**Mom:** What will you say to her?

**Jeremy:** I'm not sure.

**Mom:** You said you don't know how to do things the way she wants them done. What do you think about explaining that to her, telling her you want to do the job right, and asking for guidelines?

**Jeremy:** That might work.

**Mom:** Are you comfortable with that idea? (*Step 1*)

**Jeremy:** Not really.

**Mom:** Would you be willing to experiment with it and see what happens? (*Step 5*)

**Jeremy:** I've got nothing to lose.

**Mom:** When will you ask for the appointment?

**Jeremy:** I'll ask tomorrow.

**Mom:** After your appointment, would you like to talk about how it went? (*Step 5: Setting a time for evaluation*) .

**Jeremy:** Okay.

Jeremy's mother began by listening and showing that she understood. Her reflective listening skills encouraged Jeremy to explore alternatives with her. She used a variety of techniques to stimulate his thinking: she explained the concept of brainstorming and got Jeremy's agreement; she asked him to pretend to give advice to a friend; she used suggestions carefully, and only when there appeared to be nothing else to do. To show she understood and to avoid rushing to a solution, she backed up to Step 1 and used reflective listening. She could have suggested role playing: she could have played Jeremy and he could have played the boss. Finally, Jeremy's mother got a specific commitment from her son. She asked what he would do and when he would do it. They planned a time to evaluate his efforts. Assuming the talk with the boss went well, Jeremy and Mom may want to plan another conversation in a few days to see if he's getting along better with his supervisor.

Timing is very important in deciding to explore alternatives. We suggest that you stay with reflective listening until your teen seems to feel comfortable about sharing feelings. If you try to explore alternatives before your teenager is ready, it may seem that you're prying into personal affairs. Increased sharing is a signal that your daughter or son is feeling safe about opening up to you. When this happens, your teen is probably ready to explore alternatives.[5]

Like any method, exploring alternatives can be misused. Teens may discover that having problems is a way to gain parental attention, sympathy, and reassurance. They may use the process to try and prove that parents can't really help them. If your teen seems to be sharing problems for any of these reasons, state firmly but kindly that you're willing to get involved only if your teen really wants to solve the problem.

# Exploring Alternatives When You Own the Problem

I-messages can resolve lots of problems parents have with their teenagers. But sometimes they don't work. When they don't, you may want to enter into negotiation. The same five steps can be followed:

**1. Understand and clarify the problem.** When you have a problem you want to discuss, it's best to approach your teen when the two of you aren't at odds with one another. Choose a time when your teen is not involved in anything else. Begin the conversation with an I-message and be prepared to use your reflective listening skills. If questions are necessary, ask open ones. Make clear your desire to reach a mutually agreeable solution. Admit your mistakes.

**2. Explore alternatives through brainstorming.** Ask your teen for ideas about how the problem can be solved. If necessary, explain the brainstorming process. Join in the brainstorming if you need to—after all, you own the problem. But do get your teen's ideas first, and be careful not to attach a judgment to *any* suggestions. Write down all ideas.

**3. Evaluate proposed alternatives.** Go through the list, asking your teen to give her or his opinion first. Then give your own, phrasing it in a direct way: "I like this idea because _____." "I'm uncomfortable with this idea because _____." Cross off ideas that one or the other of you is not willing to consider.

**4. Choose a solution.** At this point decide together which idea or ideas you're both willing to follow through on. You could simply ask, "Which idea do we want?" Ideas can be modified or combined.

**5. Make a commitment and set a time for evaluation.** Summarize your agreement, ask if your teen is willing to follow the plan, and then show that you're willing to live up to it as well. Decide together how long you will experiment with the plan and when you'll meet again to discuss it.

It may be necessary to discuss and establish consequences of an agreement being broken. You can introduce this idea by saying, "If for some reason you decide not to follow our agreement, what would be a fair consequence?" Your teen may jump to the conclusion that you don't trust her or him. If so, explain that it's not a question of trust, it's more like an insurance policy. You might add, "None of us is perfect, including me!" Be sure to talk about the consequences of *your* failing to live up to the agreement. This is only fair. Negotiation works only if it's between equals!

To make sure agreements are understood and remembered, write them down and have each person sign the agreement. This may sound a bit formal, but we've found that putting agreements on paper is very effective.

When negotiating with your daughter or son, keep in mind these four essential principles of problem solving:[6]

*Establish mutual respect.* In any conflict, disrespect can destroy the chance for cooperation. If you take the initiative and show respect for your teenager, chances are your teen will return that respect. First, of course, you need to respect yourself. Mutual respect is established when you decide to neither fight nor give in, but to seek a solution that both you and your teen are willing to live with. To help establish mutual respect, use reflective listening, ask open questions, and share your feelings.

*Keep the real issue in focus.* In a parent-teen conflict, the real issue is rarely the topic being discussed. Neglecting chores, coming home late, and misusing the car are problems, yes. But the real issue in any conflict involves the parent's and teen's beliefs and goals—goals like winning, controlling, and being right. Identify the underlying problem and point it out: "Could it be that the real issue between us is who's going to win this conflict? I'm not interested in winning at your expense. How can we come up with a solution both of us can live with?"

*Recognize and change the present agreement.* In a conflict, opponents *do* have an agreement: they've decided to fight! But when people fight, they are trying to change each other. This is futile. The only way to resolve a conflict is to decide what *you* will do and what changes *you* will make, not what *your teen* will do. If you're willing to make changes, chances are your teen will be too.

*Share the responsibility for making decisions.* Further cooperation is more likely if you and your teen decide together how to resolve the conflict. Teens are more committed to decisions they've helped make.

## An Example of Exploring Alternatives When You Own the Problem

In the following example, Kris's father has a problem with his daughter's staying on the phone too long:

**Dad:** Kris, I have something I need to talk with you about. When you stay on the phone a long time, I get concerned because sometimes I need to make calls and I might miss incoming calls. (*Step*

*1: Understanding and clarifying the problem)*

**Kris:** I'm not on the phone *that* long.

**Dad:** You seem angry with my complaint.

**Kris:** Well, I should be able to talk to my friends!

**Dad:** You think I'm saying "don't use the phone"? Really, I'm not. I just want to work out a way we can both use it.

**Kris:** You're on the phone sometimes when *I* want to use it.

**Dad:** I guess I do talk too long sometimes, and I'm willing to change that. Are you willing to work out a solution to this problem that we can both live with? (*Step 2: Exploring alternatives through brainstorming*)

**Kris:** I guess so.

**Dad:** Suppose we brainstorm some ideas. Let's come up with as many as we can think of, no matter how wild, and not judge them until we're out of ideas. Is that okay with you? (Kris agrees) What suggestions do you have?

**Kris:** You could get me my own phone line.

**Dad:** That's one idea. I'll write it down. What else could we do?

**Kris:** That's all I can think of.

**Dad:** We could limit our time to fifteen minutes a call.

**Kris:** I don't want to do that.

**Dad:** I thought we agreed just to list all the ideas now, and talk about them later.

**Kris:** Okay . . . but why don't we set certain times each of us can use the phone? Unless we get calls, that is.

**Dad:** I'll write that down along with the other two ideas. What else?

**Kris:** I'm out of ideas.

**Dad:** Let's talk about each of these then. (*Step 3: Evaluating proposed alternatives*)

Kris and her father discuss the three ideas. Kris wants her own line and her father agrees to a private line providing she helps pay for it. Kris still objects to time limits on calls. Both Kris and Dad agree it might work to assign times each can use the phone.

**Dad:** We have two ideas we can agree on: getting you your own line and assigning times. Which one do we want? (*Step 4: Choosing a solution*)

**Kris:** I want my own line so we can both use a phone whenever we need to.

Kris and her father agree that she will get her own line and will have to share the installation bill and monthly payments. (*Step 4: Making a commitment*) They decide on the amount she'll pay. (*Step 3*) There is no need for a follow-up conversation (*Step 5: Setting a time for evaluation*) unless Kris doesn't pay her share. If this occurs, the consequences might be to subtract from her allowance the agreed-upon amount or to remove the phone from her room until she makes the payments. Dad may simply allow payments not to be made, in which case the phone company would remove the line.

At times, negotiations can break down—a mutually acceptable solution just doesn't emerge. If this happens, you may want to return to Step 2 and brainstorm again. Or, you may decide to stop negotiating altogether, until both of you have had a chance to think things over. If the problem at hand requires immediate attention and all efforts produce no results, you may have to make the decision on your own. You can offer your teen an opportunity to discuss the problem again at another time: "It seems we aren't able to come up with a solution, so I'll make the decision for now. We can talk about it again in a few days to see if we can agree." It may happen that your teen will refuse to negotiate at all. In this case too you may have to make the decision.

Exploring alternatives is a valuable skill for building an effective parent-teen relationship. Through exploring alternatives, parents and teens learn to cooperate. And teens learn a problem-solving process that is helpful for handling their own problems, for resolving conflicts with others, and for making life decisions.

# References

1. Thomas Gordon, *Parent Effectiveness Training* (New York: Peter H. Wyden, 1970).
2. Thomas Gordon, *Teacher Effectiveness Training* (New York: Peter H. Wyden, 1974).
3. Don Dinkmeyer, Gary D. McKay, and Don Dinkmeyer, Jr., *Teacher's Handbook: Systematic Training for Effective Teaching* (Circle Pines, Minn.: American Guidance Service, 1980).
4. Dinkmeyer, McKay, and Dinkmeyer, 1980.
5. Don Dinkmeyer and Gary D. McKay, *Raising a Responsible Child* (New York: Simon & Schuster, 1973).
6. Rudolf Dreikurs and Loren Grey, *Parent's Guide to Child Discipline* (New York: Hawthorn, 1970).

# Questions

1. What is an I-message? How is an I-message different from a you-message?
2. Give some examples of you-messages, other than those found in the chapter. How would you turn these you-messages into I-messages?
3. What is the three-step format for constructing an I-message? How can the format be varied?
4. How can an I-message be used to separate the deed from the doer? Why is it important to state the consequences the teen's behavior produces, rather than just dwelling on the behavior?
5. Why is it important to keep anger out of I-messages? What are some ways parents can deal with their own anger?
6. What is meant by exploring alternatives? How does this process differ from giving advice?
7. What are the differences between open questions and closed questions? Give some examples of each, other than those found in the chapter.
8. Why is it important to ask teens to experiment rather than just "try" an idea?
9. What are some specific situations in which you could use exploring alternatives to help your teen with a problem? to negotiate with your teen when you own the problem?
10. What are four essential principles of problem solving?
11. What can parents do if negotiations break down?

## Activity for the Week

1. Practice sending I-messages. Be prepared to use your reflective listening skills.

2. If you think your teen is ready, practice exploring alternatives. If you decide to explore alternatives to negotiate a problem between you and your teen, have in mind:
   • when you will talk with your teen
   • how you will begin
   • what concessions you are willing to make
   • what you will do if agreement is not reached

# Personal Development Exercise

## Formulating I-Messages

Write I-messages for the following situations. Use the "When _____, I feel _____ because _____" format and compare your I-messages with the ones suggested below.

**Problems**

1. You discover your son has been smoking in bed before going to sleep. He often falls asleep while reading in bed late at night, and you're concerned about fire. _____

_____

2. Your daughter keeps borrowing your hairdryer and doesn't return it to the place you normally keep it. You often have to search her room to find the dryer. _____

_____

3. Your teen snacks heavily after school and doesn't eat the dinner you've taken the trouble to prepare. _____

_____

**Suggested I-Messages**

1. When I find you've been smoking in bed, I get very worried because a fire might start.

2. When I can't find my hairdryer, I feel frustrated because looking for it might make me late for work.

3. When I work hard to fix dinner and it's not eaten, I feel discouraged because it seems that you don't care about the time and effort I've put in.

Now write two situations in your relationship with your teen where you feel I-messages would be appropriate. Write the I-message you would send to your teen.

Situation 1:_____

_____

_____

_____

I-message: _____

_____

Situation 2:_____

_____

_____

_____

I-message: _____

_____

# Communication: Reflective Listening and I-Messages

This chart illustrates situations in which the parent determines who owns a problem and decides whether to use reflective listening or send an I-message.

| Situation | Problem Owner | Reflective Listening | I-Message |
|---|---|---|---|
| Teen upset about not being invited to a party. | **Teen** | You're feeling left out because you weren't asked to the party? | |
| Teen backs out of driveway too fast. | **Parent** | | When you back out of the driveway so fast, I get really scared because you could have an accident, and someone might be hurt. |
| Teen planning on having braces removed before school starts. Dentist says teen must wait two more months. | **Teen** | It must be pretty disappointing to have to wait when you were counting on having them off before school started. | |
| Teen has friends over. In order to impress friends, teen talks rudely to parent. | **Parent** | | (After friends leave) When I'm talked to that way, I feel put down because I want to be respected just like anyone else. |

# Steps in Exploring Alternatives

| Step | When Teen Owns Problem | When Parent Owns Problem |
|------|------------------------|--------------------------|
| **1.** Understand and clarify the problem. | Sounds like you're very hurt when the others laugh at you. What do you do when they laugh? What do they do when you get angry? | When you come home late, I get very worried because something might have happened to you. |
| **2.** Explore alternatives through brainstorming. | What are some other things you could do when they laugh? | You're annoyed because you think I'm overprotective? |
| **3.** Evaluate proposed alternatives. | What do you think about the first idea—laughing with them? | How can we solve this so I don't worry and so you feel in charge of your life? |
| **4.** Choose a solution. | Which idea do you think will work best? What do you think will happen if you do this? | How do you feel about calling if you're going to be late? |
| **5.** Obtain or make a commitment and set a time for evaluation. | Are you willing to laugh with them just to see what happens? It may take them a while to get used to a new response from you— would you be willing to do this several times? Shall we talk about it on _____? | It seems we're in agreement on this idea—right?<br><br>As I understand it, you'll call me if you're going to be over fifteen minutes late. Is that the way you understand it? What do you think would be a fair consequence if you decide not to call? If I slip and get angry with you what do you think should happen? Shall we do this for a couple of weeks and then talk about how it's going? |

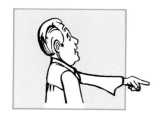

# Points to Remember

**1.** Teens may not listen to parents when parents send you-messages. You-messages accuse, blame, and criticize. They destroy communication and reinforce goals of misbehavior.

**2.** I-messages respectfully express your feelings and concerns. They don't blame or criticize. I-messages trust teens to return respect.

**3.** I-messages are often unexpected and so don't reinforce goals of misbehavior.

**4.** To formulate an I-message, use this format: "When _____, I feel _____ because _____."

**5.** An I-message delivered in anger is often a you-message.

**6.** Follow these dos and don'ts when using I-messages:

• Do be prepared to listen when you send an I-message.
• Don't overuse I-messages.
• Do use I-messages to express positive feelings.

**7.** Use the process of exploring alternatives when reflective listening or I-messages do not solve the problem. Exploring alternatives lets parents and teens look at options available for solving problems. The process can be used for both teen- and parent-owned problems.

**8.** Closed questions ask for a yes or no answer and usually begin with a verb or with *why*. They may shut off further communication. Closed questions may be interpreted as criticism.

**9.** Open questions allow for several possible responses and begin with *where, when, what, who, which,* or *how*. They don't criticize; they stimulate communication.

**10.** Use five steps to explore alternatives:

• Understand and clarify the problem.
• Explore alternatives through brainstorming.
• Evaluate proposed alternatives.
• Choose a solution.
• Obtain or make a commitment and set a time for evaluation.

**11.** When exploring alternatives, keep the following principles in mind:

• Establish mutual respect.
• Keep the real issue in focus.
• Recognize and change the present agreement.
• Share the responsibility for making decisions.

# My Plan for Improving Relationships
(An opportunity to assess progress each week)

My specific concern:

_____

_____

My usual response:

- ☐ talking, lecturing
- ☐ complaining, nagging
- ☐ becoming angry, screaming
- ☐ being sarcastic, attacking

- ☐ punishing, shaming
- ☐ giving up, forgetting because discouraged
- ☐ exerting power by removing privilege
- ☐ other_____

My progress this week:

| | I am doing this more | I need to do this more | I am about the same | | I am doing this more | I need to do this more | I am about the same |
|---|---|---|---|---|---|---|---|
| Understanding the purpose of behavior | ☐ | ☐ | ☐ | Communicating love, positive feelings | ☐ | ☐ | ☐ |
| Working on developing an equal relationship based on mutual respect | ☐ | ☐ | ☐ | Withdrawing from conflict | ☐ | ☐ | ☐ |
| Responding to emotions more effectively | ☐ | ☐ | ☐ | Preventing discipline problems by giving choices | ☐ | ☐ | ☐ |
| Encouraging | ☐ | ☐ | ☐ | Correcting discipline problems appropriately | ☐ | ☐ | ☐ |
| Appreciating and giving responsibility | ☐ | ☐ | ☐ | Arranging democratic family meetings | ☐ | ☐ | ☐ |
| Listening | ☐ | ☐ | ☐ | Being firm and kind | ☐ | ☐ | ☐ |
| Revealing my feelings without blaming or accusing | ☐ | ☐ | ☐ | Staying out of problems that are not my problems | ☐ | ☐ | ☐ |

I learned:

_____

_____

_____

I plan to change my behavior by:

_____

_____

_____

# CHAPTER 7

•

# *Discipline: The Development of Responsibility*

No task of parenthood is more challenging than discipline. Most people equate the word *discipline* with punishment. But to us, discipline is a way to help teens become mature and independent. It is not something we do to teens, but rather a system for helping them learn to lead responsible, productive lives. Providing a situation isn't harmful or self-destructive, we follow the adage "Experience is the best teacher." Discipline involves both preventive and corrective procedures for helping teens take charge of their own lives, make decisions, and learn from the consequences of those decisions.

If your relationship with your teen is generally negative, it doesn't have to stay that way. Both you and your teen can learn to respect each other. First, understand why your teen is rebelling. Rebellion usually starts brewing when teens see themselves in a master-slave relationship with their parents. Teens are struggling to establish their own identities, and they want to be treated with dignity and respect. This striving may seem a threat to parental control. If so, parents often try to reestablish authority by clamping down. Believing they don't have positive, constructive ways to be significant, teens in turn become discouraged. Many teens decide to seek recognition through misbehavior—through resistance or rebellion.

This pattern *can* be changed! By encouraging your teen, you can extinguish the fires of rebellion. This chapter and the next one present specific methods—methods that are both effective and respectful—for dealing with misbehavior and helping teens achieve independence.

Punishment is negative; discipline is not. We suggest that you think of discipline not as a way for you to be in charge or in control, but as a learning process for your teenager. The discipline that you provide can lead to self-discipline. It can guide your teen toward responsible independence.

In addition to providing discipline, parents serve as models of the mature, responsible behavior they're seeking in their teens. In simple terms, parents need to exercise self-discipline. For example, if parents who smoke are concerned about their teen's smoking, they'd better do something about their own. Parents who drink alcohol or take tranquilizers should be aware that they are modeling drug use and be careful to demonstrate moderation, restraint, and sound judgment. Actions speak very loudly.

It's essential too to include teens in decision making. This is a method of encouragement that raises self-esteem. If teens feel good about themselves, they're less likely to rebel and resist. When parents are able to offer choices, teens feel independent, valued, and responsible.

What are some choices you can offer your teen? You might give your son a clothing allowance and let him purchase his own clothes. Your daughter can decide how to spend money she earns from a part-time job. Teenagers can be encouraged to make their own decisions concerning electives to take in school, extracurricular activities, friends, hobbies, and hairstyles. They can be asked to choose which chores they are willing to do or whether they wish to accompany the family on an outing.

It's often true that "experience is the best teacher."

By providing choices that are within the limits of your teen's ability and safety (and that don't interfere with the rights of others), you can encourage your teen's cooperation. Keep in mind that teenagers are constantly making independent choices— after all, parents aren't with teens all the time! Your respectful treatment of your teenager can help foster maturity, responsibility, and a sense of self-worth.

# The Ineffectiveness of Reward and Punishment

Reward and punishment are leftovers from our autocratic past—and unappetizing ones at that. Historically, these methods haven't worked too well with teens, and they're even less effective today. They are methods that show a lack of respect for the individual. Teens who are motivated by reward or punishment eventually become dependent, fearful, and unsure of themselves; they may begin to rebel. Teens often feel they don't have control of their own destiny.

A reward is something given by someone in a superior role to someone in an inferior role. Rewards are often used as bribes, which have strings attached to them: "If you do this, then I'll do that." Remember that strings are tied at both ends—on the next occasion a teen may say, "I'll do that, if you give me this." A reward can actually set the stage for blackmail!

Consider the following situation: When Monica was twelve, her parents paid her a small amount to mow the lawn. Now that she's sixteen, Monica has told her parents, "I'll do it for the same amount a lawn service would charge." Monica hasn't learned to cooperate; she has learned only to drive a hard bargain. But life requires that we cooperate. We can't expect compensation for everything we do. Perhaps the saddest consequence of using rewards is that they teach a false value: "Never give something for nothing!"[1]

Parents usually punish when they know no other way to stop irresponsible behavior. They may criticize their children, hit them, or deny them certain privileges. All of these forms of punishment teach teens that power is what counts. They breed resentment and rebellion. As you may know from first-hand experience, teenagers—boys and girls alike—aren't willing to submit to spankings, slaps, or verbal abuse. As emerging adults, teens who live with punishment believe they have the right to punish their parents as well.

The goal of parenting is to help teenagers function responsibly on their own. Obviously, learning and growing cannot flourish when punishment is nearby. Therefore, we believe that teens don't learn constructive behavior from punishment. We suggest that instead of being punished, they be allowed to experience the consequences of their situation. Consequences—whether they're a poor grade, a scraped knee, or a hangover—are opportunities for learning.

# Natural and Logical Consequences

Some parents feel that the only alternative to reward and punishment is permissiveness. As we've said before, we think the best alternative is a relationship in which parent and teen deal with each other democratically. Such a relationship is based on equality and mutual respect. The challenge here is to find ways to cooperate and encourage each other.

How to start? Concentrate on changing yourself. If you want cooperation, be cooperative. If you want respect, be respectful. Treat your teen's friends in the same way you'd like yours to be treated. Arrange for your teen to use the family car from time to time. By demonstrating that you respect your teenager and want to cooperate, you'll be letting your teen know that you see him or her as a worthy person, equal in value to yourself.

What happens, though, when you need to step in and discipline? We believe the most effective procedure is to allow teens to experience the natural or logical consequences[2] of a situation. A consequence always relates directly to what would happen anyhow if others did not interfere. For example, if you overeat, you're likely to gain weight. If you're late to work, your pay might be docked. If you aren't on time for your flight, the plane will take off without you. If you don't pay your electric bill, service will eventually be disconnected. None of these events is a punishment; each is simply the result of violating the natural or social order. And notice the absence of hostility in these consequences. Where punishment can be angrily resisted and provoked again and again, natural and logical consequences give a matter-of-fact message that's hard to ignore.

Let your teen learn from natural consequences.

Logical consequences are a result of
violating the social order.

Parents can apply natural or logical consequences according to what a given situation needs or requires. A *natural consequence* is the result of going against the natural order of events that exists in life. For example, if a teenager misses dinner, the natural consequence will be hunger. A *logical consequence* represents a violation of the *social* order—what it takes to live cooperatively together. If your son misses dinner and therefore has to prepare his own food, he experiences logical consequences. If you say, "You can prepare your own food as long as you clean up," the logical consequence of not cleaning up could then be that your son isn't allowed to prepare food the next time he misses dinner. Silence is often a way of allowing logical consequences to happen. Instead of reminding, "It's almost time to leave for school," a parent can simply say nothing. The teen will then experience and learn from the logical consequences of being late.

Let's look at ways this method of discipline works for a specific problem:

Fifteen-year-old Juan Chavez has always received above-average grades. Now, in his second year of high school, Juan is on the football team, has joined two clubs, and is dating a classmate; his grades have dropped. Mrs. Chavez has begun continually reminding Juan to do his homework, pointing out how well he has done in the past, and nagging him to improve his grades so he can get into college.

Letting teens work out school problems for themselves is one of the greatest challenges of parenting. What is Mrs. Chavez really accomplishing by nagging and prodding? Who is taking the responsibility for Juan's schoolwork? Does Mrs. Chavez plan to go with her son to college?

It's been our experience that if parents let teens manage their own schoolwork, conflict is dramatically reduced. And teens often learn to accept responsibility for their work when it ceases to be an issue between them and their parents. Since many teens use poor school performance as a weapon, they're literally disarmed when their parents step out of the conflict. Of course, by withholding allowances, denying the use of the car, grounding, or banning TV-watching, parents may win a few temporary victories. But they may just as easily lose the relationship and destroy the possibility of cooperation.

Take yourself out of conflicts over schoolwork by saying, "I've been on your back about your schoolwork and I've decided it's really not my problem. The responsibility for school belongs to you, so I won't check up on you any more. I hope you do well, but it's up to you." Be sure you mean what you say. Be prepared for your teen to test you. Grades may drop for a while, homework may go unfinished, or your teen may find other ways to tempt you to get involved. And don't expect quick turnarounds or miracles. Your teen may have to experience some unpleasant consequences before deciding to improve school performance.

Another area of concern for many parents is their teen's friends and social life. Teens have a right to choose whom they go out with. Assuming that the friends aren't involved in illegal activities, parents can let teens choose their own friends. This goes for dating partners too. Each family will want to establish guidelines for the age when dating begins, for curfews, for use of cars, and for where teens will go on dates. Teens will learn the most about the kinds of friends they want for life by experiencing the consequences of selecting friends. Often, consequences are positive: teens discover that a friend or dating partner is compatible and stimulating. But, painful as it may be for parents and teens alike, teenagers also need to experience hurt, rejection, and what parents might consider "bad influence." These experiences help teens clarify their own values as well as discover what kinds of people they best fit with.

Another source of conflict is a teen's messy room. Yet it seems hopeless to force teens to take care of their rooms. Why not use natural consequences? A natural consequence of living in sloppy conditions is to lose things and not be able to find them when needed. If a messy room truly bothers you, you could ask your teen to keep the door closed. If dirt or odors creep into other parts of your home, however, your rights have been violated. At this point you'll need to negotiate a time for cleaning the room and the consequences for not doing so. For example, you and your teen could decide that the room is to be cleaned on Saturdays before your teen goes out. The logical consequence of not cleaning is that your teen can't leave to go somewhere.

Some parents, though, simply won't tolerate a teenager's messy room. If this is your problem (and realize that it *is* your problem), you could solve it by doing what this parent did:

Paul Hansen had four teenagers, ages eighteen, sixteen, fourteen, and thirteen. He told them that if their rooms were not straightened up by the day the housekeeper came to clean, he would ask the housekeeper to straighten as well as clean their rooms and they'd have to pay whatever extra amount the straightening cost. At first the four teenagers straightened their rooms only a bit, but not enough for the housekeeper to dust and vacuum, and so they were charged for this service. After a few times of paying the housekeeper, though, they began to straighten up their rooms once a week.

Later in this chapter we'll discuss task trading. If you don't have a housekeeper and are not willing to let your teenager's room stay messy, you could use task trading as a logical consequence.

# Differences Between Punishment and Logical Consequences

There are six major differences between punishment and logical consequences:[3]

1. *Punishment emphasizes the power of personal authority. It makes a demand.* "Sue, turn off that stereo. Your father and I are trying to sleep."

*Logical consequences express the reality of the social order. They recognize mutual respect and mutual rights.* "Sue, I realize you're enjoying that music, but Dad and I are trying to sleep. Either turn down the stereo or turn it off. You decide which you'd rather do."

SO YOU GOT GROUNDED FOR TWO MONTHS, HUH?

BOY, DID I GET GROUNDED! THEY MOVED ME TO THE BASEMENT AND TOOK AWAY MY TV!

Punishment is arbitrary or barely related to the logic of the situation.

2. *Punishment is arbitrary or barely related to the logic of the situation.* "All right, Kevin. Since you don't know how to get in on time, you're grounded and can't go out for the next two months!"

*Logical consequences are directly related to the behavior.* "Since you're not yet willing to come home at the time we agreed upon, you can't go out Saturday night, Kevin. You can try again next week." (Mother and son had previously negotiated a time to be home, and the consequences for being late. Knowing her son was expecting her to speak up, Mother said nothing when the teen arrived home late. Instead, she waited until a relaxed time the next day.)

3. *Punishment is personalized and implies a moral judgment. It equates the deed with the doer.* "You took the car without my permission! You're no better than a car thief! Give me those keys! Your car privileges are suspended indefinitely!"

*Logical consequences imply no element of moral judgment. They separate the deed from the doer.* "Since you took the car without asking permission, I can see you're not ready to follow the rules for using it, and so you may not use the car tomorrow. The day after tomorrow you can have another chance to show me you're willing to follow the rules."

4. *Punishment is concerned with past behavior.* "No you can't have a party. All you did last time was leave a big mess, and some of your friends were drinking beer."

*Logical consequences are concerned with present and future behavior.* "You can have a party as long as you're willing to clean up afterwards and you make sure there's no drinking."

5. *Punishment is a put-down that threatens to treat the offender with disrespect.* "You embarrassed me in front of my friends. You're so inconsiderate of my feelings! Just wait until the next time *your* friends come over!"

*Logical consequences are invoked in a friendly manner, after parent and teen have calmed down. They imply good will.* "Since you're not willing to act respectfully when I have guests, I'll have to ask you to stay in your room or go out next time my friends come over."

6. *Punishment demands obedience.* "You mow the lawn right now!"

*Logical consequences permit choice.* "You can mow the lawn anytime before you go out. You decide when."

# Spoiled Consequences

In addition to the clear differences between punishment and logical consequences presented above, there are subtle attitudes, feelings, and actions that can turn the best-intended natural or logical consequence into a punishment. Consequences can be spoiled by any of the following actions:

**Being inconsistent.** No one's actions can be totally consistent—we're all human! We can, however, work to respond to our teens as consistently as possible. When parents are autocratic one day, permissive the next, and democratic on another, teens never know *where* they stand. Consider this analogy: Stand-up comedians who consistently fail to get a laugh with a certain joke will drop the joke from their act. But if they *sometimes* get a laugh, they may keep the joke just in case. The same is true for teens. If, for example, teens are able to provoke arguments with their parents at some times but not at others, chances are they'll continue to try to pick fights.

**Pitying.** Overprotective parents often have a hard time following through on consequences because they feel sorry about their teenager's suffering. But pity is damaging; it implies that teens can't handle life's re-

quirements. And pity doesn't stop with the parents—it can lead to self-pity in teens. Teens may learn to feel sorry for themselves and then give up.

*Empathy* is different from pity. Empathic parents understand and care about how their teen feels, and regret that their teen has to experience the negative consequences of an action. But instead of pitying the teen, empathic parents have confidence in the teen's ability to learn from the experience. Empathy might be expressed in this way: "I'm sorry you decided to make that choice, but I'm sure you can handle the consequences."

**Being overconcerned about what others think.** Many parents don't follow through on consequences because they fear reactions from friends, neighbors, teachers, or relatives.

Fifteen-year-old Lori Jenning was caught by the police with a six-pack of beer in her possession. The authorities took Lori to the juvenile detention center and called her father to come pick her up.

Mr. Jenning felt that letting Lori spend the night in custody would help her see more clearly the consequences of breaking the law. After talking it over with the officer in charge to make sure his daughter would be safe in the facility, Mr. Jenning decided to wait and pick Lori up in the morning. Mr. Jenning's mother told him she thought it was cruel to leave Lori in "jail." But Mr. Jenning stood firm and told her, "I understand you're angry with me because you feel this experience will do Lori harm. Just the same, I feel the opposite is true, and I'm going to follow through with my plan."

Mr. Jenning showed a lot of courage in risking his mother's disapproval. He made a choice. He decided to do what he felt was best for his daughter and not yield to the disapproval of others. This is the decision we must all make as parents. After all, what's more important—developing responsibility in our teenagers, or pleasing others?

Excessive talking can lead to "parent deafness."

**Talking too much.** What's the first thing parents usually do when teenagers misbehave? Talk! Our teens expect us to lecture and nag! If we do exactly as they expect,

this only reinforces their misbehavior. In fact, excessive talking may actually create a "disability" in teens called "parent deafness."[4] There's no sense talking if no one's listening.

When your teen misbehaves, replace talk with action. If the situation doesn't require immediate attention, follow the "Silence Is Golden" rule. Discuss the situation later, when the two of you aren't in conflict. If the problem needs attention immediately, choose your words carefully: "I'm afraid the baseball may accidentally hit the window and break it. Either play catch away from the window or take the game to the park."

In deciding what things are emergencies that require immediate attention, be honest with yourself. For most misbehavior, talk can be delayed. When you do talk, be brief—too much talk can lead to reminders, hints, and threats, all of which ruin what you're trying to do. Once a consequence has been set up and your teen chooses to take that consequence, just let whatever happens happen (dangerous situations excepted).

**Using inappropriate timing.** Choose the right time to talk. As we said, most talk can be delayed until a time when you and your teen are calm. Talking in the midst of a conflict may produce hurt feelings, not a lasting agreement. The timing of a consequence is very important. By setting up consequences in advance—with negotiation conversations or family meetings—you can save yourself words and energy. Consider the following situation:

During a family meeting, thirteen-year-old Arlene agreed to feed the dog each night before she sat down to supper. For the first few nights after the meeting, Arlene remembered her agreement and fed the dog before coming to the table. One night she neglected to do the chore and sat down at the table, but found no plate or silverware at her place. With a bewildered look, she got up, went to the kitchen, and came back with a plate and utensils. Her father said, "I didn't set your place, Arlene, because you're not ready to eat yet." "Why not!" demanded Arlene. "Check the agreements we posted on the refrigerator after the last family meeting," her father replied. "Oh, yeah," Arlene said with an embarrassed look. She promptly fed the dog and returned to the table ready to eat.

**Feeling and communicating hostility.** Consequences must be applied in a firm but friendly way. If you communicate annoyance, anger, or hurt, your teen will view the consequence as punishment. Watch your choice of words, tone of voice, gestures, expressions, and body language. Remember that no matter how logical the consequence may seem, if your tone is harsh or your attitude superior, that consequence will be received as a punishment.

In Chapter 3 we discussed ways to change your usual emotional responses to your teen's misbehavior. If you're having difficulty keeping hostility out of consequences, reread that chapter and practice the suggestions.

**Having hidden motives.** When some parents first learn about natural and logical consequences, they see them as new "tricks" to enable them to get what they want. Their consequences may be very logical, but their hidden motive of control comes through loud and clear to teens.

By the same token, never use consequences to get even with your teen. If you feel like getting even, you're better off examining

the negative results of revenge than trying to use consequences.

**Playing detective.** When children in a family misbehave and parents don't know who the "guilty" party is, parents tend to put on their Sherlock Holmes outfits and try to solve the case! Parents don't have to play these detective games. While it may seem logical to discipline the one who caused the problem, this is actually an ineffective approach. Competition and rivalry among siblings increase, and cooperation among parents and children decreases. The "good" children maintain their status by making the "bad" children look bad. And the "bad" children seek to get even with their "good" brothers and sisters, and with their parents as well.

Dreikurs used to say, "Put them all in the same boat."[5] That way siblings can learn to row together or sink! This approach may seem unfair, but remember that going after the "guilty" person adds a little more shine to the "good" children's halos at the "bad" children's expense. If, for example, you come home and find mud all over the floor, have all your children share the responsibility. Don't listen to accusations and complaints. You might say: "How do I know which of you didn't wipe your feet? Frankly, I'm not interested in finding out. The point is that the floor needs cleaning. You can figure out how to get it cleaned up."

Parents who listen to tattling are also inadvertently encouraging rivalry among siblings. Respond to any tattling with silence—busy yourself with other things. Don't even say, "I don't listen to tattling," for if you say that, you *are* listening—children and teens will get the message. In situations of real danger, your children will let you know that they need to have you listen. Teenagers and even young children are smart enough to know the difference between tattling and reporting possible danger.

**Rejecting the person instead of the act.**
We've pointed out that punishment equates the deed with the doer—it says that a person is bad if he or she does a bad thing. If you communicate that a bad act makes your teen a bad person, then how can you expect your teen to behave appropriately?[6] Why would a "bad" teen decide to be "good"?

All of us behave inappropriately at times, but this doesn't make us bad people. The reverse of this is true as well—doing what is right doesn't make us good people! If we believe that people are basically worthwhile, then we're in a position to separate the deed from the doer. Choice of words, tone of voice, expressions, and motives can all communicate to a teen, "While I don't like what you're doing, I still love you."

## Guidelines in Applying Consequences

**Determine your teen's goal of misbehavior.** Regardless of the goal, parents don't have to step in and apply natural consequences—they just happen. But, parents do need to apply *logical* consequences. To apply appropriate logical consequences, parents first need to determine the goal of misbehavior.

When a teen seeks *attention,* it's best to avoid giving that attention on demand. Here's how one parent set up logical consequences:

Fourteen-year-old Brian liked to joke and clown around. His parents enjoyed his antics at times, but not when they had company for dinner. One evening before guests were to arrive, Brian's mother told

him, "I know you enjoy joking around, and often we enjoy it too. But clowning around won't be appropriate tonight. So if you decide to tell jokes, I'll have to ask you to excuse yourself from the table."

Brian needs to learn when and where his humor is acceptable. His parents also need to pay attention to him at other times, when he isn't expecting it. For example, they can show appreciation when Brian helps out around the house.

When teens seek *power,* we suggest they experience the logical consequence of having no opponent. The guideline for dealing with power seekers is to withdraw from the conflict. For example:

Whenever Tina didn't get her way, she tried to force her parents to give in by becoming very angry and accusing them of being unfair. One day Tina's father decided not to let himself be manipulated, and when Tina started her angry tirade, he simply left and went for a walk. Tina was bewildered—she didn't know what to do without her audience!

Be careful when applying logical consequences for power-seeking misbehavior. Use them only when the misbehavior is disruptive, and then only if absolutely necessary. Work on your relationship instead: listen, provide encouragement, and ask for your teen's opinions and help.

If your teen seeks *revenge,* avoid feeling hurt and make sure you don't seek revenge yourself. Instead, focus on building a trusting relationship. Here's how one family applied logical consequences:

> When Tom's teacher reported that Tom was failing in school, his parents felt embarrassed and hurt. They valued high marks, and Tom knew it. They tried to force Tom to work by suspending all his privileges until he raised his grades, but he made no improvement. Still deeply hurt and frustrated, the parents visited a family counselor who pointed out that Tom was failing in order to get back at them. Obviously their punishments were not working. There was only one thing they could do—place the responsibility for school on Tom's shoulders, wish him well, and work at improving their relationship with him. It was very difficult for them to back out of Tom's school life, but they did, and things slowly improved.

Using any type of punishment rarely accomplishes what parents want it to, and this is especially true with teens who seek revenge. Logical consequences are often seen as punishment. For example, if your teenage daughter broke a lamp during an angry argument, you'd certainly want the damage paid for. But it would be foolish to challenge her in the heat of the moment. Such an action would only increase the war of revenge. At a later time, when the two of you had cooled off, you could discuss repairing or replacing the lamp. As with power-motivated teens, parents of revenge seekers will do well to avoid applying logical consequences unless the behavior is disruptive; and even then, they need to use them cautiously. Whenever possible, work to improve the relationship through trust, mutual respect, and encouragement.

Logical consequences aren't appropriate for those teens who *display inadequacy.* Their behavior doesn't disrupt the family in any way—they've given up. In this case, don't give up, don't criticize, and don't pity. Do provide specific and regular encouragement, concentrating on what your teen can do rather than on what you see as your teen's inadequacies. When you see progress or effort, say so. By spotlighting and appreciating your teen's strengths, you can help him or her gain confidence to try in other areas.

The above guidelines for using consequences can be applied to the goals of *excitement, peer acceptance,* and *superiority* as well, since these are usually pursued along with one of the four basic goals. For example, if your son is seeking excitement by swearing when you are out together in public, he is probably also seeking power by trying to anger and embarrass you. Give your son the choice of cleaning up his language or not going out with you until he is ready to cooperate.

**Determine who owns the problem.**
When teens own the problem, *natural* consequences usually apply. As long as the consequences aren't dangerous, parents don't have to interfere. For example, if a teenager stays up late on school nights, the natural consequence is being tired the next day. Sometimes *logical* consequences also apply to teen-owned problems. For example, if your daughter misses the school bus, she'll have to find another way to get to school.

When parents own the problem, *logical* consequences are one way to take care of it. For example, if your teenage son has agreed to do certain chores but doesn't honor the agreement, you can decide to use task trading as a logical consequence. First, take an inventory of all the services you provide for your teen: laundry, transportation, cleaning, cooking, and so forth. Then withdraw these services in exchange for doing the chores he has neglected to do. The responsibility for doing the tasks you usually do for your son now belongs to him. For example, if he wants clean clothes, he'll have to wash them himself. This approach keeps you out of conflict because you can easily withdraw your services without trying to force your son to do anything. Task trading can work well with a teen who seeks power by refusing to do chores. Never use this approach as a weapon, though— use it simply as a means to share chores fairly.

When using task trading, make certain the tasks you're trading are equivalent. Otherwise you may be setting the stage for revenge. You might say to your son, "If you're not willing to shovel the snow, then I'll do that and you can take care of your laundry." Ask if he feels that's fair. If not, tell him you're willing to negotiate as long as he's willing to fulfill his agreements. If he doesn't negotiate, you'll assume he's decided to trade tasks for a couple of weeks and then reevaluate the agreement.

Keep in mind that before approaching your teen about trading tasks, it's best to work at improving your relationship. In many families, chores are a source of conflict; they're seldom a good starting point for trying to change the relationship. Encourage your teen to take responsibility for things other than chores.

**Present choices.** When applying consequences, it's essential to provide alternatives so that teens can learn to make decisions. If you give choices, recognize that there is no wrong decision, and be ready to accept whatever the decision may be.

Consider these examples: "Either put away the things you left in the family room, or I'll put them in a box in the storage room just to get them out of my way." "Either slow down, or stop the car and I'll drive." When the choice is obvious, you don't need to spell it out. If your teenager and friends are laughing and joking while you're trying to watch TV, you could say, "It looks to me like you're really not interested in this program. You may stay here as long as you're willing to be quiet so I can watch the program." If a slumber party is in the works: "You can have the slumber party here as long as you and your friends are willing to be quiet after midnight."

Some consequences are only a statement of your intentions: "I'll announce when supper's ready once. If you decide not to come, I'll assume you either don't want to eat or don't mind cold food." "I'm willing to wash only the dirty clothes I find in the hamper."

**Follow through if your teen chooses to take the consequence.** If teens choose the consequence, the decision has to stand for the moment. They can have an opportunity to change the decision at a later time, though. For instance, in the case of teens laughing and joking while you're trying to watch TV, you can give them the choice of being quiet or leaving the room. They may quiet down for a few minutes, but then return to making a disturbance. Now is the time to follow through with the consequence, assuring them of an opportunity to change their decision later: "I see by your behavior that you've chosen to leave the room. Come on back when you're ready to be quiet."

You may need to extend the time that elapses before the teens re-decide. Whenever teens fail to cooperate, they're really saying they aren't ready to be responsible. Suppose they return to watch TV in a few minutes, are quiet for a short period, but then start disrupting again. You can say, "I see you're still not ready to watch TV. You may come back in five minutes if you're willing to be quiet." If the misbehavior occurs again, say nothing except to assure the teens that they will get another opportunity to demonstrate their willingness to cooperate. The waiting time needs to be increased at this point: "I guess you've decided to leave until the program's over."

**Choose your words carefully.** Avoid *musts, shoulds,* and *have tos.* Be careful not to use phrases your teen may see as put-downs, such as, "I've told you before that . . ." Focus on the misbehavior and what the choices are. Here are some ways to apply consequences:

Either _____ or _____. You decide.
You have a choice . . .
I'm willing . . .
I'm not willing . . . *or* I choose not to . . .
I'm sorry, but . . .
You may . . . as long as you're willing to . . .
If this happens, I'll assume you've decided . . .

**Focus on positive behavior soon after correcting misbehavior.** Catch your teen being good—this helps you separate the deed from the doer. If you've applied logical consequences because your teen took the car without asking, look for positive things you can encourage: kindness to a younger brother or sister, helpfulness around the home, efforts in schoolwork or a sport.

**Negotiate consequences whenever possible.** Teenagers are more committed to agreements and consequences if they're involved in making the decisions that affect them. When discussing a problem, you might ask, "What would you consider a fair consequence for this behavior?" If your teen doesn't know, ask what the teen would do if he or she were the parent. If your teenager refuses to help negotiate a consequence, you'll need to go ahead and make a decision. After experiencing consequences, many teens are interested in negotiating them.

There will be times when negotiation isn't necessary. Perhaps the problem is minor and there's no need to make it more important than it is. Or perhaps the misbehavior is very serious and the choices are rather limited. There are many opportunities, though, to involve your teen in negotiating consequences for misbehavior. The more involved your teen can be, the more you can develop a cooperative working relationship.

Whenever you have difficulty in applying consequences, you may want to check the guidelines described above. To make sure your consequence is not a punishment, check how you're handling the following points:

• Are you showing an open attitude by giving a choice and accepting your teen's decision?
• Are you using a friendly tone of voice?
• Are you certain the consequence is logically related to the misbehavior?

A final note about logical consequences: Never try to give a choice you or your teen can't follow through on. Consequences only work when you're firm as well as friendly, when you believe in what you're doing, and when your teen, though reluctant, is willing to accept the consequences.

## References

1. Don Dinkmeyer, Gary D. McKay, and Don Dinkmeyer, Jr., *Teacher's Handbook: Systematic Training for Effective Teaching* (Circle Pines, Minn.: American Guidance Service, 1980).

2. The concept of *natural and logical consequences* is attributed to Rudolf Dreikurs. See Rudolf Dreikurs and Vicki Soltz, *Children: The Challenge* (New York: Hawthorn, 1964).

3. Rudolf Dreikurs and Loren Grey, *Parent's Guide to Child Discipline* (New York: Hawthorn, 1970) and Don Dinkmeyer and Gary D. McKay, *Parent's Handbook: Systematic Training for Effective Parenting* (Circle Pines, Minn.: American Guidance Service, 1976).

4. Dreikurs and Soltz, 1964.

5. Ibid.

6. Albert Ellis, *How to Live With and Without Anger* (New York: Reader's Digest Press, 1977).

## Questions

1. How do the authors define discipline?
2. Why is it important to involve teens in decisions that affect them? What choices can you give your teen that will help your teen feel more independent?
3. Why are rewards often ineffective? What do teens learn when parents rely on rewards?
4. Why is punishment usually ineffective? What do teens learn from punishment?
5. What is a natural consequence? Give some examples of natural consequences other than those found in the chapter. How are natural consequences different from punishment?
6. What is a logical consequence? Give some examples of logical consequences other than those found in the chapter. How are logical consequences different from punishment?
7. How can consequences be spoiled and turned into punishments?
8. Why is it important to determine who owns the problem? to identify the teen's goal of misbehavior before applying consequences? to focus on positive behavior

soon after correcting misbehavior? Why is word choice crucial?

9. How can you determine whether to negotiate consequences with your teen?

10. What do you think of some of the consequences suggested in the text?

## Activity for the Week

Choose a challenge in your relationship with your teen and practice applying consequences. Select a situation in which you believe you can be successful. If using logical consequences, negotiate consequences with your teen when appropriate.

# Personal Development Exercise

## Preventing Discipline Problems Through Giving Choices

At the beginning of the chapter we suggested some choices you could offer your teenager. What choices are you willing to give your teenager to prevent discipline problems? Include any we mentioned that seem appropriate, and add others you can think of. List as many as you can.

_____

_____

_____

_____

_____

_____

_____

By not offering meaningful choices, parents imply that teens are not able to make decisions. But in many cases, teens have more knowledge on which to base a decision, and are therefore better equipped than parents to do so. What are some areas of your teen's life in which he or she has a better knowledge base for making decisions?

_____

_____

_____

_____

_____

_____

Where will you begin this week? Consider the choices and decision-making areas you've listed, and decide on one or two specific choices you can offer your teen. As your teen becomes comfortable with this responsibility, you can gradually increase the areas.

_____

_____

_____

_____

_____

_____

Chart 7

# Major Differences Between Punishment and Logical Consequences

## Punishment

| Characteristics | Underlying Message | Likely Results |
|---|---|---|
| 1. Emphasizes power of personal authority; makes demand. | Do what I say because I say so! I'm the boss! | Rebellion. Revenge. Lack of self-discipline. Sneakiness. Irresponsibility. |
| 2. Arbitrary; rarely related to act. | I'll show you! You deserve what you're getting! | Resentment. Revenge. Fear. Confusion. Rebellion. |
| 3. Implies moral judgment; equates deed with doer. | This should teach you! You're no good! | Feelings of hurt, resentment, guilt. Desire for revenge. |
| 4. Is concerned with past behavior. | This is for what you did—I'm not forgetting! You'll never learn! | Feels unable to make good decisions. Feels unacceptable in eyes of parent. |
| 5. Threatens disrespect; is a put-down. | You'd better shape up! No son of mine acts like that! | Desire to get even. Fear. Rebellion. Guilt feelings. |
| 6. Demands obedience. | Your preferences don't matter! You can't be trusted to make wise decisions! | "Defiant compliance." Desire to get even another time. Destruction of trust and equality. |

## Logical Consequences

| Characteristics | Underlying Message | Likely Results |
|---|---|---|
| 1. Express reality of social order; recognize mutual respect and rights. | I trust you to learn to respect yourself and the rights of others. | Self-discipline. Cooperation. Respect for self and others. Reliability. |
| 2. Are directly related to misbehavior; make sense. | I trust you to make responsible choices. | Learns from experience. |
| 3. Imply no moral judgment; separate deed from doer. | You are a worthwhile person! | Learns behavior may be objectionable, but not self. |
| 4. Are concerned with present and future behavior. | You can make your own choices and take care of yourself. | Becomes self-directed and self-evaluating. |
| 5. Are invoked in friendly manner after parent and teen have calmed; imply good will. | I don't like your behavior, but I still love you! | Feels secure about parent's respect, love, and support. |
| 6. Permit choice. | You are capable of deciding. | Makes responsible decisions. Shows increased resourcefulness. |

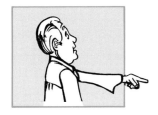

# Points to Remember

**1.** Discipline is a learning process. It involves both preventing and correcting problems.

**2.** Many discipline problems are prevented by giving teens choices within appropriate limits. Teens then experience control over various areas of their own lives.

**3.** Reward and punishment are inappropriate in equal relationships. Reward and punishment imply that the parent is superior; they stimulate rebellion and resistance.

**4.** Natural and logical consequences replace reward and punishment. They require teens to take the responsibility for their own behavior; they promote self-discipline.

**5.** A *natural consequence* represents a violation of the natural order. For example, a teen who skips lunch is hungry. A *logical consequence* represents a violation of the social order. For example, a teen who comes in too late from a date may not go out the next evening.

**6.** Logical consequences are effective only when they are logical to the teen, presented as a choice, and administered in a firm and friendly way.

**7.** Parents can spoil consequences by:

- being inconsistent
- pitying
- being overconcerned about what others think
- talking too much
- using inappropriate timing
- feeling and communicating hostility
- having hidden motives
- playing detective
- rejecting the person instead of the act

**8.** Use the following guidelines when applying consequences:

- Determine your teen's goal of misbehavior.
- Determine who owns the problem.
- Present choices.
- Follow through if your teen chooses to take the consequence.
- Choose your words carefully.
- Focus on positive behavior soon after correcting misbehavior.
- Negotiate consequences whenever possible.

**9.** Never give a choice you or your teen can't follow through on.

# My Plan for Improving Relationships
(An opportunity to assess progress each week)

My specific concern:

_____

_____


My usual response:

☐ talking, lecturing

☐ complaining, nagging

☐ becoming angry, screaming

☐ being sarcastic, attacking

☐ punishing, shaming

☐ giving up, forgetting because discouraged

☐ exerting power by removing privilege

☐ other _____


My progress this week:

| | I am doing this more | I need to do this more | I am about the same | | I am doing this more | I need to do this more | I am about the same |
|---|:---:|:---:|:---:|---|:---:|:---:|:---:|
| Understanding the purpose of behavior | ☐ | ☐ | ☐ | Communicating love, positive feelings | ☐ | ☐ | ☐ |
| Working on developing an equal relationship based on mutual respect | ☐ | ☐ | ☐ | Withdrawing from conflict | ☐ | ☐ | ☐ |
| Responding to emotions more effectively | ☐ | ☐ | ☐ | Preventing discipline problems by giving choices | ☐ | ☐ | ☐ |
| Encouraging | ☐ | ☐ | ☐ | Correcting discipline problems appropriately | ☐ | ☐ | ☐ |
| Appreciating and giving responsibility | ☐ | ☐ | ☐ | Arranging democratic family meetings | ☐ | ☐ | ☐ |
| Listening | ☐ | ☐ | ☐ | Being firm and kind | ☐ | ☐ | ☐ |
| Revealing my feelings without blaming or accusing | ☐ | ☐ | ☐ | Staying out of problems that are not my problems | ☐ | ☐ | ☐ |

I learned:

_____

_____

_____


I plan to change my behavior by:

_____

_____

_____

142

# CHAPTER 8

●

# *Discipline: Selecting the Appropriate Approach*

So far we've presented four ways to improve parent-teen relationships: reflective listening, I-messages, exploring alternatives, and natural and logical consequences. When listening, talking, negotiating, or applying consequences, be encouraging! Encouragement can prevent many discipline problems. Separating the deed from the doer and remaining both firm and friendly are encouragement skills that help teens feel accepted even though their behavior may not be acceptable. Without encouragement, any approach you decide to use is likely to fail because your teen won't feel valued by you.

If you think of discipline in a broad sense—as maintaining order and establishing mutual rights and respect—you can see that these four approaches work together to promote responsible behavior. When we listen, we help teens feel understood and clarify their concerns. I-messages not only communicate our feelings in nonjudgmental ways, they show that we trust our teens to respect those feelings. When teens need help in deciding what to do about a problem, we help them explore alternatives. We can also use the skill of exploring alternatives to negotiate when *we* have problems with their behavior. Natural and logical consequences are approaches that aid us in redirecting misbehavior and promoting self-discipline in our teens. For these approaches to work effectively, we need to know when and how to use each one.

## Guidelines for Selecting an Appropriate Approach

**Identify the goal of misbehavior.** When deciding which approach to use, first consider the goal of your teen's misbehavior. If your teen seeks attention by constantly bringing problems to you, continued use of reflective listening and exploring alternatives will only reinforce the misbehavior. If you explore alternatives when it's clear your teen has no intention of solving a problem, you may be fueling a power struggle. In fact, whenever you allow yourself to become involved in your teen's problem, you may be inviting a power conflict. Being concerned and interested is one thing, but investing your personal worth as a parent in your ability to "help" is something else! Learn to back off whenever you sense you're walking into a trap.

Power struggles and reflective listening don't mix. When your teen is hostile toward you, it's best to withdraw from the contest. Don't withdraw in a huff, though; say that you're willing to discuss the issue later when everyone's calmed down.

Power struggles and reflective listening don't mix.

If your daughter or son displays inadequacy, your reflective listening skills can be very useful. Reflective listening helps a teen clarify and understand feelings, and this understanding can pave the way for the two of you to explore alternatives. While exploring alternatives you might ask, "How did you come to the conclusion you can't do _____?" "Could it be you believe you can't do it because you think you have to do it perfectly?" Then you could encourage your teen to approach the uncomfortable task one small step at a time.

I-messages can be very effective in dealing with attention getting, power, and revenge. When your teen is seeking attention, an I-message often gives an unanticipated response. Teens expect parents to be annoyed and to remind and coax; they don't expect them simply to share their feelings. When your teen seeks power or revenge, use I-messages only during a time when the two of you aren't in conflict. Using I-messages during an argument usually intensifies the battle. Keep in mind that when you send I-messages, you may get them in return. Be prepared to listen.

A note of caution: I-messages can be overused. They may turn off some teens or reinforce the very misbehavior you'd like to change. Use them sparingly. When I-messages are ineffective, you may need to apply natural or logical consequences. As we said in Chapter 7, this approach works best when parents explore alternatives and negotiate consequences *with teens* in conversations or family meetings. But sometimes no negotiation is necessary: the problem may be rather minor, or it may be quite serious and the choices limited. And if teens refuse to cooperate in deciding on a consequence, negotiation can't be used.

Here's an example of how an I-message and a logical consequence can be combined:

> Suppose you're trying to balance your checkbook and your son and his friend are laughing and joking loudly in the next room. You say, "When I'm trying to work and there's so much noise, I get distracted because I can't concentrate." They quiet down for a few minutes, but pretty soon they're very noisy again. You could then set up a logical consequence by offering them a choice: "I'm sorry, but I can't concentrate. Either quiet down, or I'll have to ask you to leave until I'm finished." You'd then follow through if their behavior showed they'd chosen to leave: "I see you've decided to leave. Come back in an hour if you wish—I'll be through by then."

Natural consequences are usually effective with any goal of misbehavior because they require no special arrangements. You just get out of the way and let nature take its course (dangerous situations excepted). Let's say your seventeen-year-old daughter has been to a party where alcohol was served, and she got drunk on the beer she drank. A natural consequence might be the hangover she'll undoubtedly have the next morning. If the teen has a drinking problem though, natural consequences are not enough, and logical consequences could fuel the problem. Problem drinking is a case in which the teen will need professional help. (See Chapter 10 for more about teenage drinking.)

Logical consequences require your involvement and work best with attention getters. Teens seeking power or revenge may see consequences as punishment, so apply them carefully. In these cases, use logical consequences only when the behavior is disruptive, and continue to concentrate on building a more positive relationship. Logical consequences are not appropriate for teens who display inadequacy because their behavior isn't disruptive. These teens need a lot of encouragement. Recognize the slightest sign of progress.

Some misbehavior can be ignored. Ignoring misbehavior is a way of applying logical consequences: teens don't get the desired response and thus must change to get parents' involvement. If your teen calls you a name in the heat of anger, just ignore it. Note that we're *not* saying, "Ignore your teen"—just ignore the name-calling. Be sure to be generous with your encouragement at times when your teenager isn't misbehaving.

**Determine who owns the problem.** The effectiveness of the approach you select depends upon the problem at hand and whom it belongs to. If your teen owns the problem, you may decide to listen, explore alternatives, or let natural or logical consequences be experienced. Explore alternatives when *you* own the problem. I-messages and logical consequences are also helpful when parents own the problem.

**Base your decision on what the situation requires and the effectiveness of**

**the approach.** When your teen shares a problem, you may decide to use reflective listening. Or, sensing your teenager is trying to use problems to gain your attention or to engage you in a power contest, you may choose to ignore invitations to discuss problems. And if I-messages haven't worked well for you in the past, you may decide not to use an I-message and proceed directly to a logical consequence.

Sometimes combining approaches is the most appropriate thing to do. You may often start with reflective listening and move on to exploring alternatives. There may be situations that call for all four approaches. Imagine this scene:

You've explored alternatives with your daughter regarding the condition of her room, and the two of you have decided she may keep the room as she likes unless its condition interferes with your rights. By and by the odor from her dirty room becomes offensive to people passing by. You negotiate, using reflective listening and I-messages. You agree on when the room will be cleaned and discuss a logical consequence for not cleaning it. The room is to be cleaned before your daughter goes out that day. If she doesn't clean it, she'll stay home until she does.

We realize that not all of these suggested approaches will be appropriate for you and your teen. But we encourage you to experiment with all of them—give them a fair test. This will help you decide which methods work best for you.

# Selecting Approaches for Typical Teen Misbehaviors

**Arguing.** Teens often challenge parents' beliefs and attitudes. These challenges don't have to cause friction, but sometimes they do—especially when mistaken goals are at stake. When a teen wants to argue with parents about beliefs, the teen owns the problem (unless the parents decide to argue—then the parents own it!). Arguments seldom succeed in changing anyone's point of view; they usually convince each person how "right" she or he was in the first place.

How do you handle a conversation that starts to turn into a potentially disrespectful or hurtful argument? We suggest you agree to disagree. Use reflective listening and I-messages. You can say, "I understand that you believe smoking pot isn't harmful. I believe it *is* dangerous. Each of us is entitled to an opinion. I don't think we're getting anyplace with this issue, and I guess the best we can do is agree to disagree." Then change the subject. By establishing mutual respect and refusing to argue, you can avoid a losing battle and lots of grief.

If your teen wants to argue about a logical consequence you've set up, stand firm but

friendly in the choice you're giving. For example, let's suppose the family is out for dinner and your son wants the most expensive item on the menu. You feel you can't afford this, and you tell him that he can have a choice between the low- and medium-priced items. He begins to argue that he doesn't see why you can't afford it just once. You could offer to pay for part of the meal if he'll pay for the rest from his allowance. If he refuses and still insists he wants the expensive meal, you could say, "I'm sorry, but that's not one of the choices." "That's not one of the choices" is an effective way to respond when you present alternatives and your teen wants to do something else that you consider unreasonable.

For unreasonable alternatives you could say, "That's not one of the choices."

**Clothing and hairstyles.** Most teens try to establish their own identity by wearing their clothes and hair in ways that are acceptable to their friends. Think back— didn't many of us do the same thing when we were in our teens? Why do so many parents get upset over changes in fads? Parents own this problem—they are the ones who are concerned about it. We don't ask parents to *like* the way their teens dress; we just suggest that they avoid getting involved. Some parents worry about what other adults will think of their teen's appearance. One father got in a big argument with his son over wearing an old shirt to school. This man was worried about what the teachers would think of him as a parent. But teachers see all kinds of teenage garb. If the school is really concerned about it, they'll develop a dress code. What others think is *their* problem. Why make it yours?

We suggest you ignore the way your teen dresses. Don't comment on it or show disapproval—resolve to accept it. If you're taking your teen out, you do have the right to specify the type of dress you're willing to accept; but your teen also has the right to choose whether to go.

**Cleanliness.** Some teens refuse to change clothes, bathe regularly, or brush their teeth. Why? Teens may do these things to gain attention, to prove parents can't make them be clean, or to get even with parents for other restrictions. Teens really own this problem. It becomes parents' problem only when the dirt or odor interferes with them. Teenagers have the right to be dirty, but parents also have the right not to be offended by dirt or odor.

If your teen has poor grooming habits but is basically cooperative, you can use the logical consequence of having the teen stay away from you. You might say, "I'm sorry, but the odor really gets to me. Please go to another room if you choose not to bathe." Or you could say, "If you want to sit on the couch, you'll have to change out of those muddy jeans." If teens refuse to brush their teeth regularly, parents can simply inform them that not brushing is their choice, but that parents won't pay for dental problems caused by neglect.

If your teen is basically uncooperative, remove yourself whenever possible to avoid in-

creasing the conflict. This may be inconvenient, but you need to decide what you want to accomplish—do you want the conflict to increase, or would you rather solve the problem?

**Insults and vulgar language or gestures.** An angry teen may try to shock and upset parents with crude or insulting remarks and gestures. Teens often swear to create excitement or to gain peer acceptance, but when vulgarity is directed at parents, teens are usually seeking attention, power, or revenge. For example, if your daughter uses crude language, she may expect you to lecture her about obscenity. She may expect to be punished. But be aware that she owns this problem—after all, she is the one who's upset. Tempting as it may be, if you react the way your daughter expects you to, you'll reinforce the goal of her misbehavior.

One option is to ignore her vulgar language.

If you think her goal is attention, ignore her comments—be unimpressed. Or use reflective listening and, if necessary, explore alternatives to reach agreement. If your daughter is bent on power or revenge, the most effective thing, again, is to be unimpressed. Take yourself out of the situation so you won't reinforce her misbehavior. This is a logical consequence that says in effect, "I respect myself too much to be with you when you're behaving this way!"

Some parents may worry that walking away communicates to younger children who are present permission to be obscene and vulgar. Actually, the opposite is more often true: younger children see that parents can and will choose to remove themselves from such provocation. Just like teens, the younger children in a family want parents' interest and involvement— they don't want Mom or Dad to leave the scene!

Later, when your daughter has calmed down, might be a good time for the two of you to discuss the issue of vulgarity. Acknowledge her feelings and express your own. "I realize you were very angry this morning and I respect your right to be angry, but when you talk to me as you did, I feel disrespected. It seems you're not concerned about my feelings." Or, "When I hear swearing, I feel turned off because I really don't like that kind of language."

There are, of course, some teens who swear "like troopers" even when they're not angry. In this case too you can choose not to be with them when they are swearing and later communicate how you feel when they use vulgar language.

Many parents find insults and vulgarity very difficult to tolerate. They want to counterattack and order the teen never to speak that way again. But do punishments and demands really work? Do they have long-lasting results? Everyone gets angry at times, even if it's better not to. We're all capable of behaving inappropriately when we're angry. This is part of our human imperfection. Give your teen this right to be imperfect!

**Forgetting.** Like all behavior, forgetting has a purpose. It is often used as an excuse for not fulfilling responsibility. Sometimes teens get attention by forgetting. Teens may also forget in order to defeat their parents. And "I forgot" can often be an attempt to get oneself off the hook. Sometimes such an excuse is accepted. At other times it provokes a power contest: "You forgot! Don't give me that nonsense!" Forgetting can be used for revenge if forgetting a task is hurtful to parents. And teens who display inadequacy can use "forgetting" to take care of tasks they believe they can't handle.

Who owns the problem? If your teen's forgetting doesn't interfere with your rights, then your teen owns the problem. She or he will have to take the logical consequences of forgetting schoolbooks, lunch money, or personal appointments. But many parents protect their teens from these consequences by giving constant reminders. Then, of course, teens don't need to remember anything!

When the teen's forgetting causes you problems, then you own those problems. Suppose your son agrees to do a certain chore, but constantly forgets to do it. What does this behavior tell you? Obviously he has no intention of doing the chore. If you keep reminding him, you may be trapped into giving undue attention. A power contest may ensue. One alternative is to use an I-message: "When the driveway isn't shoveled, I feel frustrated, because I can't get the car out of the garage." Another possibility is to apply a logical consequence, such as task trading (see Chapter 7), if such a thing has been set up in advance. (See Chapter 9 for consequences of neglecting some typical chores.) You and your son could also enter into negotiation and make a new decision. Using I-messages, exploring alternatives, and deciding logical consequences can all be useful in these instances. Which action to use, of course, depends upon the situation and the people involved.

**Arguing and fighting among siblings.**
When sisters and brothers fight, it's usually for the parents' benefit. Squabbles trap parents' attention. Parents soon find themselves playing referee or joining in the power struggle. A son who picks on a sister or brother he considers to be a parent's favorite may be seeking revenge. Some parents believe a fair approach to arguing is to punish all contestants; but the fighters usually don't see it this way! When parents do this, at least one child will feel unfairly treated and will most likely want to get even. Whatever the misbehavior goals may be, parents reinforce those goals when they interfere or try to arbitrate.

Do parents own the problem of squabbles between siblings? Of course not! What can you do when your youngsters fight? First, think about what they will learn if you interfere. Obviously they won't learn to work out their difficulties—they'll learn to rely on a third party to resolve disputes. Fighting may be *typical,* but it's not *normal.* Children can learn to get along without

fighting. But they'll learn this only if you let them work out their problems of living together. So refuse to become involved in an argument or fight. Let the squabblers learn from the natural consequences of fighting.

Resolve to get as far away from the next fight as possible. When it happens, firmly take yourself out of the situation. Go to the bathroom (this is usually a respected place of privacy), your bedroom, or out walking. If you go to another place in your house or apartment, take along a radio or some magazines, and plan to stay away until the air has cleared.[1] If someone finds you to tattle, reply, "This is between the (two) of you. I'm sure you can work it out." Say this only once, and don't say any more. The next time someone tattles, say nothing—just take yourself out of the situation. Refuse to be involved.

In most fights no one is clearly innocent or guilty.

Many parents assume ownership of the problem of squabbling because they detest fighting or fear someone will be hurt. Certainly if you feel serious harm will come to your children, it's best to step in. But most fights among siblings don't result in real physical harm. Parents also ask if there aren't times when one person is an innocent victim. What about when Lenny was just walking down the hall and his brother hit him? In most fights no one is clearly innocent or guilty. Who knows what the seemingly "innocent" Lenny may have done earlier to provoke his "guilty" brother? And, even if Lenny is a victim, how will he learn to protect himself in similar situations if you step in to protect him?

When you first begin to withdraw from fights, you may find that the fights actually intensify for a while. This invariably happens when parents change their approach to any misbehavior. A teen who is used to a particular response will keep trying to get that response until convinced the game is over. And if you remove yourself to the bathroom or bedroom, you may find that the fight too has been moved—to right outside your door! This is a sure sign that the fight is at least partly for your benefit!

**When older and younger children fight.** If there is a large difference in age and size between contestants, the younger or smaller one could get hurt. In this case, you'll need to step in. But realize that younger or smaller siblings can take advantage of their older sisters or brothers by getting you to protect them. If seven-year-old Audra and fifteen-year-old Ryan are getting too rough, simply tell Audra respectfully, "It's time to quit," and remove her from the room. In this way you don't punish either person, and Audra takes the logical consequences of being removed.

**Boys against girls.** Some people apply the old saying "boys will be boys" when boys fight with one another, but feel boys should not hit girls. We question this double standard. Think of the advantage it gives to a girl! She can do whatever she wants to her brother, but he can't fight back. If anyone, male *or* female, decides to get involved in a fight, why shouldn't that person take the consequences?

**Times when the contestants need to change the battleground.** Removing yourself is the ideal thing to do when siblings fight. But if their fight is endangering family property, they'll be the ones who need to leave and fight elsewhere. By the same token, if for some reason you *can't* leave the area, the squabblers will need to leave. In this case you can use a logical consequence: "Either stop fighting or go outside and fight." Your children's behavior will let you know their decision.

**The teen who doesn't accept criticism (and the parent who doesn't know how to give it).** Teens—like many adults—can be very sensitive to criticism. After all, who enjoys being criticized? When we are criticized, we often equate our personal worth with the negative response to our behavior. We end up feeling like worthless or stupid people!

Parents often criticize out of annoyance, anger, or their own hurt. But criticizing reinforces a teen's goal of attention, power, or revenge. The attention seeker would rather be criticized than ignored. Power-driven teens use criticism as fuel to keep their "war" going. And parents' critical counterattacks give those teens who seek revenge reasons to keep getting even. The wounded reactions to criticism displayed by some overly sensitive teens may leave parents afraid to say anything. And, of course, criticizing teens who display inadequacy drives the teens further into their shells. A teen who has a strong desire to be perfect or "good" will be especially sensitive to criticism; this teen will view any critical remark as total rejection.

Teens who are sensitive to criticism own the problem of how they feel when they are criticized. Yet, it is the parents' responsibility to be encouraging even when it's necessary to criticize. How can this be done? First of all, criticize the act, not the person. Make sure the criticism is truly constructive. True constructive criticism shows concern and respect for the person to whom it's directed; its purpose is to be helpful.

When your teen's behavior interferes with your rights, using I-messages can be an effective way to give constructive criticism. By telling your teen that a certain behavior is unacceptable and giving a choice between changing the behavior or accepting the consequences, you can use logical consequences as constructive criticism. Whether using I-messages or logical consequences, keep the behavior, not the person, as the critical focus. And there's another way to give constructive criticism: Simply point out what you see. You might begin by saying, "This is merely an observation, not a criticism. I notice that you _____."

Let's say your teenage daughter complains that people don't like her. She has no idea why. You might tell her you've observed that she often involves herself in arguments with the people around her. You could suggest that others might find this uncomfortable. Or you could point out possible consequences of arguing. You could help your daughter explore alternatives by asking, "What do you think will happen if you do it this way?" Or you can make a suggestion: "Would you like to experiment with doing it this way and see what happens?" "If you do it this way I think it will work better for you, because _____." You have the right to make such comments. But keep in mind that whether your daughter accepts your comments is still her choice.

Be generous with your encouragement and positive interactions with your teen; keep your criticisms to a minimum. When things aren't going well between you, ask yourself if you're focusing too much on problems, and not enough on building a positive relationship. It's important to focus on only one or two problems at a time. When you begin new approaches, start where you feel you can be successful. Don't start with the problems that bother you most, unless potentially serious consequences make them extremely pressing.

**Smoking.** People smoke for a variety of reasons: for oral gratification, for pleasure, to relax, to achieve an image. Teenagers may believe smoking gains them acceptance with their peers. They may see smoking as a way to exhibit adult behavior. Some smoke to rebel against their parents, or to get even. And teens may also find smoking exciting—they may enjoy the fear of being caught or feel a sense of danger. Most teens who smoke do so for a combination of the above purposes.

There are some areas in which your influence with your teen is rather limited, and smoking is one of them. Teens who smoke actually own this problem. Even though health problems may develop later in life, smoking usually doesn't present a situation of immediate danger. Naturally, many parents are concerned when their teen takes up smoking. Some may demand, search the teen's clothing and room, or try to smell the teen's breath. Others may lecture or plead with their teen to stop smoking. But such responses are futile. They usually drive the teen to smoke more, and they damage the parent-teen relationship in the bargain.

If your teenager smokes, about the only thing you can do is express your concern for her or his health. If you are concerned about the health of others in your home who are exposed to the smoke, you can ask your teen not to smoke in the house. Some parents, though, prefer not to make this request, because they don't like to have their teen "sneaking off" for a cigarette. If you are a smoker, realize that you are modeling smoking as appropriate adult behavior. But even if you are a nonsmoker and an assertive antismoker as well, there is no guarantee your teen won't smoke.

**Dating.** Parents of teenagers have many questions and concerns about dating. "At what age should my daughter date?" "What time should I expect my son to be home?" "What if my teenager wants to date someone I don't approve of?" "What about going steady?" And, the big question: "Will my teen be sexually active?"

The appropriate age to begin dating depends upon the maturity level of the individual teenager. If your son is interested in dating and you think he is too young, consider the purpose of his desire to date. Perhaps many of his friends date or are interested in dating, and so your son wants to gain peer acceptance. He may want to act more grown-up—this is a form of seeking power through asserting his independence. And dating may appear exciting to him.

Here is a case in which you own the problem—you're the one who's concerned about it! If you feel your son is too young to date, you have the right to say no. Give your reasons firmly and respectfully; and be prepared to hear some objections. Using your reflective listening skills will give your son a chance to express any negative feelings he may have.

Some parents worry because their teen does not date. A teen who doesn't date may simply not be ready. Teens may also use nondating to rebel against parents. For example:

> Knowing her parents want her to date, a teenage girl may decide not to in order to assert power. The parents own the problem here. Their best approach will be to completely quit pressuring their daughter to date. Most teenagers will begin to date when they feel ready.

Some teens may not date because they have problems forming or keeping peer relationships. While the teen owns this problem, parents have an obligation to help, and in many cases counseling may be needed.

Establishing curfews is always a challenge. Most teens want to be independent—to come and go as they please. But parents have a responsibility for their teen's safety, and so parents own this problem. To establish a curfew with your teenage son, ask him what he considers a reasonable time to be home. If you disagree, negotiate a time. Once a specific time has been agreed upon, ask your son what he thinks would be a fair consequence if he decides to arrive home late. Since unforeseen circumstances can occur, you might work out an arrangement for him to phone home if he knows he'll be late. Again, agree upon specific consequences for not calling. If you then begin to receive frequent phone calls and suspect your son is simply stretching the curfew, some renegotiation may be needed.

UH, DAD ... WE'RE GOING TO BE A LITTLE LATE ... GENE'S CAR RAN OUT OF GAS.

There are times when parents disapprove of their teenager's dating partner. If you don't approve of someone your teen wants to date, examine your reasons for disapproving. Are you prejudiced against the person's social, ethnic, or religious background? Are you afraid the dating partner will exert a bad influence on your teen? Perhaps you feel the person is too young or too old for your teen. Consider too your teen's purpose in choosing a dating partner of whom you disapprove. It's quite possible your teen is asserting power: "I'll date anybody I want, and you can't stop me." Do you feel hurt? If so, perhaps your teenager is trying to get even with you. Some teens will choose partners at the risk of their parents' disapproval if they feel the partner will give them status in their peer group, or if they think the partner will be exciting.

Regardless of the teen's purpose, if you disapprove, you own the problem. You have the right to express your feelings. You also have the right to say no. Forbidding your teen to date a certain person, however, cannot guarantee that the dating won't take place. Ask yourself whether you trust your teen to make responsible choices. Might your teenager recognize in time that a mistake has been made, and break off the relationship? The bottom line is to have faith and trust in your teenager!

Going steady is another tough issue for parents. But going steady is an activity many parents of teens should expect. In teenage peer groups, going steady is often the expectation. This activity also fulfills a desire to have an exclusive relationship with one person. If you feel your teen is too young to go steady or hasn't known a dating partner long enough to do so, you own this problem. By all means, state your feelings. But, again, realize that even if you forbid it, the couple can still go steady unofficially.

The fear of sexual intimacy between teenagers is common to most parents. While we will say more on this subject in Chapter 10, we want for now to stress the importance of open, honest discussions with your teen about sex. By communicating your beliefs, listening to your teen, and providing factual information, you can set the groundwork for your teen to make carefully thought-out, responsible decisions. Of course, you can't monitor every move. Like it or not, the decision about sexual intimacy is one your teen must make. Open communication, faith, and trust are the best approach to dealing with this issue.

## Relating to Other Adults Who Have Problems with Your Teen

Often parents ask, "What can I do when other adults complain to me about my teenager?" All of us have been in this uncomfortable position at one time or another. It's actually a perfect opportunity to use some of your new communication skills!

When your teen has a problem with another adult, the teen owns the problem. If you interfere in your teenager's relationships, how will your teen learn to deal with problems she or he experiences with others? There are, of course, some exceptions to this. For instance, you'll need to get involved in areas where your teen or others may be endangered. But such cases are rare.

Suppose you've decided to turn your daughter's school life over to her. When her counselor or teacher calls you about failing grades, what can you do? First, use reflective listening regarding the caller's feelings about your daughter's performance: "I imagine it's very frustrating for you to see students who don't live up to their potential." In this way you communicate your understanding and begin to establish mutual respect. If the caller asks you to get involved in trying to make your teen study, state your beliefs and intentions: "I understand

that you'd like my help. But I believe if I get involved, my daughter may become more resistant, and things may get worse. I think it's best if she accepts the responsibility and any consequences that may come from the school." Express your confidence in the school personnel. If the caller persists, respectfully stand firm. "I'm sorry, but I'm not willing to try to push her. You'll have to decide to do what you think is best."

You may sense that the caller is open to suggestions. If you have one, you could share it and explore alternatives: "I've found _____ to be effective with her at home." Realize that school personnel call or send notes out of frustration. They need your understanding and support. But you don't need to agree to step in when you believe the problem should be worked out between your teen and the school.

No doubt you've heard your own parents criticize your teen and the parenting methods you use. "We didn't raise you that way and you turned out all right!" Parents who say this don't understand that family relationships are different than they once were. They may view your different approach to parenting as a rejection of their own skills as parents. When this happens, listen to your parents' feelings, and state your own. Explain why you are doing things differently. Reassure them that your methods are not meant as a rejection of them as parents. But remain firm in your convictions. Although it can be particularly difficult to act in a way that displeases parents, what's best for your teenager has to be your primary concern.

If grandparents or other relatives complain about your teen's misbehavior, suggest they deal with the teen directly. You could share this book with them or make some suggestions of your own. But give them the right to make their own choices.

Let's say a neighbor, Mrs. Kamm, complains about something your daughter has done. Again, use your reflective listening skills to show you understand how the woman feels. "I can see you're very angry that Bonnie trampled your flowerbed." Explain that you feel it would be best for her to deal directly with Bonnie in making arrangements for Bonnie to take care of the problem. If the neighbor agrees, you can ask Bonnie to talk with her. If Mrs. Kamm insists that you do something about the problem, though, you may decide it's best not to push the issue further. After all, you have to live in the neighborhood, too. You can ask Mrs. Kamm what she thinks should be done and decide whether you want to do it. Or you could suggest some action you're willing to take and explore alternatives with her. Perhaps Bonnie could spend a weekend taking care of the damage, or could pay for it out of her allowance. These would both be logical consequences for such behavior.

When discipline problems arise, reflective listening, I-messages, exploring alternatives, and natural and logical consequences can all be used to relate to teenagers effec-

tively and positively. And don't forget encouragement—the most important ingredient in any approach!

## Reference

1. Rudolf Dreikurs and Vicki Soltz, *Children: The Challenge* (New York: Hawthorn, 1964).

## Questions

1. How can identifying the goal of misbehavior and determining who owns the problem help parents choose the most effective approach to discipline?
2. Why is encouragement essential to any approach? How can you demonstrate an encouraging attitude when dealing with discipline problems? Give examples other than those found in the chapter.
3. What are some goals for which reflective listening would be appropriate? inappropriate? Give some examples of how you have used reflective listening effectively.
4. What are some goals for which I-messages can be effective? ineffective? Give some examples of how you have used I-messages effectively.
5. What kinds of situations call for a combination of approaches?
6. How do the authors suggest parents deal with arguments? with matters of clothing, hairstyle, and personal grooming? What is their reasoning for making these suggestions?
7. How can parents deal effectively with insults and vulgar language or gestures?
8. What can you do when your teen forgets things that don't involve you? that do involve you? Give examples other than those found in the chapter.
9. What can parents do when siblings fight among themselves? Why do the authors suggest parents stay out of such arguments?

10. How can parents criticize in an encouraging way?
11. When a teen smokes, who owns the problem? What do the authors suggest parents do if their teenager smokes?
12. How can you apply the authors' suggestions about dating to the circumstances in your own family?
13. What do the authors suggest parents do when teens have problems getting along with other adults?

## Activity for the Week

Practice selecting and applying the appropriate approach to a challenge with your teenager. Remember that encouragement is essential to any approach.

# Personal Development Exercise

## Assessing the Effectiveness of Different Approaches to Discipline

Answer the following questions about *each* of the four approaches to democratic discipline: reflective listening, I-messages, exploring alternatives, and natural and logical consequences.

1. What are some typical situations in which you've used the approach?

2. Give a specific example of a situation in which you've used the approach.
   Who owned the problem? How did your teen respond? If the situation did not go well, why do you think the approach was ineffective?

3. Which approaches have been most effective for you?

4. Would you be willing to give some or all of the approaches more emphasis?

5. How will you proceed?

Chart 8

# Effective Approaches to Problems

| Approach | Purpose | Example |
|---|---|---|
| Reflective listening | Showing you understand teen's feelings. Used when teen owns problem. | You're very worried about the semester exam? Sounds like you're feeling discouraged because the job's so difficult. |
| I-message | Communicating your feelings about how teen's behavior affects you. Used when you own problem. | When I'm ill and the dishes are left for me to do, I feel disrespected because it seems no one cares about me. When you borrow tools and don't return them, I feel discouraged because I don't have the tools I need when there's a job to do. |
| Exploring alternatives | Helping teens decide how to solve problems they own. Negotiating agreements with teen when you own problem. | What are some ways you could solve this problem? Which idea appeals to you most? Are you willing to do this until _____? What can we do to settle this conflict between us? Are we in agreement on that idea? What would be a fair consequence if the agreement is broken? |
| Natural and logical consequences | Permitting teens within limits to decide how they will behave and allowing them to experience consequences. Natural consequences apply when teen owns problem. Logical consequences apply when either parent or teen owns problem. | Natural: Teen who forgets coat on cold day gets cold. Teen who skips lunch goes hungry. Logical: Teen who spends allowance quickly does not receive any more money until next allowance day. Teen who neglects to study for a test gets low grade. |

# Points to Remember

**1.** The four approaches to democratic discipline are reflective listening, I-messages, exploring alternatives, and natural and logical consequences.

**2.** Encouragement is important to any approach if it is to be successful.

**3.** Use the following guidelines to select the most effective approach:

• Identify the goal of misbehavior.
• Determine who owns the problem.
• Base your decision on what the situation requires and the effectiveness of the approach.

**4.** Avoid arguing. Arguments usually leave each party more convinced that she or he is right. Use reflective listening and I-messages; agree to disagree.

**5.** Permit your teen to choose how to dress. If your teen is to accompany you, then you have a right to specify a preferred style of dress.

**6.** Your teen needs to be responsible for personal cleanliness. If dirt or body odor offends you, request that the teen go to another area of the home, or remove yourself. Teens who refuse to brush their teeth can pay their own dental bills.

**7.** Either ignore insults, vulgar remarks, and gestures, or use reflective listening to show you understand the anger. At a calm time, express your feelings about vulgarity.

**8.** When your teen's forgetting doesn't affect you, your teen owns the problem. If the forgetting does affect you, use I-messages, explore alternatives, and apply logical consequences.

**9.** Arguments and fights among siblings are usually not the parent's problem. Take yourself away from the squabblers and out of the role of referee.

**10.** Keep criticism to a minimum. If you feel criticism is necessary, criticize the act, not the person. I-messages and logical consequences are two positive approaches to criticism.

**11.** A teen who smokes owns the problem. The best parents can do is communicate concern for their teen's health.

**12.** Parents own most concerns they have about their teen's dating. To deal with these concerns, use your communication and negotiation skills.

**13.** Teens own most of the problems between themselves and other adults. They need to learn how to deal with other adults without parents' help or interference.

# My Plan for Improving Relationships
(An opportunity to assess progress each week)

My specific concern:

_____

_____

My usual response:

- ☐ talking, lecturing
- ☐ complaining, nagging
- ☐ becoming angry, screaming
- ☐ being sarcastic, attacking

- ☐ punishing, shaming
- ☐ giving up, forgetting because discouraged
- ☐ exerting power by removing privilege
- ☐ other _____

My progress this week:

| | I am doing this more | I need to do this more | I am about the same | | I am doing this more | I need to do this more | I am about the same |
|---|---|---|---|---|---|---|---|
| Understanding the purpose of behavior . . . . | ☐ | ☐ | ☐ | Communicating love, positive feelings . . . . . . . | ☐ | ☐ | ☐ |
| Working on developing an equal relationship based on mutual respect . . . . . . . | ☐ | ☐ | ☐ | Withdrawing from conflict . . . . . . . . . | ☐ | ☐ | ☐ |
| Responding to emotions more effectively . . . . . . . | ☐ | ☐ | ☐ | Preventing discipline problems by giving choices . . . | ☐ | ☐ | ☐ |
| Encouraging . . . . . . . . | ☐ | ☐ | ☐ | Correcting discipline problems appropriately . . . . . | ☐ | ☐ | ☐ |
| Appreciating and giving responsibility . . . . . . . | ☐ | ☐ | ☐ | Arranging democratic family meetings . . . . . . . | ☐ | ☐ | ☐ |
| Listening . . . . . . . . . | ☐ | ☐ | ☐ | Being firm and kind . . . . | ☐ | ☐ | ☐ |
| Revealing my feelings without blaming or accusing . . . . . . . . . . | ☐ | ☐ | ☐ | Staying out of problems that are not my problems . | ☐ | ☐ | ☐ |

I learned:

_____

_____

_____

I plan to change my behavior by:

_____

_____

_____

# CHAPTER 9

●

# *The Family Meeting*

A democratic family thrives on making decisions together. But, you may be asking, who has the time to get together every time a decision has to be made? If STEP/teen is to work for you, you'll want to take time to allow your family to function democratically. Family meetings give children and teens opportunities to participate in decision making and to learn the democratic process.[1]

The family meeting is a regularly scheduled meeting of all family members. Its purpose is to make plans and decisions, provide encouragement, and solve problems. In contrast to an informal or emergency meeting, the regularly scheduled family meeting assures all family members that they'll have a forum in which to be heard at a definite time each week. Plans and decisions made during a meeting stay in effect until the next family meeting. And family members know exactly when they'll have a chance to discuss and change a decision they've found hard to live with. If anyone has a complaint that doesn't require immediate attention, you can simply say, "Bring it up at the next family meeting, and we'll talk about it."

Unlike the negotiations described in Chapter 6, family meetings serve to do more than just solve problems. In fact, if the meeting focus is mainly on problems, interest is likely to dwindle rapidly. Family

meetings provide the following opportunities for each person:

• to be heard
• to express positive feelings about other family members
• to give encouragement
• to agree upon fair distribution of chores
• to express concerns, feelings, and complaints
• to help settle conflicts and deal with recurring issues
• to participate in planning family recreation

## How to Have Effective Family Meetings

To make your meetings productive and satisfying, we suggest you follow these guidelines:

**Establish a specific weekly meeting time.** The time and place of meetings is something for all family members to decide together. If democratic decision making starts even in the planning stages, all members will feel their opinions are truly important. Keeping the time and place consistent from week to week will establish the meeting as a regular part of family life. Any changes in meeting times are also made by consensus.

If some family members decide not to attend family meetings, decisions can still be made by those present. The absent member(s) will have to live with the decisions made by those who came.

**Rotate chairperson and secretary.** Parents and children alike need the opportunity to lead family meetings. Usually a parent chairs the first meeting in order to make sure everyone is heard, to structure the meeting so members know the procedures, and to demonstrate democratic decision making.

After the first meeting, family members can decide how to rotate the chair. Some families rotate by age, alphabetically, or by drawing names out of a hat.

If your family includes young children, you may wonder how old a child should be in order to be chairperson. School-age children are usually capable of being chairpersons—with a little parental assistance! Although you may occasionally have to remind younger children of the procedures, give a hand only when it's needed. Always allow the child serving as chairperson to address the group.

Family meetings require a secretary who keeps minutes so members have a record of what decisions were made. Here too family members can decide how the position should be rotated. The secretary posts the minutes in a place where all members can see them. Some families teach young secretaries to operate a tape recorder.

**Establish and stick to time limits.** Time limits are decided by the family. Be aware that without time limits, meetings may drag on until members lose interest. One hour is long enough for adults and teens; twenty to thirty minutes is a safer limit for a family with young children.

The chairperson has the responsibility of beginning and ending a meeting on time. Family members will learn the importance of showing up on time; they'll see there's only so much time in which to get things done.

**Make sure all members have a chance to offer ideas.** While everyone has the right to offer opinions and suggestions, it's best to let children and teens speak first.

Be careful not to let anyone dominate a meeting.

Parents can then add ideas only if necessary. This is especially true in early meetings. If parents lead off with a lot of suggestions, children may feel the real purpose of the meeting is for parents to impose their ideas. You might ask, "Who has an idea?" "Bill, we haven't heard from you. Have you anything to suggest?"

After meeting successfully several times, parents can feel freer to give ideas because a democratic atmosphere will have been established. Don't, however, let *anyone* dominate a meeting.

**Encourage everyone to bring up issues.** If the meetings are to be of interest to everyone, then each person must have the opportunity to have his or her concerns discussed. Some families establish an agenda book. Sometime before the meeting, members write down items they want discussed. Then, during the meeting, the chairperson proceeds down the list of items. Things that aren't discussed in one meeting are placed first on the agenda for the next meeting.

**Don't permit meetings to become gripe sessions.** Constant complaining can destroy family meetings. If it becomes a problem, you may have to insist that a member who complains be prepared to seek a solution. "I can hear you feel _____ about this. What suggestions do you have to solve this problem?" You may want to ask others in the family to contribute ideas. When problems come up, keep the focus on solutions.

**Distribute chores fairly.** Forgetting or refusing to do chores is usually a sign that chores have been arbitrarily assigned by parents. Solve the problem by asking the family what chores need to be done. Make the list together. With the group, determine which chores can be shared and which can

be accomplished by one person. Decide how chores will be chosen and rotated. You might ask, "How can we fairly distribute the chores?"

WHAT THE HECK... I'LL SPLIT THE WOOD, SCRUB THE TOILET, AND CLEAN THE OVEN!

Parents may be surprised at the effectiveness of the volunteer method.

Some families write each chore on a slip of paper and place the slips in a "job jar."[2] Each week, family members draw chores out of the jar. Another idea is to have everyone volunteer for chores. When first beginning the process, parents can model cooperation by volunteering for unpleasant chores. But make sure no one—including yourself—is always stuck with unpleasant chores.

**Plan family fun.** Each week, plan an enjoyable activity for the whole family to do. Perhaps you'll want to have a picnic, play a game, work on a project, see a movie, go to a flea market—there are probably a number of things your family likes to do. If the activity will involve chores, decide who will do what. Sometimes teens will choose not to join in family fun. Let them make that decision, but always make sure they're invited.

**Use your communication skills.** Make use of reflective listening to show you understand feelings and to clarify issues. Using open questions will encourage people to contribute. Exploring alternatives and brainstorming will stimulate thinking. You could ask, "What shall we do about this?" or "Who has an idea?" Send I-messages to express your feelings and beliefs. And make sure to focus on the real issue: "It seems to me we're all trying to get our own way. Is this going to help us solve the problem?"

In your family meeting, it's important to make decisions by consensus—by getting general agreement rather than majority approval. If there's a deadlock, either brainstorm again or table the issue to give everyone a chance to think. Avoid voting. Voting creates winners and losers and can actually hamper cooperation. If the deadlocked situation requires immediate action, you may need to make the decision yourself: "It looks as if we're not willing to agree on this issue right now. Something has to be done, so I'll make a temporary decision. At the next meeting we can discuss it again." Use this procedure only as a last resort, after you've looked carefully at the issue and have seen that it definitely warrants immediate attention. Never make such a decision in anger or for revenge. And if you find you do have to make a decision, make sure it fits the needs of the situation; otherwise you're inviting resistance.

When the family is ready to make a commitment, the chairperson summarizes what's been decided and asks if everyone is willing to accept the decision. A final summary of the meeting reminds members of all decisions that have been made.

**Evaluate the meeting.** At the close of each meeting, ask family members how they felt about the meeting and what suggestions they have for improving meetings in the future. Seek consensus; it's impor-

tant to be continually looking for ways to encourage cooperation.

**Evaluate decisions at the next meeting.** When discussing old business, be sure to have the family evaluate any commitments made at the previous meeting. The family can then decide whether to keep the decision or change it. Who wants to stick with a plan that no one likes?

## How to Start Family Meetings

A typical family-meeting format runs like this:

1. Share warm and pleasant feelings about good things that have happened over the past week. Send positive I-messages to family members about how they've cooperated. You could say, "I appreciated it when _____ because _____."

2. Read and, if necessary, discuss the minutes from the previous meeting.

3. Discuss old business.

4. Bring up new business, focusing on family fun as well as on plans and problems.

5. Summarize and evaluate the meeting.

Successful family meetings require plenty of cooperation. With this in mind, initiate the first meeting only after you feel your relationship with your teen and other children is one of mutual respect and honesty. If you've begun to use the various skills presented in STEP/teen and have gained more cooperation, your family is probably ready.

You might start by calling the family together and presenting the idea of meeting regularly. Some children and teens respond well to formal procedures; others need a bit of time to warm up to them. Here's how one couple introduced formal family meetings: "We've been thinking about all the things that need to be done around home and how we parents usually decide who'll do what and when it will be done. We've also been thinking about how it might feel to have parents make all the decisions about what you do around the house. We thought all of you might like to help decide what needs to be done and who will do it when. We'd like to start having regular family meetings each week where we can make these decisions together. And maybe in our meetings we can also help each other solve problems and plan some fun things to do together."

After presenting the idea, explain the meeting format and name some general kinds of things the family could discuss together— for example: family fun, chores, problems. Ask how each person feels about the proposal. If there's agreement, begin the meeting format by sharing positive feelings about things that have happened recently. Then proceed to new business. New business in this first meeting would include when and where to meet, rotation of chair and secretary, time limits, and any questions about setting up meetings. Take time to plan some family fun.

If family members have questions or comments about family meetings, delay using the format until these issues are discussed. You may have to wait until the next meeting to use the format.

What if you aren't able to get the whole family together to introduce the idea? You might bring it up to each person individually. And it's not necessary to wait until everyone is ready. If most people are, begin. Others may decide to join in later, after they've seen the benefits of participation.

## Leadership Skills for Family Meetings

The following group leadership skills will help you conduct more effective family meetings. As you model the skills, other family members will probably begin to use them too. And teens can be encouraged to read this section to gain a better understanding of the skills.

**Structuring.** Structuring simply means keeping the meeting on target. Without an identified structure, groups tend to wander. Basically, structuring involves keeping the meeting focused on the topic under discussion, following established procedures, and sticking to established time limits. Here's an example:

The Carlsens were spending a great deal of time on one topic. Several items on the agenda had not yet been addressed.

Mr. Carlsen asked the family how much more time they wanted to spend on the topic. The family agreed that if the issue was not resolved within five minutes, it would be tabled until the next meeting.

**Universalizing.** Members of a family may not always recognize that they have mutual concerns. To universalize a concern, the chairperson might say, "Who else feels this way?" or "It looks like you and Mom feel the same about this. Is that right?"

**Redirecting.** The chairperson needs to be constantly calling for opinions from group members. "Who has an idea on this?" "Janet, how do you feel?" Questions directed to the chair can also be redirected to the group: "I'll be glad to give you my opinion, but I'd like to hear from others first." Redirecting in these ways helps get all family members involved in the discussion. It also ensures that the meeting won't be monopolized by one person or another.

**Brainstorming.** Brainstorming encourages a free exchange of ideas. Group members can share all ideas, even those that seem remote or outlandish. Discussion or judgment of suggestions is suspended until brainstorming is finished.

**Summarizing.** Summaries may be needed at any time during a meeting—not just at the end. For example, if the family has had a lengthy discussion on a topic, a summary of the major points is helpful before moving on. Summaries following disagreements will serve to clarify points of view.

**Obtaining commitments.** The chairperson obtains commitments by asking group members if they are willing to carry out agreed-upon decisions during the week. Since commitments are recorded in the minutes, everyone can refer back to them during the week.

Sometimes family members will talk to each other through the chairperson.

**Promoting feedback.** Sometimes it's necessary to let family members know how their behavior may be affecting others in the group. Feedback can be given in I-messages. The chairperson might also ask members to report how they feel when someone in the group behaves in a certain way. Focusing attention on the real issue is another way to promote feedback: "It seems we all think we're right. I wonder how this will help us solve the problem?"

**Promoting direct interaction.** Sometimes one family member will talk to another through the chair. This is especially true when the chairperson is a parent. To avoid the role of "translator," remind members to speak directly to each other. "Joyce, will you please tell Gary directly how you feel."

**Promoting encouragement.** Yes, here it is again—the cornerstone of all the skills! Without encouragement, the family meeting will fail. Family members can build each other's self-esteem by focusing on contributions and strengths. Tell the whole group what you appreciate about them. If things have been running more smoothly during the week, say that you appreciate how everyone has pitched in.

# An Example of a Family Meeting

How do family meetings work? What do they sound like? To give you an idea, we've included the following example involving a mother, a father, and two teenagers, four-teen-year-old Paul and sixteen-year-old Brenda. Brenda is the chairperson for this meeting. As you read, note the use of specific communication and leadership skills.

**Brenda:** Dad, you're first in the agenda book—something about "messy bathroom." (*Structuring*)

**Dad:** Yes, I'm concerned about the condition of the bathroom after you two use it. I find towels thrown around, hair in the sink, and clothes, combs, and the hairdryer left lying around.

**Paul:** Talk to Brenda—she's the one who never cleans up!

**Dad:** I guess I'm not concerned about who leaves the mess. Mom and I've been cleaning it up, and I don't think that's fair to us, what with all the other things we have to do. (*Providing feedback through an I-message*)

**Paul:** I still say it's Brenda who's leaving the mess.

**Brenda:** I am *not*. You're not the neatest person in the world!

**Mom:** Sounds to me like you two are pretty touchy about this. I wonder if the problem will get solved if everyone's just interested in blaming? (*Reflective listening to help clarify feelings; feedback to identify the real issue*)

**Brenda:** Well, I'm tired of being called the resident slob!

**Dad:** I can see you feel picked on, Brenda, but that's not what I'm doing. I don't want to play detective—I just want

this problem solved. (*Structuring by clarifying both positions through reflective listening and I-message*)

**Paul:** But *she's* the one who makes most of the mess!

**Mom:** Paul, I don't think blaming is going to help us solve this problem. (*Structuring by focusing on the topic through an I-message*)

**Paul:** And I don't see why I should have to share this problem when she leaves the mess!

**Brenda:** I told you—

**Mom:** Whoa! Just a minute, please. Brenda, let me answer Paul. (*Structuring the meeting*) Paul, you don't think this is your problem and so you feel it's unfair to involve you in it, is that right? (*Clarifying through reflective listening*)

**Paul:** Right!

**Dad:** Well, what do you suggest we do about it then? (*Structuring by bringing the focus back on the topic*)

**Paul:** Make her clean it up!

**Brenda:** But I don't make *all* the mess. You do your share!

**Paul:** Yeah, but you make most of it!

**Dad:** You both seem to have a problem deciding who makes what mess. (*Universalizing and clarifying*) (Jokingly) Should we label each sock, comb, towel, and strand of hair?

**Paul:** (Smiling) That might not be a bad idea. (Silence)

**Mom:** Well, what can we do about this? Brenda, you're the chairperson. Want to call for some ideas? (*Structuring*)

**Brenda:** Oh, all right—who has an idea? Dad? (*Redirecting*)

**Dad:** How about you and Paul working together on cleaning up?

**Paul:** I will if she will.

**Mom:** How about it, Brenda?

**Brenda:** Well, okay, but how do we make it fair?

**Dad:** I'm not sure yet, but I think if the four of us put our heads together, we can figure it out.

**Paul:** What if whoever uses the bathroom cleans it up and calls you or Mom to check it before the next person uses it? That way, whoever makes the mess cleans it up.

**Dad:** That's one idea. I have another. Suppose Mom or I inspect the bathroom when you're both finished and then, if it's messy, the two of you will have to take care of it.

**Paul:** Why do that? Then you can't tell who made the mess.

**Mom:** Brenda, are we finished brainstorming, or are we discussing the ideas? (*Reminding the chairperson of the structure of the meeting*)

**Brenda:** Oh, yeah. Any more ideas? (Silence) Okay, let's discuss them. How does everyone feel about Paul's idea?

**Dad:** I'm uncomfortable with it because it makes Mom and me "bathroom police." That's why I suggested the second idea. I'm willing to inspect the bathroom once, but twice is too much for me. I don't know how Mom feels about it.

**Mom:** I agree.

**Paul:** But how will you know who made what mess?

**Mom:** I really feel the two of you can work together to take care of the problem. I don't think Dad and I need to get involved. (*Encouraging by showing faith in teens' ability*) Brenda, how do you feel about Dad's idea?

**Brenda:** I'll go along with it.

**Paul:** Well, I don't like it!

**Dad:** What shall we do? (Silence)

**Mom:** I'd like to suggest we try out Dad's idea until the next meeting just to see how it works. We can always change it. Paul, I know you don't like the idea, but would you be willing to use it this week? (*Obtaining a commitment*)

**Paul:** All right . . . I guess so.

**Dad:** I'm glad we came to at least a temporary agreement on this. (*Encouraging*) Are we ready to go on with something else? (*Structuring*)

This was a difficult issue. Obviously, each teenager wanted to shift the responsibility (and the blame) to the other, putting their parents in the middle. Mom and Dad stood firm, stating their own beliefs and feelings and showing understanding of how Paul and Brenda felt. Paul probably sees himself as the "good" teenager in the family—the one who always does the right thing. Brenda, then, takes the role of the "bad" one, or at least the messy one in this instance. The two may not sound very cooperative, but they are cooperating in this situation to get their parents to place blame. Paul worked very hard to shine his own halo and polish Brenda's horns. But it didn't work. Brenda was quick to agree with her father's solution because she saw that it wouldn't single her out as the messy one. Paul was reluctant because it would be more difficult for him to blame Brenda for the mess.

What will happen over the coming week? Brenda may try to get even with Paul by continuing to leave a mess that Paul will have to help clean up. And Paul may try to get even with his parents by continuing to complain about how unfair he thinks the arrangement is. But if the parents are willing to let the two teens own the problem, Brenda and Paul have a good chance of working it out.

# Frequently Asked Questions About Family Meetings

Every family has its own way of holding meetings—no two families are alike! Over the years, though, we've found that parents ask similar questions about family meetings.

**What if my spouse isn't interested?**
Without the cooperation of your spouse, can you still have effective family meetings? Definitely. Family meetings can involve all who are interested. If your spouse doesn't want to attend, you and the rest of the family can still make decisions about issues between you and them. We've discovered that reluctant spouses often decide to attend when they see how family meetings generate cooperation.

If yours is a single-parent family, we recommend that you discuss topics involving you and your teen, not those involving your teen's relationship with an absent parent. Issues involving an absent parent are best talked over at other times. The exception to this is when your teen's behavior relating to that parent affects your relationship with your teen in some way. For example, if your teen leaves chores till the last minute, and the absent parent arrives at the door, ready for an outing, you have a problem to talk over.

The same procedures apply to blended families. Keep the issues in family meetings restricted to the family that lives in the household. Issues involving absent parents or siblings should be dealt with directly with those people, and outside of the regular family meeting.

**How can I include my young children?**
Young children who can communicate are ready for family meetings, even ones that focus on teenage concerns. They may tire and want to be excused early—that's okay. Encourage young children to take part.

**What if my teen won't participate?** If your teenager doesn't wish to take part in family meetings, you and the others can still make decisions about issues between you and them. As in the case of a reluctant spouse, a teenager may come around after seeing how the rest of the family is responding to the system. Often a teen will hold off for a while and then join in. After all, it's not much fun to be on the outside of something others seem to find rewarding!

**Must children and teens be involved in all family decisions?** This is up to you. You may decide that some things are the parent's prerogative. Taking a new job, buying a new car, or moving to a different town may or may not be issues you want the entire family to help decide. When your teen brings up an issue you feel is yours to handle, simply say: "This is my decision" or "Mom and I are going to decide that." Do use the family meeting for most decisions, though, or you're likely to lose your teen's cooperation. Some issues that could involve the entire family include family outings, menu planning, allowances, vacations, conflicts concerning most or all family members, chores, planning for visitors, and family finances (what is affordable and what isn't).

**What can be done about broken agreements?** Right when agreements are made is the best time to discuss and settle on what will happen if they're broken. Follow the procedure suggested in Chapter 6: build in logical consequences. With chores, for example, family members need to decide when a task will be done and what will happen if it's not done by the agreed-upon time.

Here are some possible consequences for breaking typical household agreements. Some of these consequences may inconvenience you, but they'll help your teen learn to take responsibility seriously. Compare this temporary inconvenience with the prolonged inconvenience of nagging and arguing!

**Messy kitchen.** If the kitchen is messy, you can delay meal preparation until it's cleaned up. You have a right not to cook in a messy kitchen—it's inconvenient and unpleasant. Apply the same procedure if dishes are left undone, if the table isn't set, or if the kitchen trash is overflowing. Chances are the full trash can will be as smelly and unpleasant to your teen as it is to you.

**Empty gas tank.** In the family meeting, establish a policy for keeping gas in the car. For example, you and your teen can agree that you'll each always leave a quarter of a tank of gas for the next person who will drive the car. If your son or daughter leaves the car with little or no gas, you might decide to let natural consequences occur by not using the car yourself, therefore leaving it for your teen to buy gas

when he or she wants to drive again. But if you think natural consequences are likely to be too inconvenient, or if you find they don't solve a recurring problem, use the family meeting to decide logical consequences. Then, the next time your teen leaves the gas tank empty, he or she will have to accept the agreed-upon consequences: "I'm sorry, Margaret, but, as we agreed, you'll either have to give me money for a quarter tank of gas or plan not to drive at all for the next week."

**Routine chores.** Washing the car, cutting the grass, caring for pets, and running errands can all be handled by agreeing on a time limit. If they're not done by that time, you can interrupt your teen's activities to have them taken care of. (Reminders such as this are part of the logical consequence of not doing the chore. They are not nagging.)

If after a reasonable length of time natural and logical consequences haven't worked, it's time to reconsider the agreements. Your teen may be unwilling to keep certain agreements. If this is the case, it may be effective to change jobs. Or you can use task trading (see Chapter 7).

## The Potential of Family Meetings

We urge you to initiate regular family meetings in your home. These meetings are a must if families are truly to function democratically. And they're especially important for families with teenagers. Teens want to make as many of their own decisions as they can. When they can't do so by themselves, they need to participate in decisions that affect their lives. Involvement in family meetings is an essential ingredient of living cooperatively with teens.

While family meetings are by no means a panacea for family conflict, they do provide opportunities for open, honest communication. They establish a structure through which parents and teens can learn to treat each other with mutual respect. They provide a forum not only for problem solving, but also for cooperative planning and shared encouragement. Family members are more likely to be willing and eager to follow through on plans that they've helped to form. Although family meetings aren't easy in the beginning, a commitment to meeting and working together in an atmosphere of mutual concern and respect can have lasting benefits for your family.

## References

1. Rudolf Dreikurs and Vicki Soltz, *Children: The Challenge* (New York: Hawthorn, 1964).
2. Don Dinkmeyer and Gary D. McKay, *Raising a Responsible Child* (New York: Simon & Schuster, 1973).

## Questions

1. What is the purpose of the family meeting?
2. What format do the authors recommend for the family meeting?
3. What are some guidelines for family meetings?
4. Why is it important to operate by consensus, rather than by voting?
5. How are the following leadership skills applied to family meetings: structuring, redirecting, brainstorming, and summarizing?
6. How can you use your communication skills in family meetings?
7. In your family, what are the major challenges to effective family meetings?

## Activity for the Week

Plan to conduct a family meeting. Afterward, evaluate and write down what you think were the strengths and weaknesses of the meeting.

# Personal Development Exercise

## Planning Your First Family Meeting

1. How will you begin? Plan exactly what you will do and say. _____

_____

_____

_____

_____

_____

_____

_____

2. Are there any particular problems you anticipate with some family members? Indicate the problems and what you'll do if they arise. _____

_____

_____

_____

_____

_____

_____

_____

3. When will you hold your first family meeting? _____

_____

4. What family-meeting guidelines do you think are most important for your family? _____

_____

_____

_____

_____

_____

_____

Chart 9

# Leadership Skills for Effective Family Meetings

| Skill | Purpose | Example |
|---|---|---|
| **Structuring** | To set purpose and limits of the meeting. To keep meeting focused on topic. | "We seem to be off the subject." "We were talking about _____." "How much more time do we want to spend on this?" |
| **Universalizing** | To help family members recognize shared concerns. | "Is anyone else concerned about this?" "It seems you and Tracy feel the same way about this. Is that right?" |
| **Redirecting** | To get *all* family members involved in discussion. Helps keep members from dominating meeting. | "What do the rest of you think about this?" "Jane, we haven't heard from you. What do you think?" |
| **Brainstorming** | To encourage family members to generate alternatives. | "Let's think of as many ways to solve this problem as we can. We won't react to any of them until we've run out of suggestions." |
| **Summarizing** | To clarify what has been said and decided. | "What have we said about this issue?" "What have we decided to do about this?" |
| **Obtaining commitments** | To develop specific commitments for family members to carry out. | "Are we all willing to do this until the next meeting?" "Jack, you said you would _____, is that right?" |
| **Promoting feedback** | To let family members understand how other family members see and hear them. | "I wonder how Kristin feels when you say that." "I wonder if that comment will be helpful to John." "I appreciate your helping us solve this problem." |
| **Promoting direct interaction** | To get family members to speak directly to each other when appropriate. | "Would you tell Vickie directly what you think about her comment?" |
| **Promoting encouragement** | To help family members increase each other's self-esteem and self-confidence. | "What does Doug do that you like?" "Thank you all for cooperating in getting the chores done this week." |

# Points to Remember

**1.** In a democratic family, decisions that affect the entire family are made cooperatively. Time needs to be set aside to discuss such issues.

**2.** The family meeting is a regularly scheduled meeting of all family members. Its purpose is to make plans and decisions, to provide encouragement, and to solve problems.

**3.** Plans and decisions made during a family meeting remain in effect until the next meeting.

**4.** Family meetings provide opportunities for:

• being heard
• expressing positive feelings about one another
• giving encouragement
• distributing chores fairly
• expressing concerns, feelings, and complaints
• settling conflicts and dealing with recurring problems
• planning family recreation

**5.** Use the following guidelines for effective family meetings:

• Establish a specific weekly meeting time.
• Rotate chairperson and secretary.
• Establish and stick to time limits.
• Make sure all members have a chance to offer ideas.
• Encourage everyone to bring up issues.
• Don't permit meetings to become gripe sessions.
• Distribute chores fairly.
• Plan family fun.
• Use your communication skills.
• Evaluate the meeting.
• Evaluate decisions at the next meeting.

**6.** Begin family meetings only after you feel your relationship with your children is one of mutual respect and honesty.

**7.** A typical family-meeting agenda might be:

• Share positive feelings about good things that have happened during the week.
• Read and discuss the minutes from the previous meeting.
• Discuss old business.
• Bring up new business (focusing on family fun as well as on plans and problems).
• Summarize and evaluate the meeting.

**8.** Follow through on agreements. At the time agreements are made, build in logical consequences for broken agreements.

**9.** All members participate in family meetings as equals.

**10.** Family meetings are essential if families are truly to function democratically.

# My Plan for Improving Relationships
(An opportunity to assess progress each week)

My specific concern:

_____

_____

My usual response:

- ☐ talking, lecturing
- ☐ complaining, nagging
- ☐ becoming angry, screaming
- ☐ being sarcastic, attacking

- ☐ punishing, shaming
- ☐ giving up, forgetting because discouraged
- ☐ exerting power by removing privilege
- ☐ other _____

My progress this week:

| | I am doing this more | I need to do this more | I am about the same | | I am doing this more | I need to do this more | I am about the same |
|---|---|---|---|---|---|---|---|
| Understanding the purpose of behavior | ☐ | ☐ | ☐ | Communicating love, positive feelings | ☐ | ☐ | ☐ |
| Working on developing an equal relationship based on mutual respect | ☐ | ☐ | ☐ | Withdrawing from conflict | ☐ | ☐ | ☐ |
| Responding to emotions more effectively | ☐ | ☐ | ☐ | Preventing discipline problems by giving choices | ☐ | ☐ | ☐ |
| Encouraging | ☐ | ☐ | ☐ | Correcting discipline problems appropriately | ☐ | ☐ | ☐ |
| Appreciating and giving responsibility | ☐ | ☐ | ☐ | Arranging democratic family meetings | ☐ | ☐ | ☐ |
| Listening | ☐ | ☐ | ☐ | Being firm and kind | ☐ | ☐ | ☐ |
| Revealing my feelings without blaming or accusing | ☐ | ☐ | ☐ | Staying out of problems that are not my problems | ☐ | ☐ | ☐ |

I learned:

_____

_____

_____

I plan to change my behavior by:

_____

_____

_____

# Special Challenges

In previous chapters you've learned concepts and skills to help you relate more effectively with your teen. In this final chapter we'll discuss how to apply this information to various parenting situations and special teenage problems. We ask that you not read this chapter until you've read, understood, and practiced what's been presented in previous chapters. You need a firm grasp of those concepts and skills in order to apply them to the special challenges in this chapter.

## When Your Spouse Doesn't Agree with Your Methods

Suppose you've found the information in STEP/teen just what you're looking for, but your spouse doesn't agree. Do you scrap the whole approach? No. You don't have to give up just because your wife or husband doesn't agree. First of all, keep in mind that couples seldom agree completely about child-rearing. While it's certainly very helpful for your teen, your spouse, and you to be in agreement, it's not absolutely necessary.

You have to decide how you want to relate to your teen. Let your spouse do the same. Your spouse may try to sway you from your chosen path, but you don't have to leave

that path if you don't want to. You control your own behavior.

If you and your spouse don't see eye-to-eye on STEP/teen's democratic approach, you can agree to disagree. Continue to take care of problems between you and your teen, and let your spouse do the same. Even if you feel your spouse's effect on your teen is negative, you'll still be able to influence your teen in positive ways. Teens know how to deal with a negative person.

When parents argue, they both lose.

Above all, don't interfere in your spouse's relationship with your teen.*

Don't try to sway your spouse to your way. If you establish a respectful relationship with your teen and positive changes occur, your wife or husband may decide to adopt your approach—as long as you don't try to make your success a testimony to your spouse's failure.

## The Effects of Divorce on Children and Teens

There are a lot of myths about the effects of divorce on children and teens. The major myth is that children are irreparably damaged by divorce. It's true that divorce presents challenges for most children, but children are not passive puppets who have no control over themselves. Often, some of the most damaging effects of divorce are due to well-meaning friends and relatives who feel sorry for children. Children and teens on the receiving end of such pity may come to believe that they are powerless to handle a tough situation.[1]

Guilt can also discourage children of divorce. Divorced parents often feel guilty, and this guilt may motivate them to try to "make it up" to children. The children in turn are often sensitive to the parents' guilt and use the guilt feelings to their own advantage. No one can afford to be glib about divorce, but if you regard it as unfortunate rather than catastrophic, you can prevent guilt from eating away at family relationships.

Children and teenagers whose parents get divorced may feel guilty on their own. They may believe that if only they had been better behaved, the parents would still be together. Such children need to understand that divorce is nobody's fault. It doesn't signify failure. Divorce is a difficult decision to change a situation; it's one alternative to a discouraging relationship.

Everyone's feelings about the divorce need to be openly discussed. Children and teens may want to talk about feelings and facts over and over. Emily and John Visher, authorities in working with stepparents, suggest that you be patient if this happens. It takes time to sort out feelings.[2] Use your reflective listening skills to help children and teens clarify and understand their feelings. But if you find your child is using feelings of guilt, anger, depression, or blame to manipulate you, it's time to stop responding to those feelings. Get on with life and expect your daughter or son to do the same.

Unfortunately, some divorced parents use their children as a weapon against each other. This can have very discouraging effects. Caught in the middle in this way, children and teens often feel they're being forced to make a choice. Remember that while you may no longer love your ex-spouse, your children still do. The relationship between you and your ex-spouse is your responsibility, not your children's. The more cordial the two of you can be to one another, the better off your children and teens will be. If they feel free to love both

---

*One exception to this is the presence of child abuse. Teens, as well as younger children, can be subjected to physical, verbal, or psychological abuse. If you feel that your spouse is abusing *any* of the children in your family, you'll need to seek help. If you live in the United States, check with your county's Department of Social Services or Public Health Nursing Services. For more information write to Parents Anonymous, 6733 S. Sepulveda Blvd., Suite 270, Los Angeles, CA 90045; or call (213) 410-9732 or (800) 421-0353. In Canada, write to Parents Anonymous of Calgary, 204601 Seventeenth Ave. S.W., Calgary, Alberta T2S LB3; or call (403) 265-1117. In Australia, write to Parents Anonymous, 1st Floor, 156 Collins Street, Melbourne, Victoria 3000; or call 03-654-4654.

parents and are able to develop a relationship with each one, their adjustment to the divorce will be much more positive.

# Single Parents

If you're a single parent, you have a very challenging task. There are times when you may feel lonely, isolated, and trapped. Without minimizing your task, we think there is also an advantage to your situation: you're in complete charge of your children. You can decide, without interference, how you want to raise them. Many couples don't have that advantage—they're busy disagreeing about how the children should be raised.

But, you may be thinking, when the children visit my ex-spouse, my efforts are undone. We don't agree. Given the opportunity, your children's other parent may attempt to spoil your efforts, but you don't have to cooperate. Let your ex-spouse deal with the children as she or he sees fit. Do your best to relate positively and democratically with your children when you're with them. They can learn from your example and influence. And don't give up if your children are with their other parent more than they're with you. A few hours of positive contact, no matter how infrequent, can do a lot to help children and teens feel good about themselves. Keep in mind too that children learn to adjust to different expectations. In fact, they deal with differences among family members, friends, and teachers every day.

Sometimes children try to play one parent off the other. For example:

> Your teen may tell you, "But when I'm at Mom's, she lets me stay out till midnight." Don't become trapped in arguments and hurt feelings. Show you understand how your teen feels, state

> your limits, and refuse to argue: "I know you stay out later when you're with your mom, and that's up to you and her to decide. But when you're here, I'll expect you to be in by eleven, as we agreed."

Avoid criticizing your ex-spouse in front of teens and children. Criticizing an absent spouse puts children in an uncomfortable, discouraging position. Instead of condemning the rules in the other household, simply say that you don't agree with the rules, but that all people have the right to make decisions and form opinions for themselves.

Sometimes children invite criticism by complaining about problems they have with their other parent. If this happens, resist the temptation to side with your children. By the same token, you needn't defend your ex-spouse. Instead, use your reflective listening skills and explore alternatives to help children and teens learn what they can do to effectively deal with the situation.

As a single parent, you may find that your social life is a source of conflict. Some single parents are reluctant to date, or feel guilty when they do. If your children don't like the fact that you date or don't approve of your dating partners, that's their problem. You can help by taking time to listen and understand their feelings. Then tell them, kindly but firmly, that while you understand their feelings, you have a right to make decisions about your personal life.

# Stepparents

Being a stepparent is an extremely challenging task. Stepparents usually enter a family whose relationships are already well established. They have to "fit in."

Many stepparents are so anxious about being accepted by their new families that they have trouble establishing healthy, effective relationships. But the more anxious you are about winning the love and respect of your stepchildren, the more conflict you're likely to encounter. Children and teenagers can sense this anxiety. They may learn to play it against you. You in turn may try harder to please them. Eventually, when you become tired of this, you'll probably decide it's time to exert your authority. This is the road to trouble! Trying to please and trying to control are different sides of the same coin. Some stepparents try to take the place of the children's absent parent. We believe this is also a mistake. Most children and teens love their absent parent. They're sure to reject a newcomer's efforts to act as a replacement.

Often, stepparents try too hard to please their new children. This is the road to trouble.

There are times when the shoe is on the other foot. The children and teenagers are so eager to be accepted and loved by their new parent, they bend over backward to please. At first, this may flatter some stepparents, but most eventually tire of being courted in this way. Knowing the children are not for real, a stepparent in this position becomes uncomfortable and confused.

A stepparent who enters a family with teenagers needs to realize that adolescents aren't children anymore—they're in the process of separating from the family to establish their own identities. Also, the young adults may have played special roles in the family during the time they had only one parent at home, perhaps taking on many adult responsibilities. If you step in and start performing all these duties, the teens may feel displaced. They may resent your presence. Let teenagers continue to assume the responsibilities they're accustomed to. Acknowledge their importance to the family.

If you and your spouse have different ideas on how to raise children, understandings and agreements need to be reached. Some negotiation may be necessary; perhaps the two of you will decide that each parent will deal with the children as she or he sees fit. If so, you'll also need to agree that one will not interfere with the other and that you won't let children and teens play you off against each other.

Family meetings or negotiation conversations with all family members can really help a blended family learn to get along together. They provide a forum where feelings can be expressed and agreements can be reached. We suggest you review Chapter 9 to see how regular meetings can strengthen the bonds within your blended family.

The Vishers point out some things to keep in mind about your stepchildren and your role as a stepparent:[3]

*Realize that many children don't see a stepparent's entrance into the family as the gain of an additional parent.* They may see the arrival as an intrusion into their relationship with their natural parents. And they may have a sense of loss—a sense of being deserted by their noncustodial parent and of being neglected by their custodial parent.

*Be aware that some stepchildren worry that if they don't behave properly, they might be responsible for a second divorce.* They may feel guilty and fearful. If you understand this, you're in a better position to respond positively to any misbehavior associated with these feelings.

*Get to know your stepchildren and establish a positive relationship with them by offering them an opportunity to do things with you.* Arrange private time together for activities that are of mutual interest. Take time, too, to do some things together as an entire family. Encourage your stepchildren's natural parent to spend some private time with them as well. This will make sharing the natural parent less stressful for your stepchildren.

*Make your role in the family one that is unique, and noncompetitive with the children's natural parent.*

*If you have some contact with your stepchildren's absent parent, try to establish a congenial relationship.* Remember, the children love this person. It won't help your relationship with them if you are inconsiderate toward their other parent.

*Don't try to hide from the children any negative feelings you may have about your spouse's previous mate.* Hidden feelings are expressed through gestures, tone of voice, and facial expressions, not just through words. Your stepfamily will know how you feel. If you don't like something the absent parent does, say so, but not in a critical way. Simply state your feelings in the form of an I-message. And, if possible, don't forget to express positive feelings you may have.

# Special Problems with Teenagers

**Lying.** Most parents see lies as a sign their children don't trust them. Yet many parents actually train their teens to lie. Certain kinds of "little white lies" may be a part of family life that children know about and learn from. Have you ever said, "Tell him I'm not home" when the phone rings and you don't want to talk? If someone invites you to a party and you don't want to go, is that what you tell the person? Did you ever try to pass off your thirteen-year-old as an eleven-year-old to get a cheaper movie ticket? Parents need to be aware that practices such as these model lying as acceptable behavior.

Lying, like all misbehavior, serves a purpose. Teens may exaggerate to gain the attention of parents or peers. If parents can't catch them in a lie, teens may use lies to defeat parents. Lying can also be used to escape punishment, to seek revenge, to generate excitement, to gain acceptance from peers, or to give teens a feeling of superiority.

Who owns the problem when lies are told? It depends on whom the lying affects. If teens exaggerate to gain attention, peer recognition, or superiority, then they own the problem. Parents can help a teen stop lying by being unimpressed. They can simply listen, without acknowledging that they know the teen is stretching the truth, and without challenging the facts. Later, parents can find ways to give their teen positive attention, by looking for assets and planning ways for the teenager to use those assets to contribute to the family. The teen will then see no need to use falsehoods to impress others.

If you find that silence doesn't stop the lying, you can discuss the situation with your teen. You might say, "Could it be you want to impress me with these stories?" Then discuss why your teen feels the need to impress you. Listen and explore alternatives to help your teen find ways to gain a sense of importance in the family.[4]

If your teen's lying affects you, then you certainly own the problem. Before we suggest what you can do in this case, we want to list some don'ts. First of all, don't set up unrealistic expectations. For example, too many *can't*s almost guarantee lying. "You can't go to that movie." "No, you can't ride with Kate." "You can't play those records in this home!" A teen on the receiving end of too many commands like this will likely feel there's no choice *but* to lie.

Teenagers need a certain amount of freedom and a lot of trust and confidence from their parents. Don't play detective by asking questions like "Where did you go?" "Whom were you with?" and "What did you do?" Too many questions delivered in the third degree may induce lying. Don't make telling the truth more dangerous than lying; if you do, your teen will lie for self-protection. And don't set up situations to

try and catch your teenager in a lie, as in the following example:

> Mr. Thompson didn't trust his son Sam to tell him the truth about where he was going. One night Mr. Thompson set a trap: Sam told his father he was going to visit his friend Toby, and late in the evening Mr. Thompson called Toby's mother and found that Sam had not been there. When Sam came home, he found his father waiting up for him. "You liar!" Mr. Thompson confronted his son. "Where were you? You weren't at Toby's because I checked! You're grounded for a month!"

While one would hope Sam would be willing to tell his father where he was, Mr. Thompson's basic distrust of Sam certainly won't encourage him to be truthful in the future.

Finally, don't overreact if you happen to discover your teen has lied to you. Telling a few lies does not make a person a pathological liar! But mistrusting, playing detective, and overreacting can keep the lies coming.

Follow these suggestions to help curb lying:[5]

- Use an I-message to show you're disappointed: "When you don't tell me the truth, I feel really disappointed because I've always been able to depend on what you say to me." In this way, you make your feelings known and also appeal to your teen's sense of self-respect.
- Show that you appreciate your teen's willingness to tell the truth: "I'm not willing to accept what you did, and we'll need to discuss what to do about it. But I know it took real courage for you to tell me this, and I'm glad you told me."
- When you know your teen has lied, don't make an accusation. Just deal with the specific situation. If necessary, use logical consequences: "Diane, I know you had

your friends in while we were gone, because beer is missing from the refrigerator. So the next time we go out, you'll have to go with us or go to your grandparents'."

The more accepting, encouraging, and trusting your relationship is with your teen, the less likely it is that she or he will feel the need to lie. Lying is a signal that there is distrust in your relationship. If you discover your teen is lying to you, closely examine the relationship. Work to open up channels of communication.

**Stealing.** To understand why a teen might steal, think in terms of purposive behavior: stealing is aimed at a goal. In fact, it could be aimed at attention, power, revenge, excitement, peer acceptance, or superiority. Obviously, the person whose possessions are taken owns the problem. This may be you, other family members, or people in the community.

**When a teen steals from parents.** If your teen has stolen something of yours, check your feelings to determine the purpose of the stealing. If you're merely annoyed, the stealing is probably designed to trap your attention. But if you're angry or hurt, the purpose is power and revenge. Excitement is often mixed with power, and so you're likely to feel angry if the goal of excitement is involved. If you're puzzled and frustrated because you can't find the thief, superiority may be mixed in.

When you encounter stealing, the worst thing you can do is lecture and moralize. You don't have to tell your teen that stealing is wrong—everyone knows that! And lectures, name-calling, and punishments will reinforce the misbehavior and increase the likelihood of future stealing.

Teens who steal to trap their parents' attention want to be caught. If you simply take the items back without comment, your teen will receive no attention for stealing. Make sure you give positive attention at other times by noting contributions and assets. Teens who steal to gain power or to seek revenge may also want to be caught. In this way they show parents who's in control. Again, don't lecture or moralize. Take the items back. You may also want to put them away so your teen can't steal them again. If your daughter or son is stealing money, choose a quiet time to discuss ways to earn extra money instead. You could begin by saying, "It appears you feel you need some extra money. Would you like to talk about how you could earn some?"

When your teen has hidden your possessions, you can ask for their return. If you get a denial, resist the temptation to argue. Simply state that if the items aren't returned, they'll be paid for from the teen's allowance. Leave the choice to your teen.

Parents can offer teens responsible use of power. They can put teens in charge of some aspect of family business: for example, buying household items or making sure the car has gasoline and proper fluid levels. If excitement is part of the goal, parents might want to help the teen find excitement in more socially acceptable ways. Families can do exciting things together—go to a play, a car race, or a rock concert, for example.

If you suspect your teen is stealing from you to demonstrate superiority, encourage using a talent to help the family. If your teenage son enjoys cooking, invite him to plan and prepare some of the family meals.

What if something is missing and you don't know who the culprit is? In this case, inform your children that you aren't interested in who took it—you just want it back. Provide a place and time where the item can be returned anonymously. Then, if it isn't returned, it becomes the children's problem. They'll have to figure out how to find it or replace it.

**When a teen steals from the community.** Unless you find objects in your teen's possession that you can't account for, you may not be aware that stealing is taking place. Should you find what you suspect are stolen items in your teen's possession, ask where they're from. Give the teen a choice: "Either you return those items, or I will." If the police become involved, don't panic. Let your teen take the consequences society provides. Where attorneys' fees and restitution are involved, you'll need to discuss with your teen how she or he will help pay for these.

One final word about stealing. If it becomes a persistent problem, you and your teen may need to seek professional help from a qualified family counselor or psychologist.

**Sexual activity.** Many parents are anxious about their children's sexual maturation—sex is a very difficult and complicated issue! Parents worry that teens may be sexually active, that they might be hurt emotionally, physically, or both. Parents also fear the possibility of pregnancy and venereal disease. They are concerned that their teens may have to make agonizing decisions with little or no experience and guidance.

Sex is broadcast to teens every day—from movies, books, magazines, billboards, TV, radio, and peers. Some parents may actually expect their teenagers to be sexually active. And teens may perceive such an expectation as tacit permission to do so. Amidst this confusion of standards, teenagers must make decisions about sex.

Every teenager has sexual feelings and must decide what to do about them. Sexual choices are just that—choices that each person must make. Teenagers are in control of sex just as they're in control of any other behavior. Sex does not control teenagers.

And, like all behavior, sex has a purpose. One purpose of having sex is obvious—pleasure. Another purpose is to experience and express love. But teenagers can use their sexuality to pursue other goals. Teens may become sexually active to rebel against strict, moralistic parents. They may engage in sex to seek revenge against parents, to gain peer acceptance, or to seek superiority. Teenagers own their sexuality and the problems associated with it, unless the consequences, such as venereal disease or pregnancy, affect parents or other people.

How you feel about masturbation, birth control, petting, and premarital sexual intercourse is dependent on your religious and moral beliefs. We don't intend to tell you what to believe. We do hope, however, that you were willing to talk about sex to your child early on, and that you gradually expanded conversations about sex as your daughter or son grew older. As your children move through adolescence, you need to continue these talks, and to share as well your values about sex. We hope these will be friendly and open discussions, not a list of dos and don'ts. Taboos, regardless of their intent, are rarely effective. An open, honest exchange of opinions is the best way to help teens make responsible decisions about sex. Trust and confidence in your teen's good judgment is the best gift you can give.

Many parents who had little or no trouble explaining sex to children find discussing the subject with early adolescents a bit more difficult. You may want to go to your local library or bookstore or talk to teachers to find age-appropriate materials that will help your teen learn about body maturation, feelings, and decisions. Sometimes a book can say better what you find difficult to give words to. Nevertheless, discuss the book with your teen; don't just hand it over. Most of all, be available when your teen wants to talk about sex, love, and intimacy.

Be sure to discuss the books with your teen—don't just hand them over.

**Anger and violence.** Anger and violence serve a purpose, though not a positive one. They enable a teenager to be challenging and to feel in control. One of the problems with anger is that it usually influences the person on the receiving end to withdraw or attack.

If your teen's anger is directed at you, you own the problem. In the case of a temper tantrum, you needn't become involved. You can leave the room and let your teen calm down. But when the anger is accusatory, it's important to show that you hear it: "You sound very angry with me because you feel I'm unfair?" At times using reflective listening skills when your teen is angry may only increase the anger. In such instances it may be best to withdraw until tempers have cooled. Discuss the issue at a calmer time. Once your teen is aware that

you hear the anger and that you're willing to work out the problem, alternatives can be explored: "I understand your anger, but I don't feel it's unfair for me to expect that your overnight ski trip be chaperoned. How can we work it out so we're both happy?"

In any conflict, the first step is to identify whether people are acting respectfully. Then identify the real issue or the goal that is the purpose of the anger. Next, note your response to the anger. Consider how you can change, perhaps by doing the opposite of what you're inclined to do. For example, if you feel like lashing out, walk away instead. If you leave, the anger will not be effective. For some teens, expressing anger is a way of being heard. If you often respond by arguing and yelling, listen instead. Defuse your teen's anger by being understanding and showing you hear it.

Always look for any encouraging aspect of the anger. Yes, look for something positive! Anger usually demonstrates that teens are taking a stand for what they believe in. It also shows they respect their parents enough to let the parents know how they feel. For some teens it is the only way they know of being independent. Such teens may need to find other forms of self-expression. I-messages and reflective listening will be helpful. One of the most effective procedures is to help your teen explore alternative ways to solve a particular problem. Keep in mind too that anger is preferable to apathy because it's active. As you recognize and accept the positive aspects of anger, you help your teen redirect these strong feelings toward more constructive goals.

Of course, if your teen is violent and tries to attack you physically, you will have to protect yourself. Breaking family possessions is a form of violence. Violence toward you or family property is a sign that

185

professional help may be needed. If you are experiencing these problems with your teen, consider family therapy.

**Dependency.** Dependent teens turn their parents into servants. Parents are the ones who check the homework, supply all the money, select all the clothing, and wake teens up in the morning. Dependent teens act as if they're incapable, and their parents usually feel very discouraged.

When you provide special services for your teen, your intention may be to help, but the result is that your daughter or son becomes less effective and feels inadequate. If teens are to develop self-respect, they must be encouraged to function on their own steam.

Dependent teens turn their parents into servants.

What purpose does dependency have? A dependent teen may be looking for attention. Or the goal may be to display inadequacy in order to be excused from functioning as a regular member of the family. Some teens actually use dependent behavior to demonstrate power. It's as if they're saying, "I'll force you to do it for me." Dependent teens are the ones who own the problem. If parents stop serving their teen, the logical con-

sequence is that the teen must learn to function independently.

Encourage a dependent teen by recognizing assets and minimizing mistakes and weaknesses. Small positive steps can lead to independence. As you decline to be involved in confirming inadequacy, your teen will begin to learn from the consequences of failing to function. She or he will have to choose between similar future consequences or different circumstances that will result from self-reliance. For your part, be patient at this point. The teen has spent a lot of time and energy being dependent. It won't be easy to give up this role. Be supportive, and focus on any effort or positive movement you see.

Consider this example:

> At the family meeting, Martha Rizzo told her thirteen-year-old son, Ron, that she planned to start doing the grocery shopping regularly every Wednesday evening. If there was anything Ron wanted from the store, he was to tell her about it sometime before she left for work on Wednesdays. Ron wanted a certain brand of cereal, peanuts, oranges, and some English muffins. Unfortunately, he neglected to tell his mother. As he helped her unload the grocery bags, he realized none of his favorite foods was there. He began to complain, and Martha told him, "I'm sorry you forgot to tell me what you wanted. I'm sure you'll remember next week."

**Alcohol and other substance abuse.** Teens who abuse alcohol or other drugs may be seeking excitement or trying to escape boredom. They may use drugs to rebel—to show that parents and other adults can't control them. Teens may also abuse drugs to gain peer acceptance, for revenge against parents, or to avoid dealing with life.

Certainly parents will want to communicate feelings and concerns about the use or abuse of alcohol and other drugs. Parents have the right to insist the drugs not be used in their home. As a legal adult and head of a household, a parent can be held liable if illegal substances are found or used on the parent's property.

It's important first of all to distinguish between *occasional* use of alcohol or marijuana and *habitual* use. It is equally important to ascertain whether hard drugs or toxic substances are being used. Even though you may disapprove of occasional drinking or pot smoking, this in itself may not be a real problem. But regularly using these substances, or using hard drugs even experimentally, makes matters more serious. The family and the teen will need professional help.

If there is substance abuse in your home, you know you own the problem. While the abuser has a major problem, the behavior overlaps into so many facets of life that you cannot overlook it. A teenager with a drug or alcohol problem desperately needs your help.

How can you tell if your teen is abusing drugs? Unless the abuse has reached a very advanced stage, there are no sure signs that would be noticed in day-to-day family living. Certain changes in behavior may take place: there may be changes in choice of friends, a lowered performance in school or at work, frequent mood swings, or changes in truthfulness and honesty. Changes in goals and attitudes may also occur.[6]

Instead of looking for specific symptoms of drug abuse, be aware of changes in your teenager. Is your daughter or son losing weight? Is your teen keeping strange hours? Has your teenager begun to neglect basic grooming habits? Has she or he become secretive or withdrawn?[7] Of course, such changes do not automatically indicate that drug abuse is taking place.[8] In fact, many of these changes are somewhat typical in adolescents from time to time. You know your teenager. If you've noted a combination of several puzzling or unusual behaviors, you'll at least want to consider that alcohol or drug abuse could be the problem.

Teenage drug abuse can cause family heartbreak—it's extremely difficult for parents to deal with a teen who they feel is disrespecting self, family, and all the family believes in. In some cases, parents feel completely powerless. Rather than look for a reasonable course of action, these parents despair. But neither anger nor despair can do much to help a teen who is abusing a drug. Whether a teen is seeking power, revenge, excitement, or some other goal, substance abuse indicates a lack of self-esteem and self-worth. By communicating respect, you can provide a start in building a discouraged teen's self-esteem.

Perhaps the most difficult challenge is for parents to change their attitude toward both the teen and themselves. Many adults are appalled at the use of alcohol, marijuana, and other drugs. They often feel challenged, and become determined to "stamp it out." But this action invites rebellion and, possibly, the establishment of a drug habit. If parents persist in attacking and arguing, the teen will be forced into a defensive position. If parents engage in self-blame, they will not be able to do anything constructive. While parents certainly share in the responsibility for the problem, the teen also has a responsibility for drug abuse. Blaming *anyone* is a dead-end street. If parents can accept that the teen is alcoholic or dependent on another drug, and start to look for resources to meet this challenge, they will have initiated positive movement.

The teen who uses substances to escape or to create excitement often feels she or he is not accepted, is not heard, is not even listened to at home. Start by building this teenager's self-esteem. Find any strength or positive behavior and point it out. Help the teen to have a sense of belonging. Most important, don't nag and criticize. Don't lecture, plead, or bribe. Do not rescue the teen from teachers or employers. Instead, help your teen experience the logical consequences of the abusive behavior. Help explore alternative, less destructive, ways to take a stand and seek excitement.

Be aware that alcohol and drugs are easily available to most teenagers. In many circles their use is considered acceptable; in some, it's the expected norm.[9] To learn about the drug scene in your community, contact your school district, county social service office, or a local hospital to find what classes or materials are available for parent education.

If the problem of alcohol or other drug abuse becomes too much for you and your family to handle, you'll need to seek professional help. A school counselor, member of the clergy, family doctor, or social referral agency can help guide you to a competent chemical-dependency counselor or treatment program.

**Pregnancy.** There are a variety of reasons why teens become pregnant, including lack of information, the need for love and acceptance, and rebellion against family values. As with any problem, parents will need to examine their own feelings, the family relationship, and the individual situation.

The problem belongs to both the pregnant teen and the young father. But the girl is the one who is pregnant, and she is ultimately the one who must live with this fact. As her parent, your first feeling may be shock or rejection. This is something you're not ready to accept. But rejecting your daughter will not cancel the pregnancy. She needs your understanding and support—perhaps more now than ever before.

You and your daughter can seek guidance from a doctor, family therapist, member of the clergy, counselor, or social service agency. Such outside assistance can provide greatly needed support at a time when logic may easily give way to emotions and irrationality. It may be appropriate to meet with the boy and his parents to discuss the problem openly and honestly.

The major change required of you is attitudinal: you must begin to understand and accept what has happened. If your attitude communicates acceptance, you will have established an atmosphere for problem solving. Don't lecture or moralize. Avoid using the words *should* and *must*. Listen to your daughter's feelings. If you hear fear, loneliness, or rejection, reflect the feeling and investigate it. By understanding how she feels about the pregnancy, you will establish mutual respect. By listening to your daughter's point of view, you will increase her self-esteem and sense of self-worth. You can then begin to help her explore alternatives, and together you can weigh what will be best for her and for the baby.

But what if you are the parent of the boy? What do you do? Use your communication skills to explore his feelings and intentions. Together, explore ways that he can act responsibly and realistically.

**Early marriage.** The goal in early marriage may be to escape the supervision and controls of home. To teens raised in an autocratic home environment, marriage may appear to be a freeing, attractive alternative way of life.

Your teen owns the problem of wanting to marry at an early age, not you. Remember that by fighting against the marriage, you are likely to provide the resistance that could make the prospect even more attractive. Again, begin by listening. Listen to the couple's opinions and help them understand their feelings. It is difficult to show respect if you believe an early marriage is not desirable. Yet, you can be a resource by being empathic and helping the teens clarify their goals. By hearing their feelings and accepting their beliefs, you will provide a climate in which a more reasonable decision can be made.

This is a time to utilize your human-relationship skills. Help the couple clarify their reasons for marrying now. Encourage them to explore alternatives. For example:

If it's their goal to be free of parental supervision, there are other avenues open besides marriage. You could say, "It seems you both want more freedom. What are some other things that might make you feel more in charge of your own lives?"

By listening, understanding, and exploring alternatives you will provide a nurturing atmosphere in which the teenagers have the opportunity to make a responsible decision—for *or* against an early marriage.

Each of the problems discussed in this chapter provides a difficult challenge. Each situation will require courage, patience, and careful application of your new skills. You can't expect simple answers or immediate success. Many of the situations require a long-term investment of your love, encouragement, and personal self-esteem.

In this chapter, we've often suggested a possible need for family counseling. We want to emphasize that if, after applying the procedures in STEP/teen, you are still encountering major problems in *any* area of your relationship with your teen, family therapy may be in order. In most cases, it would be ideal to involve the entire family if counseling is to be effective. Realistically, however, some family members, including your teen, may refuse counseling. If this is the case, the teen can still benefit from your involvement in counseling.

## The Challenge of Building and Maintaining Your Self-Confidence

In all your relationships, and particularly in those with your teen, the only person you can change is *you*. You may have been attracted to STEP/teen in the hopes that you could change your teen. But by now you are aware that you can only influence others as you change yourself.

If you are going to be effective in your relationship with your teenager, you need to establish some realistic goals for yourself. Probably one of the most important goals for the parent of a teenager is to develop the courage to be imperfect. Many of us tend to push ourselves and our teen to be perfect. While our intentions may be good, the results are often exactly the opposite of what we have in mind. As you become comfortable with the idea that mistakes are really guidelines for learning, you will exert less pressure on yourself and your teenager. You'll feel better about yourself, and you'll no doubt find your teen more cooperative and self-reliant.

Bear in mind that your teen is in the process of growing up. Allow this maturing to happen and don't expect it to happen overnight. You too are in the process of changing. Again, this is not something that will

take place quickly or easily. Patience and a sense of humor can do much to keep you going when things seem bleak or discouraging.

In STEP/teen you have learned about the vital role of encouragement. It is important to recognize how significantly your expectations influence all your relationships. Learn to encourage not only your teen, but yourself as well. Look inside yourself to see what gives you satisfaction. Recognize where you feel respected and valued. And remind yourself of the progress you are making toward building a more satisfying relationship with your teenager.

The teen years are a time of challenge. Your teenager is trying out a variety of new tasks and attempting to develop a unique human identity. Don't take every move toward independence as rebellion. Instead, see these moves for what they really are: ways of asserting self. The evidence is that there is no stage called "teens." Whatever happens during those years is often dependent upon the relationship between teenagers and parents. If you have courage, hope, and creativity, if you focus on

Avoid the tendency to push your teen to be perfect. The result is often the opposite of what you intend.

encouragement and cooperation, there are no relationships that cannot be improved.

## References

1. Rudolf Dreikurs and Vicki Soltz, *Children: The Challenge* (New York: Hawthorn, 1964).
2. Emily B. Visher and John S. Visher, *Stepfamilies: A Guide to Working with Stepparents and Stepchildren* (New York: Brunner-Mazel, 1979).
3. Ibid.
4. Don Dinkmeyer and Gary D. McKay, *Raising a Responsible Child* (New York: Simon & Schuster, 1973).
5. Myrtle T. Collins and Dwane R. Collins, *Survival Kit for Teachers (and Parents)* (Santa Monica, Calif.: Goodyear, 1975).
6. Sidney Cohen, *The Substance Abuse Problems* (New York: Haworth Press, 1981).
7. Marsha Manatt, *Parents, Peers, and Pot* (U.S. Department of Health and Human Services; Alcohol, Drug Abuse, and Mental Health Administration; Prevention Branch, Division of Resource Development, National Institute on Drug Abuse; 1980).
8. Cohen, 1981, and Manatt, 1980.
9. Manatt, 1980.

## Questions

1. What are some issues regarding your teen about which you and your spouse have different opinions? Have you resolved the differences? How? If not, how might you begin to do so?
2. What are some special challenges of being a single parent or a stepparent? What are some ways the authors suggest parents handle these challenges?
3. What are some ways parents can deal with lying?
4. What are the special challenges you face regarding sexual activity and your teenager? How have you approached these challenges? What are some other approaches you might take?
5. What are the signs that a teenager might be abusing drugs? How can parents help a teen with a drug-abuse problem?
6. What are the specific ways you intend to build and maintain your self-confidence?

# Personal Development Exercises

## Identifying Your Progress*

Spend some time identifying your progress. Whenever you become discouraged, review your list. (Example: I am *using reflective listening* and as a result *my teen is sharing feelings with me*.) Don't limit yourself to the space provided. Keep going!

I am _____ and as a result _____

I am _____ and as a result _____

I am _____ and as a result _____

I am _____ and as a result _____

I am _____ and as a result _____

Making a Contract for Change**

When you wish to improve something about your relationship with your teen, follow these steps. Be careful not to place unrealistic expectations on yourself. Plan to make a little progress at a time.

1. Problem: _____

2. My teen's goal: _____

3. Who owns the problem? _____

4. My plan (keep it specific and manageable): _____
_____
_____

5. If I'm not careful, I might sabotage my plan by (for example: feeling guilty, over-talking, sending inappropriate nonverbal signals): _____
_____

6. I will evaluate my plan on: _____

**Tips for Success**

• Make a chart of your daily progress. Focus on the positive.
• Don't evaluate the plan before the date set in Step 6.
• Use your plan throughout the set test period.
• When you evaluate your plan, focus on positive progress. If you aren't pleased with your progress, ask yourself why: Did you expect too much of yourself or your teen? Did you sabotage your plan?
• Decide whether to continue, modify, or discontinue the plan.

---

*Adapted from Don Dinkmeyer, Gary D. McKay, and Don Dinkmeyer, Jr., *Teacher's Resource Book: Systematic Training for Effective Teaching* (Circle Pines, Minn.: American Guidance Service, 1980).
**Adapted from Gary McKay, *The Basics of Encouragement* (Coral Springs, Fla.: CMTI Press, 1976) and Dinkmeyer, McKay, and Dinkmeyer, 1980.

Chart 10

# Democratic and Positive Parenting of Teens

| Challenge | Autocratic Response | Permissive Response | Democratic Response |
|---|---|---|---|
| Teen stays out too late. | Lecture, ground teen. | Express wish that teen come home on time, but do nothing. | Agree in advance on time to come home. Apply logical consequences (teen can't go out next night). |
| Teen does not do chores. | Demand, order, name-call. | Do chores for teen. Stop assigning chores to teen. | Use family meeting to make agreements about chores and consequences for not doing them. |
| Teen expresses anger toward parent. | Threaten, counterattack. | Accept responsibility for teen's feelings. | Use reflective listening and I-messages; explore alternatives. Or decide to ignore attack and discuss problem at calmer time. |
| Teen has improper diet. | Lecture, try to make teen eat properly. | Ignore teen's eating habits completely. | Include teen in meal planning. Make nutritious snack items available. |
| Teen is failing in school. | Try to force teen to study. Punish, lecture, bribe. | Show no interest in teen's school performance. | Give responsibility for school to teen. Focus on teen's efforts, improvements, and strengths. |
| Teen has minor accident in family car. | Become angry. Lecture. Deny teen use of car and/or make teen pay for damage. | Be overly sympathetic. Assume responsibility for teen. | Let teen pay for any damage not covered by insurance. Express confidence in teen's ability to drive. |

# Points to Remember

**1.** If you and your spouse don't see eye-to-eye on STEP/Teen's parenting methods, permit your spouse to decide how she or he wants to relate to your children. You decide how you will relate.

**2.** Divorce presents challenges for children and teens, but it does not have to do permanent damage. To deal with your children if you are divorced:

• Avoid pity.
• Don't feel guilty.
• Openly discuss their feelings about divorce.
• Don't use your children as a weapon against your former spouse.

**3.** Some guidelines for single parents are:

• Let your ex-spouse decide how to relate to your children when she or he is with them.
• Don't let children and teens play one parent against the other.
• Avoid criticizing your ex-spouse in front of your children.
• Don't take sides with your children against your ex-spouse.
• You have a right to make decisions about your personal life.

**4.** Stepparents need to establish their own relationship with stepchildren, rather than try to take the place of the absent parent. Some guidelines for stepparents are:

• Accept your new stepchildren as they are.
• Don't expect to be accepted and loved immediately.
• Allow teenagers to continue to assume the responsibilities they're accustomed to.
• Arrange private time together with stepchildren to do things that are of mutual interest.
• Maintain a congenial relationship with your stepchildren's absent parent.

**5.** Lying may be a signal that there is distrust in the parent-teen relationship. If lying is discovered, deal with the situation and not the offender. Show appreciation when your teen tells the truth.

**6.** If your teen steals from you, take the items back or ask for their return or equivalent payment. If your teen steals from the community, allow logical consequences to occur.

**7.** Help your teen make wise decisions about sex through open discussion in which you listen to your teen and clearly communicate your own feelings.

**8.** If your teen is angry, identify the purpose of the anger and consider how you can change your own response.

**9.** Avoid providing teens with special services. Let dependent teens learn from the consequences of failing to function.

**10.** In cases of substance abuse, avoid power struggles. Find ways to communicate respect and build self-esteem. If necessary, seek professional help.

**11.** A pregnant teen needs understanding, support, and help in deciding what to do. Involve the teenage father in the decision-making process as much as possible.

**12.** When teens wish to marry early, help them clarify their goals and purposes in order to make a responsible decision.

**13.** One of the most important goals for the parent of a teenager is to develop the courage to be imperfect.

**14.** Learn to encourage not only your teen, but yourself as well.

# My Plan for Improving Relationships
(An opportunity to assess progress each week)

My specific concern:

_____

_____

My usual response:

- ☐ talking, lecturing
- ☐ complaining, nagging
- ☐ becoming angry, screaming
- ☐ being sarcastic, attacking

- ☐ punishing, shaming
- ☐ giving up, forgetting because discouraged
- ☐ exerting power by removing privilege
- ☐ other _____

My progress this week:

| | I am doing this more | I need to do this more | I am about the same | | I am doing this more | I need to do this more | I am about the same |
|---|---|---|---|---|---|---|---|
| Understanding the purpose of behavior | ☐ | ☐ | ☐ | Communicating love, positive feelings | ☐ | ☐ | ☐ |
| Working on developing an equal relationship based on mutual respect | ☐ | ☐ | ☐ | Withdrawing from conflict | ☐ | ☐ | ☐ |
| Responding to emotions more effectively | ☐ | ☐ | ☐ | Preventing discipline problems by giving choices | ☐ | ☐ | ☐ |
| Encouraging | ☐ | ☐ | ☐ | Correcting discipline problems appropriately | ☐ | ☐ | ☐ |
| Appreciating and giving responsibility | ☐ | ☐ | ☐ | Arranging democratic family meetings | ☐ | ☐ | ☐ |
| Listening | ☐ | ☐ | ☐ | Being firm and kind | ☐ | ☐ | ☐ |
| Revealing my feelings without blaming or accusing | ☐ | ☐ | ☐ | Staying out of problems that are not my problems | ☐ | ☐ | ☐ |

I learned:

_____

_____

_____

I plan to change my behavior by:

_____

_____

_____

196

# To Learn More About Parenting

- STEP/teen—for parents of junior high and high school youth
- STEP—for parents of preschool through middle school children (also available in a Spanish-language edition, PECES—Padres Eficaces Con Entrenamiento Sistemático)
- Early Childhood STEP—for parents of infants, toddlers, and preschoolers
- The Next STEP—for parents who wish to extend the skills taught in the other STEP programs

The STEP programs focus on group discussion and are based on democratic principles of mutual respect, cooperation, and open communication between parents and children. In an atmosphere of mutual support, STEP group participants learn how best to encourage their children . . . how to get their children to assume responsibility . . . how to identify the goals of children's misbehavior . . . and how to redirect their children toward positive ends.

Parents who have taken part in STEP programs have reported several benefits, including
- increased knowledge of parenting
- improved relationships in their families
- improved communication with their children
- less conflict in their families

For many parents, joining a STEP *support group* has led directly to improved parenting skills. By discussing the principles of STEP with other parents and the group leader, they have received support and encouragement from new sources. In one study, *over 93 percent* of the participants in STEP groups said they would indeed recommend the course to other parents.

If you are interested in joining or leading a STEP, STEP/teen, Early Childhood STEP, or Next STEP group, many organizations in your community might be able to give you information. Check to see whether STEP groups are being offered by local schools, community centers, health centers, churches and synagogues, adult education programs, counseling centers, civic groups, psychologists, social workers, or the military.

For more details about any STEP groups near you, or for information about how to start a group yourself, write to the publisher:

**AGS**®

American Guidance Service
Publishers' Building
Circle Pines, MN 55014-1796

**In Canada, write to:**
Psycan Corporation
P.O. Box 290, Station V
Toronto, Ontario M6R 3A5

**In Australia, write to:**
Australian Council for Educational
 Research Ltd.
P.O. Box 210
Hawthorn, Victoria 3122